Ideology and Cultural Identity

Ideology and Cultural Identity

Modernity and the Third World Presence

JORGE LARRAIN

Polity Press

The right of Jorge Larrain to be identified as author of this work has been asserted in accordance with the Copyright, Designs and Patents Act 1988.

First published in 1994 by Polity Press in association with Blackwell Publishers.

Editorial office:
Polity Press
65 Bridge Street
Cambridge CB2 1UR, UK

Marketing and production:
Blackwell Publishers
108 Cowley Road
Oxford OX4 1JF, UK

238 Main Street
Cambridge, MA 02142, USA

ISBN 0 7456 1315 2
ISBN 0 7456 1316 0 (pbk)

A CIP catalogue record for this book is available from the British Library and the Library of Congress.

Typeset in 10 on 12 pt Palatino
by Graphicraft Typesetters Ltd, Hong Kong
Printed and bound in Great Britain by Hartnolls Limited, Bodmin, Cornwall

This book is printed on acid-free paper.

Contents

Preface and Acknowledgements

This book completes the ideas presented in earlier volumes on *The Concept of Ideology* and *Marxism and Ideology* by addressing more contemporary authors and intellectual currents, with especial emphasis on the irrationalist, poststructuralist and postmodernist theories or critiques of ideology. However, one of the objectives of the book is to present these ideas in a wider, global context which, first of all, takes into account the Third World presence and, second, opens itself up to issues of cultural identity. My attempt to deal with these connections has been greatly influenced by the intellectual atmosphere, the teaching and the discussions which take place in the Department of Cultural Studies at Birmingham University. In particular, I think I owe an important intellectual debt to Richard Johnson on issues related to cultural identity, although he may not be aware of it and cannot be made responsible for any shortcomings of my book. I would also like to thank Tony Giddens, not just because as an editor he proposed changes which greatly improved the book, but also because my understanding of modernity and postmodernity has been greatly enhanced by his ideas. I am very grateful to many people at Polity Press and Blackwell Publishers who so efficiently dealt with the problems of producing this book while I was abroad. A special mention must be made of Linden Stafford for her excellent copy-editing, which greatly improved the text. None the less, I should be held responsible for the remaining oddities of my English.

The author and publishers are grateful for permission to reproduce materials already published by the author: 'Ideology and its Revisions in Contemporary Marxism', in Noel O'Sullivan (ed.), *The Structure of Modern Ideology* (Aldershot: Edward Elgar Publishing, 1989); 'The Postmodern Critique of Ideology', *The Sociological Review*, vol. 42, no. 2 (May 1994); 'Classical Political Economists and Marx on Colonialism and "Backward" Nations', *World Development*, vol. 19, nos 2–3 (February/March 1991), pp. 225–43, with kind permission from Pergamon Press Ltd, UK; 'Stuart Hall and the Marxist Concept of Ideology', *Theory, Culture and Society*, vol. 8, no. 4 (November 1991), pp. 1–28.

Introduction

This book has several objectives and different dimensions. Generally speaking it seeks to explore the relationships between three important concepts, ideology, reason and cultural identity, which are at the centre of contemporary discussions about modernity and postmodernity. It tries to carry out such an exploration not merely in the context of European thought, but also in a dialogue with the realities of the Third World, especially Latin America. The book also seeks to expound and critically analyse the theories of ideology which inform or derive from currents of thought opposed to modernity, from Schopenhauer to postmodernity. But at the same time it will try to define and use a concept of ideology, derived from but not entirely coincident with Marx's concept, in order to assess both the problems of irrationalist theories of ideology and the shortcomings of the universalistic theories including Marx's. Additionally, the book wants to discuss more specifically some issues concerning the concept of cultural identity and the way in which it stands in relation to personal identity and the process of globalization. Finally, an important aim of the book is to explore some European conceptions of the Third World, particularly Latin America, in order to establish some relationships between both universalistic and historicist theories, and specific manners of constructing the other. A comparison between universalistic and historicist theories leads to different relationships between reason and racism.

I shall start in chapter 1 with the idea that the very concept of ideology was born in the context of the emergence of modernity and the triumph of instrumental reason. Thus the most powerful theories of ideology are those developed implicitly or explicitly by the big theories of development such as Marxism, classical political economy and Weberian theories of modernization which believe in reason and progress. The closeness between reason and ideology in the origins of modernity has direct consequences in the construction of the 'other' and the treatment of other cultures. The big representative theories of modernity tend to be universalistic, to disregard difference, to reduce the specific to the general. Thus, although some of these theories bequeath important theoretical contributions such as the very theory of ideology, they have difficulties in understanding other societies where instrumental reason has not entirely triumphed and where the universal schemes of progress seem to work less perfectly. This is the reason why they easily justify colonialism and European tutelage over other parts of the world and sometimes fall into blatant racism. I explore these issues in relation to classical political economy, Marx and Hegel in chapter 1. I also try to go further in order to discover whether there is a sort of a relationship between the most typical philosophy of the Enlightenment, empiricism, and racism.

All this leads me to try to find a concept of ideology which takes into account these other forgotten aspects which have to do with colonialism and the cultural identity of Third World areas. The almost exclusive focus on the capital/labour contradiction in Marx's theory of ideology leaves aside other conflicts which have also been shown to be relevant to the maintenance of the capitalist system, this time in its global dimension. Thus the concept with which I shall operate, although derived from Marx, will be wider in scope in that it will consider conflicts other than class antagonisms, especially racial and colonial divisions, which are also masked or explained away in the interest of the capitalist system. At the same time, the capitalist system which is at stake will be taken to go beyond the narrow boundaries of nation-states, to constitute an international system in which any of its spatially integrated parts could be affected by events elsewhere.

The opposition to and critique of universalistic theories of modernity have been carried out by historicist and irrationalist theories which attack the Enlightenment's trust in reason, progress and universal truth. Such a critique can be considered as an ideology critique, although many of these authors try to rid themselves of the concept of ideology which they find too closely attached to the rationalistic spirit and epistemological absolutism of modernity. Still, it is my contention that in spite of their formal protest and rejection of the concept of ideology they end up reintroducing it through the back door.

An important part of the book will therefore be concerned with those theories and conceptions of ideology which stem from the overrating of the role of the irrational in human life and society. They tend to doubt the value of rationality in history and society and they are sceptical about the possibility of reaching the truth. Truth becomes relativized, and every institution, epoch, nation or culture is said to have its own regime of truth. Truth acquires a discursive character because it can be constructed in different discourses which are incommensurable. This relativization of truth started with German philosophical historicism and has culminated in contemporary times with postmodernism. Reason is downgraded to being a servant of power, of the struggle for life, and ceases to be a principle which informs history and the organization of society. What characterizes the human being is the predominance of an irrational will and its drives. Reason becomes subordinate to will. Thus it is not surprising that the concept of power, as an expression of this irrational will, plays a central role in all these theories. If social life is seen as a kind of struggle where the will uses reason for its own purposes, then power becomes central.

The book will try to show that these conceptions tend to use, implicitly or explicitly, a critical notion of ideology; that is to say their aim is to criticize ideology, to expose doubtful values, to unmask traditional principles. But the main ideological culprit is almost always reason itself, or its reduction to instrumental reason. Most irrationalist theories have an acute sense of the connections between knowledge and power and therefore tend to accept that power is usually maintained by knowledge. Machiavelli and Hobbes are the intellectual ancestors of these theories. They tend to have a pessimistic idea about human nature. They criticize dogmas and superstitions, but they still think that they are necessary to keep society in order. Ideas are thus judged by their usefulness to power, not by their truth content. Irrationalist theories accept that human beings inevitably fall into distortions and false beliefs, but because these are prevalent and inevitable they should be taken advantage of, either to keep a strong central power (Pareto) or to prevail in the struggle for life (Nietzsche). So they separate the intellectual value of certain ideas from their usefulness for the exercise of power. Most attacks on reason criticize the rational masks which conceal domination and the exercise of power (Foucault, Adorno, Horkheimer), but some go beyond and tend to glorify the exercise of power as a necessity (Nietzsche, Pareto).

In chapter 2 I shall deal with some of these theories, especially Schopenhauer, Nietzsche, Pareto, Adorno and Horkheimer, trying to establish how they carried out ideology critique and assessing their contributions and problems. However, my interest in them is also instrumental in that they constitute the antecedents of more contemporary developments to be found in poststructuralism and postmodernism which are the topic of chapter 4. However, in order to get to the analysis of poststructuralism and postmodernism, in chapter 3 I take a detour through Althusserianism and its most important strands. This may seem strange but it is justified by my belief that postmodernism and poststructuralism are as much related to the development and dissolution of the Althusserian school as they are to the historicist tradition and Nietzsche. Foucault, Baudrillard and Lyotard, not to speak of Laclau and Mouffe, and Hindess and Hirst in Britain, were all originally Marxists of an Althusserian persuasion, and in order to understand them it is necessary to explore the way in which the Althusserian problematic, radicalized and with some Nietzschean inputs, became poststructuralist and postmodernist.

It will be my contention that the theories opposed to modernity right down to postmodernism are themselves ideological because in criticizing the role of reason they displace the focus of attention from, and thus tend to conceal the main problems of, capitalism. And yet, as Lukács has argued, such theories usually emerge as a reaction to some major crisis related to the emergence or progress of the capitalist system. Thus, for instance, the French Revolution, the Paris Commune, the Russian Revolution, the Second World War and, I would add, the revolt in France in 1968 constitute important events around which the thought of some irrationalist thinkers has crystallized. The first early forms of irrationalism were a reaction against the new capitalist system while socialism and the class struggle were not yet well developed. Other forms of irrationalism mirror the irrationalities which creep in during the phases of crisis in the development of capitalism, but constitute a reaction against the perceived threat of socialism which challenges the survival of capitalism. Once socialism is no longer seen as an international threat, there still subsists a potential revolutionary charge which threatens a system that is inevitably contradictory.

I shall argue that these theories may also become ideological in the sense that under the cover of respect for cultural differences, pluralism and relativism they sometimes construct the 'other' as having so little to do with the European mainstream culture as to be inferior, or at least regard it as sufficiently different to make it necessary to take some protective measures against it in order to safeguard a supposedly threatened cultural identity.

Chapter 5 is devoted to the critical analysis of perhaps the only all-encompassing and strikingly original contemporary social theory which consciously explores the issues arising in the tension between universalistic pro-modern and historicist anti-modern theories and proposes an original synthesis based on a new concept of rationality and ideology reformulated in terms of a theory of communicative action. I refer, of course, to Habermas. This chapter examines Habermas's theory of ideology and his proposal of a new, more encompassing, communicative rationality which allows both the critique of modernity and the defence of its positive sides. Habermas's notion of communicative rationality, coupled with an epistemologically universalistic stand, has important consequences for understanding some issues relating to ethnocentrism and cultural identity. Of particular relevance is his proposal for a post-national and more universalistic type of cultural identity. And this sets the stage for the last chapter.

The book ends with a more specific analysis of the concept of cultural identity in chapter 6. This exploration combines a brief historical account of the evolution of the concept of personal identity during modern times with some discussion of various positions which define such an identity in particular ways and which connect with some of the theories analysed in previous chapters. More specifically, the issue of globalization becomes a crucial point in the discussion, which shows how it has shaped cultural identities from the beginning of modernity. The distinction between centre and periphery plays an important role here.

The book argues against an essentialist and monolithic conception of identity and for a historical version. At the same time it warns against conceiving of identity as having well-demarcated and universally agreed limits, so that instead of one received version of identity there are always various versions, corresponding to the outlook of different social groups, which are highly selective in the features they choose and exclude. In this sense it is argued that, precisely because some versions of identity may conceal the cultural diversity in the interest of a dominant group, they may become ideological. On the other hand, however, they may also serve as forms by means of which oppressed groups or nations resist their cultural assimilation by more powerful groups or nations. In this sense it is crucial to understand identity not just as a construction coming from the past but also, as Habermas proposes, as a project. This allows the process of selection which all versions of cultural identity perform, to decide how to continue with a certain tradition, which ideological elements to root out, which valuable elements to keep and which elements from other traditions to adopt.

1

Ideology, Reason and the Construction of the Other

Introduction

The recent emergence of postmodernism has put at the centre of contemporary philosophical discussions the value of modernity and the problem of instrumental reason. However, it would be a mistake to believe that it is only with postmodernism that a thorough critique of the Enlightenment and its absolute trust in instrumental reason has been developed. From the very beginning, the belief in science and reason has been accompanied by critical theories, sometimes called historicist,[1] which have emphasized the values of cultural relativism and have criticized the many problems created by the blind use of instrumental reason. While the typical theories influenced by the Enlightenment are universal theories of development which emphasize the identity of goals and the similarity of means in the course of history, the theories critical of modernity emphasize cultural differences and historical discontinuities.[2] Although both types of theories have explicitly or implicitly developed their own critical conceptions of ideology, they do it in different ways. Theories that consciously want to develop the principles of modernity tend to criticize all obstacles – social, economic and philosophical – which stand in the way of reason, science and progress. Theories that regard modernity with suspicion tend to criticize reason and science themselves as ideological.

It is possible to argue as well that these two types of theories have a different approach to the cultural 'other'. While universalistic total theories have difficulties in understanding otherness and difference and see history as a series of stages through which everybody has to go, historicist theories have difficulties in understanding common problems and the forms of equality which stem from a shared humanity. To them, history is not a universal but a segmented process whose understanding requires empathy with the different cultural essence which each nation develops. Universalistic theories look at the 'other' from the perspective of the European rational subject; they tend to apply a general pattern which postulates its own absolute truth, thus reducing all cultural differences to its own unity. Historicist theories look at the 'other' from the perspective of its unique and specific cultural set-up, thus emphasizing difference and discontinuity. There are dangers implicit in both positions. While the emphasis on absolute truth and historical continuity may lead to reductionism and neglect of the other's specificity, the emphasis on difference and discontinuity may lead to the construction of the other as inferior. Two forms of racism may be the result of these extremes: whereas universalistic theories may not accept the other because they cannot recognize and accept its differences, historicist theories may dismiss the other because it is constructed as a different, inferior being.

These two types of theories have, tendentially, different conceptions of history and cultural identity. Universalistic theories tend to conceive of history as universal, unilineal, teleological progress, whereas the historicist approach conceives of history as a goalless, discontinuous and segmented process which has no universal direction. Paradoxically, the emphasis on historical specificity leads historicist theories to conceive of cultural identity ahistorically, as an essence, as an immutable spirit which marks an unbridgeable difference between peoples and nations. The emphasis on history as unilineal progress, on the contrary, may disregard historical specificities, but usually accepts a notion of cultural identity as a process of construction and reconstruction which cannot be reduced to an essence.

Some good examples of what I have called the typical universalistic theories of modernity are classical political economy, Marxism, Weberian modernization theory and neo-liberalism. They constitute important totalizing theories of development which possess an underlying theory of history and propose a universal road to progress to all countries. Although some of them go back to the eighteenth or nineteenth century, they have been very influential world-wide until today. In spite of their many differences, some of their essential underlying philosophical assumptions are very similar. These theories take different angles to see and approach the big project of modernity which had its roots in the European Enlightenment. They all start from a firm belief in instrumental reason and in science, in the idea that we can understand reality and transform it, thus improving our lives. Reason for them is no longer autonomous, beyond the power of human beings; it is an instrument of control and domination of nature, an auxiliary means of production, a way of manipulating means to achieve our ends. Common to these theories as well is the assumption that they can diagnose and analyse undesirable social situations and do something about them. Hence the importance of ideology critique for all of them. They believe that it is possible to establish by means of rational argument that certain prevailing ideas are distorted or wrong.

Hence, all traditional theories of development typical of modernity adhere to a particular notion of reason and conceive of history in terms of the deployment and progressive success of certain forms of agency which specifically express the progress of reason. From the vantage point of such conceptions of historical reason it is possible to ascertain erroneous forms of action and distorted ideas which represent obstacles to the progress of reason. Thus specific forms of ideology critique are developed. Theories of development entail theories of historical reason and theories of ideology.

For example, classical political economy argued in favour of private property, free trade and the establishment of market forces in all the domains of the economy. The entrepreneur became the main agent of progress as the producer of wealth and development. Historical reason was deployed in the free and continuous advance of productive forces and material wealth achieved by market forces. Hence the remnants of feudalism became the main object of ideological critique. Feudalism encroached upon production, and did not allow free trade and free labour. It had, then, to be dismantled so that reason and science could be applied to the productive process. Marxism in its turn makes a case for the socialization of the means of production and considers the proletariat, the direct producer, as the agent of historical reason which will be fully realized in classless society. From this position Marx develops a concept of ideology with which he criticizes the dominant political ideas of capitalism for concealing forms of inequality and exploitation. However, in proposing socialism as a road to the further development of productive forces, Marxism reaffirms a process of change and instrumental rationalization, but in a more radical manner and by the utilization of different means.

Modernization theory, drawing on the ideas of Max Weber, sees society in transition to modernity, in a process of increasing rationalization, a process whereby the traditional absolute forms of rationality typical of aristocratic and religious ideas must be criticized and set aside. Absolute reason fixed legitimate ends and means without regard to their productive usefulness, thus hindering progress and change. So it had to be replaced by new forms of instrumental rationality which maximized control, adaptation and productivity. However, an important difference between Weber's theory and the post-war modernization theories must be noted. Whereas the latter see in the process of rationalization and secularization not only a necessity but also the fulfilment of human hopes for a better life, the former is aware of the grave risk that human beings will be increasingly dominated by the 'iron cage' of bureaucratized structures and reified relationships. Still, both see the process as ineluctable. Neo-liberalism, in its turn, constitutes a recent revival of Adam Smith's ideas which consider free market and free trade as the panaceas which bring about the wealth of nations. The main historical difference from classical political economy is that the ideological critique has shifted from feudalism to Marxism and socialist ideas of the interventionist state. The problem is no longer seen as mercantilism but the more recent Keynesian policies which, according to neo-liberalism, lead to protectionism, excessive state expenditure on welfare, and the excessive power of trade unions, all of which result in poor economic growth.

Ideology and Reason

The concept of ideology was born in the context of the early bourgeois struggles against feudalism and the traditional aristocratic society. These struggles were very much the backcloth of the eighteenth-century Enlightenment, which is, more precisely, the cultural and philosophical environment within which the concept of ideology was generated for the first time. This historical context helps us understand why the concept of ideology emerged, first, as a science of ideas which entailed a deep trust in reason and, second, as a critical weapon to be used in the struggle against the old regime. Both aspects were inextricably linked. It was precisely the belief that truth could be rationally and scientifically achieved, and that armed with it society could be rationally reconstructed, that provided the Enlightenment with the confidence to criticize irrational, metaphysical and religious ideas. Not only were these forms of knowledge deemed to be distorted and superstitious but by spreading ignorance and error among the masses they worked in the interest of, and buttressed, aristocratic power. As the unhappiness of humankind was believed to be related to ignorance and prejudice, rational and lay education was thought to be the liberating solution. Ideology as a science thus entailed a renewed optimism and confidence in progress, reason and education; it believed in the emancipation of humankind.

The belief in reason, especially the belief in instrumental reason, is closely tied up with a critical concept of ideology. Everything that appears traditional or backward, everything that does not lead to progress, is the opposite of reason, is ideology. Ideology is a notion that is used to defend reason, to criticize all those ideas which are not progressive, which do not help control nature to the benefit of human beings. Instrumental reason is anthropocentric and subjective. The human being is the centre, the measure of all things. Instrumental reason is the tool that allows us to control and dominate, the tool that introduces calculability, cost and benefit. Instrumental reason therefore tends to reduce that which is good for humankind to that which increases productivity. Reason becomes an auxiliary means of production, and ideology becomes its critical weapon.

The spirit of modernity was imbued with these ideas: progress was material progress; it was growth in the production of material goods. In so far as metaphysics, religion and mythology did not help to control nature, to increase production, they had to be attacked as ideological forms. So there is a close relation between the belief in instrumental reason and the critical concept of ideology as the opposite of science or reason. In this sense there is a common thread from the French Enlightenment philosophers of the eighteenth century to the neo-liberal thinkers of today: they all wage battle against ideology as the antithesis of reason. The close historical relationship between reason and ideology makes an implicit reference to agency, that is to say, there are agents of reason and ideology. The former are for progress, the latter oppose it. At the beginning of bourgeois struggles they were synthesized in the bourgeoisie versus the feudal lords but could also be symbolized in the scientist-educator versus the priest.

With the development of bourgeois society and the expansion of capitalism, serious problems, irrationalities and contradictions inherent in the system came to the fore. Two theoretical possibilities emerged to confront them. On the one hand, by taking as a model the bourgeois critique of metaphysics and religion, Marx developed his concept of ideology in order to unmask the new forms of domination and exploitation. Ideology was no longer a science but a kind of distorted consciousness which masked the contradictions of society, thus contributing to the reproduction of the system. Marx strongly believed in reason, but for him the new proletarian class rather than the bourgeoisie was to be its bearer in order to liberate humankind. The agent was changed but the belief in emancipation was kept. Thus Marx accomplished the first important transposition in the meaning of ideology, from a science to a specific kind of distortion, but maintained the belief in reason and emancipation and the need to criticize those ideas which, by concealing the real problems of society, put obstacles in the way of the emancipatory forces.

Marx and Ideology

Marx's early critique of religion first outlines such a mechanism: religion compensates in the mind for a deficient social reality; it reconstitutes in the imagination a coherent but distorted solution which goes beyond the real world in an attempt to resolve the contradictions and sufferings of the real world. As he put it, '*religious* suffering is at one and the same time the *expression* of real suffering and a protest against real suffering. Religion is the sigh of the oppressed creature.'[3] Religion appears as an inversion because God, being a creature of the human beings' mind, becomes the creator, and the human beings, who create the idea of God, become the creatures. But this inversion in the mind responds to and derives from a real inversion: 'this state and this society produces religion, which is an *inverted consciousness of the world*, because they are an *inverted world*.'[4]

When Marx criticizes the German philosophers and left Hegelians, the same mechanism of inversion is present. The German ideologists believed that the true problems of humankind were mistaken and religious ideas which they could destroy by criticism. They forget, Marx and Engels aver, that 'to these phrases they themselves are only opposing other phrases, and they are in no way combating the real existing world.'[5] Their ideological inversion consists in their starting from consciousness rather than material reality; instead of looking at German reality 'they descended from heavens to earth.' Again, this mental inversion responds to a real inversion in reality: 'If the conscious expression of the real relations of these individuals is illusory, if in their imagination they turn reality upside-down, then this in its turn is the result of their limited material mode of activity and their limited social relations arising from it.'[6]

Similarly, when analysing the capitalist mode of production, Marx distinguishes the sphere of appearances (the market) from the sphere of inner relations (production), and argues that there is a basic inversion at the level of production, namely, the fact that past labour dominates living labour (the subject becomes an object and vice versa), and that this inversion 'necessarily produces certain correspondingly inverted conceptions, a transposed consciousness which is further developed by the metamorphoses and modifications of the actual circulation process'.[7]

These examples, taken from Marx's analyses at different points in his intellectual evolution, show a consistent pattern in spite of their different nature. In all of them there is a reference to an 'inverted consciousness of the world' which corresponds to an 'inverted world'. This inverted world is practically produced by a 'limited material mode of activity' as a contradictory world and is simultaneously projected into distorted forms of consciousness which conceal and misrepresent that contradictory reality. The role of ideology is to help reproduce that contradictory world in the interest of the ruling class. But ideology is not the result of a conspiracy of the ruling class to deceive the dominated classes, nor is it an arbitrary invention of consciousness. It is rather a spontaneous or elaborated discursive attempt to deal with forms of oppression and contradictions which is unable to ascertain the true origin of these problems and therefore results in the masking and reproduction of those very contradictions and forms of oppression.[8]

The contradictions Marx refers to in his treatment of ideology within capitalism are all derived from or express an aspect of the principal contradiction of capitalism, namely, the contradiction which is constitutive of the very essence of the capitalist mode of production, the contradiction between capital and labour. These two poles relate in a contradictory way because they presuppose and negate each other. As Marx puts it, 'capital presupposes wage labour; wage labour presupposes capital. They reciprocally condition the existence of each other; they reciprocally bring forth each other.'[9] But this mutual conditioning engenders mutual opposition because 'the working individual *alienates* himself; relates to the conditions brought out of him by his labour as those not of his *own* but of an *alien wealth* and of his own poverty.'[10] Live labour engenders capital (dead labour), but the latter controls the former; capital reproduces itself by reproducing its opposite, wage labour. It is this contradictory process of continuous reproduction whereby capital reproduces itself by reproducing its opposite that explains the origin and function of ideology. The process, in so far as it is contradictory and alienates the worker, needs to be concealed in order to be able to continue to reproduce itself.

The way in which ideology is produced as part of the process of reproduction of the capitalist main contradiction can be ascertained by focusing on the way in which the two poles, capital and labour, relate to each other. Although the production and appropriation of surplus value occur at the level of production, capital and labour first come into contact through the market. This contact through the market appears perfectly fair and equitable, for capital and labour exchange equivalent values. So the process of production and extraction of surplus value is concealed by the operation of the market, which becomes the source of ideological representations such as the idea of a 'fair wage', equality, freedom, and so on. According to Marx, the labourer's 'economic bondage is both brought about and concealed by the periodic sale of himself, by his change of masters, and by the oscillation in the market-price of labour-power.'[11] Because the exchange of equivalents by free individuals in the market is seen on the surface of society and conceals the hidden extraction of surplus value in the process of production, it naturally tends to be reproduced in the minds of both capitalists and labourers as equality and freedom, the linchpins of capitalist ideology.

Ideology, Globalization and Other Forms of Oppression

I have briefly dwelt upon Marx's theory of ideology because it provides the first and most important model of a critical concept of ideology on which I shall draw in order to carry out the analyses and sustain the main theses of this book. This does not mean, however, that I shall use Marx's concept of ideology in exactly the same sense as Marx, without alteration. From the brief account I have given of it is possible to ascertain that Marx's concept was designed to operate, on the one hand, as a critical weapon in the context of class oppression and the main contradiction between capital and labour, and, on the other, as an analytical tool within the boundaries of nation-states, where class domination typically takes place. Although I shall be focusing on the role of ideology in the process of reproduction of the capitalist system, which is, of course, very much a part of Marx's concept, my interest will not be centred mainly and directly on the national ideological processes that sustain class domination, but rather on the transnational ideological processes that sustain other forms of power and domination, which also have as a result the maintenance of capitalism as a global system.

This means taking Marx's concept of ideology beyond the class and national context in which Marx primarily used it, but keeping both its ultimate function, which is the maintenance and survival of the capitalist (international) system and its negative connotation. J. B. Thompson has made one of the first attempts to defend a negative concept of ideology which both owes something to the work of Marx and seeks to widen its scope beyond class domination. For him, to study ideology 'is to study the ways in which meaning (or signification) serves to sustain relations of domination';[12] or, to put it more succinctly, ideology is *'meaning in the service of power'*.[13] Wherever there are asymmetrical relations of power there is a situation of domination, and therefore ideology helps sustain not only class domination but also a variety of relations of domination between ethnic groups, between nation-states, between sexes, and so forth.

I fully sympathize with Thompson's intention of defending a critical concept of ideology which is able to cover all forms of domination beyond class domination. However, I have two observations to make about his definition. First, although I accept that different situations of domination are ultimately irreducible to one another, I am especially interested in establishing connections between them. My proposition is that ideological forms which sustain types of domination other than class are, or may be, also connected with the survival of capitalism as an international system.

Second, in so far as the negative connotation of ideology is concerned, Thompson seems to assume that to analyse ideology in terms of the relation between meaning and domination is to give the concept an essentially negative and restrictive sense 'which owes something to the work of Marx'.[14] I want to argue that in contrast with Marx's conception Thompson's notion of ideology does not necessarily entail a negative connotation. In effect, as he himself recognizes, meanings which support domination may well not be inherently distorted at the epistemological level. Furthermore, according to Thompson, the study of ideology does not of itself entail a critique of domination although it may facilitate it. Thus, to show how meanings are mobilized to sustain a form of domination does not necessarily entail that this form of domination is unjust or wrong![15] Thus Thompson separates from domination all elements which could be epistemologically and morally negative. It is true that Marx did not conceive of ideology as a mere error opposed to truth or as a mere moral mistake, but he certainly did more than link meanings in general to domination in general: he specified a particular kind of distortion – the masking of contradictions – which stems from and conceals an 'inverted' reality in which the real subjects are treated as objects. In this sense Marx did not totally separate the fact of domination from epistemologically and morally negative considerations.

So, although I adopt a concept of ideology which is wider than Marx's in that I take into account forms of domination other than class, I would like to keep both the reference to the international capitalist system and the negative connotation. Ideology thus remains a kind of distorted thought which seeks to mask reality, but it disguises not just forms of class domination but other forms too such as racial, gender and colonial oppressions. This does not mean that such ideological processes are disconnected from or have no bearing upon particular forms of class domination – the colonial ideological construction of colonized peoples as inferior clearly plays an ideological internal role in deceiving the dominated classes of the colonial power – but they can be analytically distinguished. Thus ideology conceals not merely class antagonisms but also forms of gender, racial and colonial domination which affect women, ethnic minorities and Third World peoples. Because the relationships between all these dimensions are not always articulated, it is possible to find theories which are unmasking and critical in one dimension and ideological in another dimension. I hope to show in the next section that this is true even of Marxism.

It can be argued that in so far as the reproduction of the capitalist system is concerned class contradictions cannot be put on the same level as other conflicts emerging from gender, race and colonial divisions. The contradiction between the two main classes of the mode of production is the only one which is constitutive of and essential to the capitalist system, in the sense that it is the only contradiction without which the capitalist system cannot survive. Gender, racial and colonial forms of oppression are not indispensable to the survival of the capitalist system. I accept that in this sense the concealment of class contradictions constitutes a privileged role of ideology. But this does not mean that the masking and/or justification of other types of conflicts has not had historically a direct bearing on the maintenance of capitalism. Nobody could deny how important colonialism and the slave trade were to the development of Western capitalism. They may not have been indispensable in principle, but they did play an important role in practice.

The other aspect which is necessary to emphasize is that, with the increasing internationalization of capitalism and the widening of the processes of globalization,[16] ideology, even in its original relation to class contradictions, cannot continue to be analysed within the narrow space of national boundaries. Even in the time of Marx and Engels, philosophy was already an international phenomenon which Marx analysed not just in relation to national class struggles, but also in relation to situations in other countries. Thus, for instance, Marx explained the problems of German philosophy on the one hand as a consequence of 'German petty bourgeois conditions',[17] but on the other as the result of Germans taking French and English ideas not 'as the expression and the product of a real movement but as purely theoretical writings which have been evolved . . . by a process of "pure thought" '.[18] In other words, German philosophy was partly explained by a negative relationship to German material practices (economic backwardness and petty-bourgeois conditions) and partly by a positive relationship to the bourgeois achievements of France and England. If this applied to German Idealism, it should also be possible to analyse German historicism and later forms of irrationalism in the wider context of European and world capitalism – except that the positive–negative relationship is inverted. Whereas Hegel had idealized the French Revolution, the romantic historicist reaction and the irrationalist aftermath were appalled by it.

Georg Lukács has rightly maintained the thesis that irrationalism is an international phenomenon which is closely related to major social crises. The first wave arose at the end of the eighteenth and beginning of the nineteenth century, partly as the result of the social upheaval caused by the French Revolution and the industrial revolution in England.[19] F. W. J. von Schelling was its main representative. Behind the philosophy of most irrationalists major crises loomed, such as the Paris Commune for Friedrich Nietzsche, the Russian Revolution for Vilfredo Pareto and also for Theodor W. Adorno and Max Horkheimer; more recently one could add Paris 1968 for postmodernism. All these events have represented major crises for the capitalist system and have had wide international repercussions which went beyond the locality where they occurred. One cannot of course reduce philosophical theories, even irrationalist theories, to nothing more than results of particular crises. But they are not entirely disconnected phenomena either. The opposition to socialism is a constant in Nietzsche, Pareto and postmodernism. However, this kind of connection, of itself, does not determine the positive or negative character of the content, which has to be analysed each time on its merits. It is here that I would like to use the concept of ideology in order to perform such an assessment. The analysis will be carried out in chapters 2 and 4.

For the time being I can only repeat in anticipation of such analyses that one of the main theses of this book is that the irrationalist reactions against the modern prevalence of instrumental reason, and against the universalistic pretensions of its typical theories of development, have performed from the beginning the ideological role of sustaining capitalism especially in its moments of deep international crisis. Some of the theories that question the universality of reason and truth reject the very notion of ideology as typical of modern totalitarian theories which are certain of possessing a vantage point from which to pass judgement upon all theories. Yet I shall try to show that implicitly all theories that reject the idea of a vantage point operate with a concept of ideology which seeks to unmask, sometimes with success, the totalitarian and reductionist features of universalistic theories. However, this is never consciously recognized. My point is that these theories are themselves ideological.

They are ideological, first, because they help to defuse the revolutionary pressures emerging from deep crises in the capitalist system by highlighting the wrong causes and the wrong solutions to the emerging problems and contradictions. The general ideological mechanism operates by arguing that if there is a crisis it is because the very project of modernity with its trust in truth and reason is faulty. Blaming modernity or reason in general causes the problem to be displaced and the more specific contradictions of the capitalist system to be concealed. The relativism and general scepticism about reason propounded by these theories undermine the belief in the possibility of any rational solution and thus discourage people from engaging in any process of change. Mongardini has shrewdly noted that 'the mainstays of modernity, the industrialists, politicians and technologists, know nothing or pretend to know nothing of postmodernity: because postmodernity is the ideology that dams up the psychological unease of modernity.'[20] Indeed capitalists need not know anything or be bothered about postmodernity, because what is being protected and never questioned by such an ideology is ultimately what they do.

Second, these theories are ideological also in the sense that by overemphasizing difference and discontinuity they help to blur the common elements of humanity in the construction of the other. This is just the reverse of understanding cultural identity as an incommensurable essence which cannot be altered or receive new inputs. Both these aspects facilitate the emergence of certain specific forms of racism. Third, the ideological character of these theories is compounded by their refusing to validate their own positions. They doubt the truth value of all other theories, but they refuse to account for the validity of their own. Worse still, they reject universal truth and the concept of ideology but they end up reintroducing both through the back door without ever recognizing that they do it. They implicitly assume their own validity and from that vantage point pass ideological judgement on other theories, especially those closely connected with the values of modernity.

And yet the fact that irrationalist theories are ideological in these senses does not fully prevent them from being able to unmask some ideological features of their adversaries. This happens mainly in relation to some reductionistic features of universalistic theories and their inability to understand differences. Thus, for instance, these theories have difficulty in understanding events in Third World countries as historically and locally specific and become dismissive of such countries and their cultures when they do not fit into a general historical scheme. Paradoxically, then, the very concept of ideology, which was born so closely connected to reason and the main projects of modernity, can be turned as a critical weapon against them, not in the general sense of reason becoming ideology, as in the work of Herbert Marcuse, but in a more particular sense which, while respecting the original mechanism, extends it to include the concealment of racial and colonial forms of oppression. Thus, for instance, Marx's analyses were fiercely critical of all theories which blurred or concealed the primacy of the British working class in the struggle for world socialism but can, in their turn, be criticized for abetting or justifying forms of colonialism when the interest of the European proletariat was at stake. In the next section some of these features will be explored.

Reason and the Reduction of Difference

An important characteristic of universalistic theories typical of modernity is the fact that no nation can escape from the universal path of development which the particular theory has proposed, once the major obstacles have been dismantled. Yet, when confronted with especially difficult cases which seem to deviate from the universal norm, some of these theories, especially the nineteenth-century ones, unable to assimilate those cases, end up excluding them or constructing explanations for their peculiarities which border on racism. It is thus instructive, for instance, to establish what some of these theories thought of what they called 'unimproving' or 'backward' nations. Through these analyses a particular way of constructing the 'other' can be detected.

According to most political economists, colonialism was necessary in order to help backward nations to break away from their old patterns of stagnation and bring about progress. J. B. Say, for instance, distinguished 'enlightened nations' possessing a 'superior civilization' from 'savage nations' possessing an 'inferior civilization'. The individuals of the latter were rather passive and resigned, had a marked preference for leisure and were incapable of any rational reflection and scientific activity. The enlightened European countries had the duty and the right to help the savage nations to become civilized.[21] Malthus in his turn clearly preferred British rule to Iberian colonialism, which he accused of cruelty, violence, maladministration and other vices,[22] but he was equally critical of the indolence, ignorance and improvidence of the South American Indians. These bad habits were fostered by the natural richness and fertility of the soil in those countries. The easier it was to make a living, the greater was the tendency to leisure.[23] According to J. S. Mill, backward societies had a very weak 'effective desire' to accumulate, to work harder and to save. Like Malthus he attributed this lack of motivation to the favourable natural conditions which generated the development of only limited needs in the population.

Similarly, in his *History of British India*, James Mill took the view that India, China and other Asiatic societies were uncivilized by comparison with Britain. In describing the moral character of Indians and Chinese he maintained that 'both nations are to nearly an equal degree tainted with the vices of insincerity; dissembling, treacherous, mendacious, to an excess which surpasses even the usual measure of uncultivated society.'[24] David Ricardo, impressed by Mill's account, wrote to him exclaiming: 'What a frightful obstruction to improvement does the immoral character of the people of India present!'[25] The only possibility of changing this picture was, for Mill, the benign and enlightened tutelage of Europeans, even if they had to resort to some form of authoritarianism.

In his *Lectures on the Philosophy of World History*, Hegel described South America as 'physically and spiritually impotent', a place where 'even the animals show the same inferiority as the human beings', who, in their turn, are considered to be 'obviously unintelligent individuals with little capacity for education'. 'Their inferiority in all respects, even in stature, can be seen in every particular' – for instance, in Paraguay 'a clergyman used to ring a bell at midnight to remind them to perform their matrimonial duties, for it would otherwise never have occurred to them to do so.' The natives are compared to 'unenlightened children, living from one day to the next, and untouched by higher thoughts or aspirations'; they inhabit a world where events 'are but an echo of the Old World and the expression of an alien life'.[26] The Latin American Creoles descended from the Spanish conquerors did not fare any better in Hegel's description. Their character was linked to that of the Spanish:

> Living far away from the mother country on which they depended, they had more scope to indulge their arbitrary inclinations. . . . The noble

and magnanimous aspects of the Spanish character did not accompany
them to America. The Creoles, who are descended from the Spanish
immigrants, lived on in the presumptuous ways they had inherited,
and behaved in an arrogant manner towards the natives.[27]

What in the classical political economists was a mere pragmatic
argument about the flaws of character and the necessary dependence
of non-European nations became in Hegel an important distinction
which underpinned his philosophy of history and influenced authors
as different as Schelling and Marx. In effect, in his *Lectures on the
Philosophy of World History*, Hegel distinguished between world-
historical peoples, who were culturally developed and capable of
building a strong state, thus contributing to the progress of world
history, and peoples without history, who were spiritually weak and
unable to build a strong state, thus having no civilizing mission to
carry out in history. The latter had to submit to the former. Thus, for
instance, China represented for Hegel a stationary nation which did
not contribute to the progress of world history. His description of
South America clearly shows that for him it had no autonomous role
to play in the development of the human spirit either; and that, on the
contrary, it constituted a world where events were a mere echo of
the Old World.

It is rather surprising to find that Marx's systematic critique of Hegel
and of classical political economy did not really include a specific
critique of their views about backward societies. On the contrary, it is
possible to argue that, somehow, Marx and Engels shared with them
the belief in the world mission of European capitalism, and that, in the
course of their historical analyses, they occasionally showed similar
prejudices as well. Hegel's remarks on the Latin American Creoles
seemed to have been closely followed by Marx when comparing the
Mexicans with the Spaniards:

> the Spaniards are completely degenerated. But in the presence of a
> Mexican a degenerated Spaniard constitutes an ideal. They have all the
> vices, arrogance, thuggery and quixotism of the Spaniards to the third
> degree, but by no means all the solid things that they possess.[28]

It is not usually known, for instance, that at an early stage in their
careers Marx and Engels condoned the forcible subjection of backward nations for the sake of progress. Thus for Engels the conquest
of Algeria by the French was 'an important and fortunate fact for
the progress of civilization' as it was also fortunate that 'magnificent
California was snatched from the lazy Mexicans, who did not know

what to do with it'.[29] 'It constitutes progress', Engels writes, 'that a country torn apart by perpetual civil wars and prevented from all development . . . that such a country be thrown by means of violence into the historical movement. It is in the interest of its own development that Mexico will be in the future under the tutelage of the United States.'[30]

Contrary to the consistently optimistic view of classical political economy which emphasizes the civilizing mission of capitalist expansion and colonialism throughout the world, Marx and Engels changed their position from a positive assessment of colonialism (for instance, in the case of India[31]) towards a more pessimistic and critical view after 1860 (for instance, their views on Ireland). Marx's early optimistic vision that colonial capitalism, even against its avowed intentions, could not but 'create the material basis of the new world'[32] gave way to a more cautious approach which was aware of the possibility that imperialist countries might succeed in keeping colonies in their rural backwardness. However, this crucial change of perspective did not seem to affect their references to Latin American nations, which followed a different pattern. Marx and Engels did not extend to Latin America the new thoughts they developed on Ireland and Asia after 1860, and abstained from any class analysis of that region's social and political processes.

If in the case of Ireland but not Latin America Marx and Engels changed their minds and argued against colonialism, it is not so much because they saw important differences between the Irish and the Latin American nations themselves (for instance, the idea that the Irish could develop a state whereas the Latin Americans could not) as because they saw these countries playing different roles in relation to the prospects of revolution in the most developed countries. Whereas in the case of Mexico they saw its submission as crucial for the strengthening of North American capitalism and hence for the development of the proletariat in that area, in the case of Ireland they saw its independence as crucial for the development of the English proletariat. In either case, it was the emancipation of the proletariat of the more developed nation that mattered. Marx's change of heart in respect of colonialism must therefore be qualified in that it did not necessarily mean that all former colonies have the chance to constitute themselves as viable and developing nations.

A review of Marx and Engels's writings on Latin American nations shows that they are not treated as entities with their own specificity, worth investigating in themselves. The context is frequently negative in that it tends to portray the character of Latin Americans as inherently flawed and their political processes as lacking all rationality and historical direction. For instance, Marx's biography of Simón Bolívar, the Venezuelan hero of Latin American independence, depicts him as a miserable, brutal and cowardly scoundrel.[33] This kind of abuse not only is unfortunate but also reduces the Latin American independence process to a story of personal betrayal, envy and cowardice without any analysis of the social forces operating behind the process. To this treatment of Bolívar one should add the more disturbing references to the Latin American character. Thus the Mexicans are said to be 'lazy', and to share 'the vices, arrogance, thuggery and quixotism' of the Spaniards. Even when Marx and Engels celebrated the Mexican victory over the French in May 1862, they still could not refrain from referring to the victorious Mexicans as 'les derniers des hommes'.[34] This type of abusive remark was used by Marx and Engels to refer to other backward nationalities and countries: the Montenegrins were labelled 'cattle robbers', the Bedouins were branded as a 'nation of robbers' and there was a reference to the 'hereditary stupidity' of the Chinese. But, of course, the fact that the Latin Americans were not singled out for attack does not justify the use of this kind of language.

However, I do not think that the use of abusive language, unacceptable as it is, constitutes the central issue. The main issue has to do with the fact that, even after Marx and Engels changed their approach and became critical of colonialism in the 1860s, Latin America continued to be neglected and its basic social processes tended to be regarded as arbitrary and irrational occurrences. How can this be explained? On the one hand the Hegelian influence seems quite clear: Marx and Engels considered Latin American nations as peoples without history, unable to construct autonomous civil societies and stable states. On the other hand I believe they shared with Hegel and classical political economists a form of ethnocentrism which Jürgen Habermas has characterized as the reduction of the complexity of reason to its cognitive-instrumental dimension. Because this dimension had been privileged in the modernization of Europe, they had a tendency to assess other cultures only in terms of their effective use of instrumental reason. Hence the inability to see and explain the specificity of other societies in their own terms, not as instances or failures of a supposedly universal rational pattern. This is clearly an ideological feature of such theories. True, Marx made the critique of political economy and of Hegel, but he was deeply influenced by their views and shared with them the typical nineteenth-century concern with the emancipation of humankind.

Not surprisingly the three approaches proposed different subjects which could accomplish that emancipating mission: the universal spirit for Hegel; the bourgeoisie for political economists; the proletariat for Marx. Apart from the common desire for emancipation and the search for a subject which could accomplish the mission, it is possible to detect another common element: the emancipating subjects happen to be historically and geographically located in the nineteenth century and in western Europe. For Hegel it is the Spirit as it manifests itself through the primacy of historical nations, among which the Prussian state has pride of place; for classical political economy it is the bourgeoisie as the representative of Britain, the first capitalist nation; for Marx and Engels it is the proletariat of Britain. The emancipating subjects may be different but they all represent the highest stage of historical reason as it is given in western Europe, and it is from there that they should carry out their mission. This is another aspect of Eurocentrism: the belief that the progress brought about by these new historical subjects in western Europe is inherently superior and has a historical mission which must finally prevail in the world. This common missionary conception is ideological. It first justified colonialism and continues to be at the basis of some of the problems all these theories have in understanding Third World societies.

Reason and Racism

What is it within the Enlightenment which allows such constructions of the other as the ones I have shown above? The problem is deep and goes back to the rise of instrumental reason in connection with the first enlightened philosophies. As Edward Said has pointed out, there is a close connection between the empiricism of Hume and Locke and racism.[35] One can certainly find in David Hume blatantly racist passages. See, for instance, the following:

> I am apt to suspect the negroes and in general all the other species of men (for there are four or five different kinds) to be naturally inferior to the whites. There never was a civilised nation of any other complexion than white, nor even any individual eminent either in action or speculation. No ingenious manufactures amongst them, no arts, no sciences. On the other hand, the most rude and barbarous of the whites, such as the ancient GERMANS, the present TARTARS, have still something eminent about them, in their valour, form of government, or some other particular. Such a uniform and constant difference could not happen, in so many countries and ages, if nature had not made an original distinction betwixt these breeds of men. Not to mention our colonies, there are NEGRO slaves dispersed all over EUROPE, of which none ever discovered

any symptoms of ingenuity; tho' low people, without education, will start up amongst us, and distinguish themselves in every profession. In JAMAICA indeed they talk of one negroe as a man of parts and learning; but 'tis likely he is admired for very slender accomplishments, like a parrot, who speaks a few words plainly.[36]

John Locke, in his turn, makes a point of supporting slavery by means of a convoluted argument:

having by his fault forfeited his own life by some act that deserves death, he to whom he has forfeit it may, when he has him in his power, delay to take it, and make use of him to his own service; and he does him no injury by it. For, whenever he finds the hardship of his slavery outweigh the value of his life, it is in his power, by resisting the will of his master, to draw on himself the death he desires. This is the perfect condition of slavery, which is nothing else but the state of war continued between a lawful conqueror and a captive.[37]

The question arises whether there are any specific connections between this kind of racism and the modern philosophical presuppositions from which these philosophers started. Several authors have tried to prove that connection, especially between empiricism and racism. One can cite here Max Horkheimer and more recently H. M. Bracken. Horkheimer provides the basic argument with his distinction between subjective and objective reason.[38] His argument is that the philosophers of the Enlightenment attacked religion and metaphysics in the name of reason but ended up destroying reason itself. Religious and metaphysical systems were based on objective reason: a principle inherent in reality which is concerned with the goodness, hierarchy and desirability of ends and purposes. Modern philosophers attacked objective reason in the name of subjective reason: a faculty or instrument of human beings which is concerned with finding appropriate means to an end. Reason is formalized: it is no longer concerned with ends or the desirability of purposes; it is only concerned with means. Objective reason was attacked as dogmatic and authoritarian. Subjective reason brings about tolerance and respect for different positions, whose validity and desirability cannot be decided by science.

However, the idea of tolerance is ambivalent. On the one hand it means freedom from dogmatic authority; on the other, 'it furthers an attitude of neutrality towards all spiritual content, which is thus surrendered to relativism.'[39] The domination of subjective reason means the domination of self-interest; it also means that crucial principles such as tolerance, freedom and equality can no longer be justified by principles of objective reason and therefore lose their intellectual foundation. Subjective reason or science cannot decide that a value is better than its opposite. Once the philosophical grounding of values on objective reason has disappeared, any party or group can argue that certain values are good for them but not for others, and nobody can oppose an argument based on reason. The more the concept of reason becomes instrumental and separated from the idea of a principle inherent in reality, the more it will lend itself to the most blatant lies.[40]

Horkheimer quotes Charles O'Conor, who during the American Civil War argued that 'negro slavery is not unjust; it is just, wise, and beneficent.'[41] It is because subjective reason conforms to anything that it may justify racism and slavery. Subjective reason is unable to adjudicate in issues related to absolute principles, values or morals. Hume expressed this very well when he argued that 'the rules of morality . . . are not conclusions of our reason': 'as long as it is allowed that reason has no influence on our passions and actions, it is vain to pretend that morality is discovered only by a deduction from reason.'[42] He goes on to say that 'reason can never immediately prevent or produce any action by contradicting or approving of it, it cannot be the source of the distinction betwixt moral good and evil, which are found to have that influence. Actions may be laudable or blameable; but they cannot be reasonable or unreasonable. . . . Reason is wholly inactive, and can never be the source of so active a principle as conscience, or a sense of morals.'[43] There can hardly be a clearer example of the total subjectification of reason. The result is that the whole area of morals, falling outside the field of reason, becomes relativized.

Locke in his turn distinguishes several meanings of the world reason: 'sometimes it is taken for true and clear principles: sometimes for clear and fair deduction from those principles: and sometimes for the cause, and particularly the final cause.'[44] However, all of these meanings which can be associated with an objective concept of reason he sets aside to say that 'the consideration I shall have of it here is in a signification different from all of these; and that is, as it stands for a faculty in man, that faculty whereby man is supposed to be distinguished from beasts.'[45] Reason is a faculty at the service of man, an instrument which distinguishes us from animals, but is expressly not conceived as a principle or final cause. One may arrive at final causes or principles through revelation but not through reason. Through reason one can only reach certainty about propositions 'which the mind arrives at by deduction made from such ideas, which it has got by the use of its natural faculties; viz. by sensation or reflection.'[46]

Horkheimer seems to uphold, at least implicitly, a distinction between empiricism and rationalism within modern philosophy. Spinoza and Descartes still upheld reason as autonomous. The empiricists like Locke and Hume, on the contrary, go the other way. Hume rejects the existence of universals and of causal necessity. The mind works only with what the senses and sensual experiences provide. There cannot be universal laws. Knowledge is always particular. Hume's scepticism about universal laws and causal connections affect his conception of human behaviour. In fact the strict empiricist logic leads him to limit the role of reason in socio-historical questions. Social customs, institutions, values and structures are not necessarily reasonable, that is, a product of reason, but may result from forms of behaviour which have been efficient in the past. Hume opposes the human pretension to redesign social reality in a rational way.[47] This allows one to understand how Hume can easily accommodate racism. If there is no such thing as universals, if one cannot generalize, then human beings are different, have different potentialities and fates that must be accepted. There are no such things as universal human rights.

H. M. Bracken has shown something similar in Locke's philosophy. Locke attacked Descartes's doctrine of innate ideas and the Cartesian notion that a substance may have essential properties. Like Hume, he argued that we do not know how a substance is really constituted, and what connections secondary qualities have with it, and that even if we did this would not constitute universal knowledge and would give us only the certainty of an example.[48] According to Bracken, 'it then becomes possible to treat any or no property as essential . . . it becomes more difficult to distinguish men from the other animals.' Rationalism was able to formulate what was essential to humankind: 'In so doing it provided a modest conceptual barrier to treating race, colour, religion, or sex as other than accidental.'[49] It is no wonder, then, that Locke excluded Catholics from the body politic and that, having become a Commissioner of Appeals in 1689 and a founding member of the Board of Trade in 1696, he played a large part in the shaping of the colonial system and the justification of slavery.

Historicism and the Neglect of Unity

I have already argued that the attack on instrumental reason began simultaneously with modernity, as an internal pole of criticism. Contrary to the universalistic and unilinear and unitary conceptions of history, the historicist views emphasized the differences and peculiarities of each culture which could only be understood through a sympathetic communion with the spirit of the people. Historicism is, of course, in the line of relativist, essentialist thought. Each culture has an essence which is basically different and difficult to apprehend without an act of historical sympathy, without the ability to connect with its basic spirit. This inner sympathetic connection with the spirit of a person or people is the purpose of hermeneutics:

> We would not understand either antiquity in general or individual documents and works of art 'if our spirit were not essentially at one with the spirit of antiquity, so that it can absorb into itself this spirit which is only temporally and *relatively* alien'. 'All grasp and understanding not just of an alien world but even of another person is simply impossible without the original unity and a likeness of all spiritual content and without the original unity of all things in the Spirit.'[50]

This effort of understanding requires sacrificing one's own prejudices and narrow points of view and therefore it can easily be construed as the only way of truly recognizing the other as different, not reducing the other to the parameters of one's own culture. The tendency to assess other cultures in terms of one's own culture leads to cultural arrogance. The values and ideals of different cultures are incommensurable and irreducible to one another. This is why there could be no such thing as an ideal society or culture. As J. G. Herder put it, 'the very thought of a superior European culture is a blatant insult to the majesty of Nature.'[51] There are no values which are universally valid. In understanding other cultures moral judgements and comparative assessments of values are useless because there is no common yardstick. All cultures are equally valid. Against the fundamental unity of history, Herder opposed pluralism, which stemmed from the interaction between the singularity of the human spirit and the soil. What gives people a sense of identity is a shared culture mainly manifested in a shared language. Consequent with these principles Herder opposed colonialism and the slave trade. However, Herder not only emphasized cultural diversity, but was also at pains to emphasize the fact that all human beings belonged to one and the same human species and that the very idea of race ought to be rejected:

> But thou, o man, honour thyself: neither the pongo nor the gibbon is thy brother, but the American [Indian] and the Negro *are*. These, therefore thou shouldst not oppress, or murder, or rob; for they are men like thee. . . .
> I should like to express the hope that distinctions that have been made – from a perfectly laudable zeal for scientific exactitude – between different members of the human species will not be carried beyond

bounds. Some, for instance, have thought fit to employ the term *races* for
four or five divisions to regions of origin or complexion. I see no reason
for employing this term. . . . Complexions run into each other; forms
follow the genetic character; and *in toto* they are, in the final analysis,
but different shades of the same great picture.[52]

However, although Herder minimized racial differences, he over-
emphasized cultural differences. For him, every people that spoke a
different language was a different nation entitled to its own identity
and government. The sense of collective identity was so important for
Herder as a way of reaching national happiness that, although he did
not advocate war, he felt that conflicts with other nations might have
at least the positive side of strengthening the internal cohesion, which
in itself was good. In the same vein Herder was not averse to finding
some sense in narrow nationalism and prejudice:

> If, in this development of particular national tendencies towards par-
> ticular forms of national happiness, the distance between the nations
> grows too great, we find prejudices arising. The Egyptian detests the
> shepherd and the nomad and despises the frivolous Greek. Similarly
> prejudices, mob judgement and narrow nationalism arise when the dis-
> positions and spheres of happiness of two nations collide. But prejudice
> is good, in its time and place, for happiness may spring from it. It urges
> nations to converge upon their centre, attaches them more firmly to
> their roots, causes them to flourish after their kind.[53]

These very principles led Herder into the defence of the German nationality and German language as against the encroachments of French
culture. Isaiah Berlin has argued that Herder was an ardent nationalist
but not in a political sense. He did not have dreams of domination and
he abhorred state dictatorships. Herder's nationalism would certainly
have been anti-French, but in a cultural sense: trying to salvage genuine
folk songs and the German language. Herder's freely expressed anti-
French feelings would have been a plea for cultural self-determination.
Still it is difficult not to see some of the worst implications of Herder's
nationalism. I wonder whether it is possible to deny political implications to expressions such as: 'spew out the Seine's ugly slime'; 'Better
Germans, whatever they are, than sham Greeks, Frenchmen, English-
men'; 'awake German nation', etc.[54] Even Isaiah Berlin recognizes that
'this may, indeed, have been the first stage of a development destined
in its later stages to become nationalistic and chauvinistic in the full,
aggressive sense.'[55] This shows that historicism, in overemphasizing
difference, can paradoxically lead to the construction of the other as a
menace, even if it is only in an attempt to safeguard one's own culture.

The justification of cultural apartheid is thus practically provided by such theory.

Berlin has argued that 'Herder was one of the leaders of the romantic revolt against rationalism and faith in the omnipotence of scientific method' and that he 'was a sharp and remorseless critic of the French Enlightenment'.[56] Lukács holds a more moderate view and believes that one should not reduce the historicism of Herder, Vico and Hamann to irrationalism. They did not attack reason and progress, they only looked for the development of reason in history.[57] Lukács is probably right in objecting to the label 'irrationalist' being applied to Herder, but his relativism, essentialism and emphasis on difference ended up in a form of nationalism which sometimes bordered on racism.

F. W. J. von Schelling's philosophy is more clearly one of the first cases of irrationalism which arose in response to the philosophical crisis created by the French Revolution. The irrationalism of Schelling was demonstrated in his idea that knowledge is acquired primarily through intellectual intuition and not through the concepts elaborated by reason. This was shown mainly in art, where intellectual intuition objectified itself. Aesthetics thus became the centre and the method of philosophy, the only way of penetrating the mystery of things-in-themselves. Later in life Schelling began to emphasize more the role of religion and less the role of aesthetics as the core of intuition. Whatever the differences between Herder and Schelling, the latter too ended up supporting racist ideas by the same procedure of overemphasizing difference and discontinuity. In a passage which reminds us of Hegel, Schelling argues thus:

> the human race, far from being a compact and indivisible whole, presents itself as divided into two large masses, in such a way that the human aspect seems to be only on the one side. In effect, one of these parts, the largest, finds itself excluded from the common traditions of the human species, eliminated from history, unable, from the beginning of history, to organize itself in states and peoples or to participate in the progressive work of the human spirit, unable systematically and regularly to enrich human knowledge, foreign to any art which goes beyond instinctive ability.[58]

All this is especially true of the South American and African natives. But, according to Schelling, the South American peoples are gentler and weaker and therefore sooner or later they will disappear, unable to resist the encounter with the Spanish. The human races are fundamentally unequal to the point that common standards of rationality are doubted. Schelling argues that 'differences such as those existing between *Kaffirs, Abyssinians* and *Egyptians* go back into the world of ideas.'[59] To those who might object that such views 'could finally lead to a scientific justification of slavery' Schelling responds with a rather specious argument which unashamedly uses the authority of Bishop Bartolomé de Las Casas, the great Spanish defender of the South American Indians, in order to depict black slavery as a merciful operation to save both the Indians and the black soul:

> it is not because of an evil mind or contempt of men that Las Casas conceived of and carried out the project of replacing in the exploitation of the silver and gold mines the weak American race by the strong and robust African race, a project which has had as a consequence certainly not the black slave trade, because these unfortunate people had already been victims of such trade, and under its most odious form, but the export of blacks which a compassionate spirit could see as the only means of saving this human race abandoned to terrible barbarism and these lost souls almost without hope from eternal death.[60]

Although in a footnote Schelling recognizes that Las Casas was not the first to conceive the project of replacing the Indians by black slaves in the mines, he insists that Las Casas wrote about it in 1517 and that it was from that moment that the black slave trade was organized. That Las Casas entertained such an idea is historically true. However, it is not accurate to say that it was because of his words that the slave trade was organized. When he wrote about this, the slave trade had already started. It is also disingenuous not to make it clear that later Las Casas greatly regretted having proposed such an idea. Be that as it may, Schelling's intention was clearly to justify black slavery. This shows how theories which overrate difference can also fall into racism.

It is easy to believe that racism lies only in not recognizing differences, in not accepting the other as he or she is, with his or her cultural specificities. Relativism and pluralism, therefore, seem to be the answer. What is good for Europeans is not necessarily good for Latin Americans. A truth which goes beyond the accepted cultural uses of a set of values is thus doubted, and pluralism seems to be preferable. If one asserts that some beliefs are justified not simply because they are life habits which enjoy social currency within a certain culture, but because they are based on good reasons, then pluralism goes out of the window and racism seems to creep in. I recall that viewpoint being put forward in a television programme: if one wants to uphold ethical values, then one will be a racist, because one will not tolerate other people's mistaken values. There seems to be an opposition between ethics and pluralism, between truth and good ethnic relations.

But this is only an appearance, not a real paradox which necessarily makes truth incompatible with an acceptance of the other. It is not the case that one is supposed to choose between racism and the belief in truth. In fact, I would contend that there is a deeper form of racism involved in cultural relativism. The absolute denial of a common truth and of universal values may easily lead to the denial of a shared nature among the participants of incommensurable cultures. From here it is only a small step to racism which takes the form of constructing the other as absolutely different, as having different (and usually inferior) standards of humanity. This form of racism masked as pluralism has been revealed by Edward Said to appear in expressions used by H. A. R. Gibbs, for whom 'the orientals have never understood the meaning of self-government the way "we" do', so 'to apply the psychology and mechanics of Western political institutions to Asian or Arab situations is pure Walt Disney.'[61]

Something similar was said to me by a well-meaning Englishwoman: democracy is all right for us Britons who have stable and moderate personalities, but when it comes to the passions of the Latin character you need dictators or authoritarian regimes to cope – democracy will not work in your part of the world. This is a more profound form of racism: it is to say that certain peoples cannot reach the same degree of rationality that others have; that they are too different. This example is repeated in education when, instead of preparing students from ethnic minorities for what is thought to be the standard for the majority of children, it is argued that they need other subjects which go better with their specific culture but which, if pursued to the exclusion of the official ones, will irrevocably handicap their future chances in society. The question has been well expressed by Said:

> Can one divide human reality, as indeed human reality seems to be genuinely divided, into clearly different cultures, histories, traditions, societies, even races, and survive the consequences humanly? By surviving the consequences humanly, I mean to ask whether there is any way of avoiding the hostility expressed by the division, say, of men into 'us' (Westerners) and 'they' (Orientals). For such divisions are generalities whose use historically and actually has been to press the importance of the distinction between some men and some other men, usually towards not especially admirable ends.[62]

For some ethnic minorities in Britain this question does not seems to be easy to answer in one direction because they want to be respected in their difference, they are proud to be different, they do not want to be assimilated to the mainstream culture, but at the same time do not want to be discriminated against or regarded as inferior because of that. The point seems to be that neither total identity nor total difference can guarantee the construction of a truly equal other. As Tzvetan Todorov has put it, 'we want an equality which does not necessarily entail identity, but also a difference, which does not degenerate into superiority/inferiority.'[63] In respect of this ideal the two main discourses co-existent in modernity present some dangers. If rationalistic theories have the danger of ethnocentrism (lack of respect for otherness), totalitarianism (lack of respect for difference), universalism (lack of respect for spatial and local specificities) and ahistoricism (lack or respect for historical and temporal specificities), historicism has the danger of racist particularism (overemphasizing difference), essentialism (cultural identity as an immutable spirit), relativism (truth becomes impossible) and irrationalism (attack on reason).

2

Ideology and the Assault on Reason

Introduction

From almost the very beginning of modernity the contradictions and irrationalities of bourgeois society began to erode the excessive con fidence in reason and to foster doubts about the possibilities of emancipation. Thus some currents of thought emerged, especially during the nineteenth century, which were sceptical about the supremacy of reason and which emphasized the role of irrational factors in social life. Irrationalism was therefore a response both to the optimistic bourgeois belief in reason and to the new socialist world-view of progress and emancipation. The suspicions about religion, metaphysics and the political ideas of freedom and equality fostered by the market were then transposed into suspicions about reason and its elaborate schemes which tend to conceal the real irrational forces which mobilize human beings. Thus there emerges a new kind of ideology critique which wants to unmask the passions and power drives which are disguised with a veneer of logic by reason.

In this chapter I shall discuss some irrationalist theories, starting with the relativist and pessimist philosophies of Schopenhauer and Nietzsche and ending with the more contemporary attack on reason propounded by Critical Theory. The importance of these theories, among other things, is that they prepare the terrain for the emergence of postmodernism as one of the main intellectual tendencies of the late twentieth century. These theories show that the critique of reason started very early and forms part of the very process of modernity. To the extent that postmodernism is only the last of, and has been influenced by, a series of irrationalist theories which go back to the eighteenth century, it can hardly claim a total rupture with modernity.

Lukács has argued that irrationalism is a form of reaction (reaction in the double sense of a secondary and retrograde phenomenon) tied up with major crises in the development of capitalism.[1] Thus the first period of irrationalism cropped up in the wake of the French Revolution – almost simultaneously with the emergence of the concept of ideology – and the second evolved in the context of the Paris Commune. Whereas the first period basically opposes bourgeois rationalism, the second sees a greater threat in the totalitarian rationalism of communism. The logic of the argument can be extended to subsequent crises within the capitalist world, like the First World War and the Russian Revolution, the Second World War and finally, May 1968 in France and the continuous recessions of the late 1970s, 1980s and 1990s. The latter seem to justify Fredric Jameson's idea that postmodernism is the cultural logic of late capitalism.[2] Although I am not going to try to establish a close and mechanical relationship between specific forms of irrationalism and particular capitalist crises, it is important to keep in mind that there is a connection between the two.

The Supremacy of the Will: Schopenhauer

Whereas most materialist philosophies of modernity influenced by the French Revolution and increasing bourgeois ascendancy are critical of religion in the name of reason, the novelty of Arthur Schopenhauer's philosophy is that he separates the critique of religion from trust in reason. In fact he attacks both the religious conception of the world and the rationalistic view of human nature. In doing so he inaugurates a line of thought which will culminate in Nietzsche. For these authors the opposition between science and ideology ceases to have any major significance, and reason itself becomes suspect as the source of distortions. But in order for this suspicion to be possible the role of reason must be downgraded. This process begins by emphasizing both the distinction between intellect and will and the more important role of the latter. Thus Schopenhauer relates the distinction between idea and will to the Kantian distinction between thing-in-itself and phenomenon. Ideas or representations constitute the world of phenomena, whereas the will is the thing-in-itself.[3] He wants to redress the balance between intellect and will which other philosophies had misunderstood. Human beings are governed not by their reason but by their will:

The will is always the primary fact in our consciousness and always maintains pre-eminence over the intellect, which is a secondary thing, subordinate and conditioned. . . . This needs to be demonstrated all the more, since all philosophers who have preceded me, from the first to the last, make the essence and somehow the centre of man consist in cognitive consciousness.

My philosophy is the first which has come to place the essence of man, not in consciousness, but in the will, which is not necessarily linked with consciousness. The will is to consciousness, that is to say knowledge, what the substance is to its accident, what light is to the illuminated object.[4]

The will is the primary and most essential force in the world. Its existence does not depend on knowledge, and this is shown by the fact that it is present in every blind force of nature and in all animal behaviour where it manifests itself as a 'vague and dark impulse'. The will is accompanied by intellect only in human beings, and even there it works blindly in all those bodily functions which are not controlled by consciousness. However, in its superior stages the will 'necessitates knowledge as an auxiliary indispensable for the maintenance of the individual and the propagation of the species'.[5] Knowledge and reason are conceived, then, as instruments or tools of the will which are needed to compensate for the disadvantage of the will's multiplicity of functions. Paradoxically, the presence of reason, much as it is necessary for life in its superior stages, determines also that the infallible security of the will is lost: 'Rational knowledge produces hesitation, uncertainty, error, which are obstacles to an adequate objectification of the will in acts. With reason the manifestation of the will could be falsified by error, by making apparent motives occupy the place of the true ones.'[6]

This means that knowledge can affect the efficiency of the will but, more importantly, that the operation of the will impairs our ability to know the truth. In so far as the will is 'an unconscious, blind and irresistible impulse', knowledge cannot disturb its decisions, but, by providing wrong information and data, it makes it possible for the actual action not to coincide with the will.[7] On the other hand, Schopenhauer argues:

the intelligence cannot perform its functions with clarity and exactitude unless the will remains mute and tranquil; all sensuous agitation of the will perturbs the intellectual functioning and such intrusion falsifies the results . . . the intellect, which by nature always tends towards truth, has to coerce itself and accept as true things which are not true or credible, or sometimes not possible; all that in order to amuse, calm down and make sleep the will. There you can see who is the master and who is the servant.[8]

In other words, reason, as a servant of the will, is polluted by the decisions of the will; it is frequently forced to provide the wrong or illusory motives for such decisions, but always afterwards. The intelligence cannot fully penetrate the decisions of the will; it can only provide motives and justifications *a posteriori*. Schopenhauer seeks to prove this assertion by showing how we experience this phenomenon in our daily lives:

> Love and hate entirely falsify our judgements; we see only defects in our enemies, excellence in those we love. . . . A similar influence is exercised over our judgement by our interests, whatever class they are; what is opposed to our interest we judge unjust and abominable. Hence all prejudices (class, professional, sects, religion). Any cherished hypothesis provides us with clear eyes to see everything that confirms it and turns us blind to all that opposes it. Our intelligence allows itself to be fascinated and hallucinated by the phantom of our inclinations.[9]

Hence, although reason is an indispensable instrument of the will in the maintenance of individual life and the propagation of the species, it has three important limitations. First, it cannot fully apprehend the essence of things, and is confined to the world of appearances where it can only perceive the outward relationships between things. Substances, the inner being of things, are beyond its grasp. Second, as the will is by definition the thing-in-itself, it follows that reason cannot really apprehend it. Third, although reason is inherently bent on truth, it is primarily an instrument of the will and as such it is also frequently deceived by the will and deflected from its aim, which is truth. As we have seen, primary interests from the will turn knowledge into prejudice, force the intellect to produce masks, to provide the wrong motives for actions. This is necessary because 'life is continuous pain'[10] and the will has to take harsh decisions; nobody would want to go on living if the will did not force reason to conceal that basic cruelty or, at least, did not dress that pain up as hope. Hope, Schopenhauer avers, 'consists in the will forcing intelligence, when it has not provided the desired object, to present at least its image, performing the role of consoler, as the nanny calms down the child, narrating tales which offer an appearance of truth.'[11]

Thus the third limitation points in the direction of a critical notion of ideology in the double sense of a distortion which seduces to life. First ideology is produced by reason as a consoler, as a narcotic, as a means to alleviate the pain of existence. Second, in ideology the results of knowledge are falsified by passions, interests, inclinations, drives – in sum, all the possible manifestations of the will. This implicit concept of ideology has some affinity with Bacon's theory of idols, in spite of the fact that Bacon never identified a common source of idols in the will: in both cases reason can reach the truth provided the idols or the will are quiet. However, whereas Bacon was optimistic that human beings could control the idols which crop up in the mind, Schopenhauer is rather pessimistic in his view that intelligence can never control the will. All reason can aim at is to be not affected by the will, to emancipate itself temporarily from its influence. Only exceptionally, 'in the perception of beauty, aesthetics, in the genius, we reach a state of consciousness entirely emancipated from the will, pure consciousness.'[12] This means that objective knowledge, free from deceptions, can only be attained when intellectual activity is at its highest level. This can only happen with geniuses. Schopenhauer argues:

> The form of knowledge in the genius is free from the will. When the intelligence is capable of escaping the will, sublime works can be produced. This can only happen once in a while. Mediocrity consists, substantially, in the fact that the intelligence, still too dependent on the will, works at the behest of the will, being therefore entirely at its service.[13]

If reason, even exceptionally, can reach the truth when the urges of the will are totally passive, it can presumably also uncover the false motives, lies and prejudices which are normally its own doing. It can even arrive, as Schopenhauer does, at the conclusion that reason is merely a tool of the will. But here an obvious problem arises: how can a mere instrument of the will become totally detached in order not only to criticize ideological deceptions but also to recognize its own servitude? At bottom, there is a contradiction between a conception of reason as a mere tool at the service of the will to life, and a conception of reason which can reach the truth when the will to life does not interfere. Either the will to life is true to itself and cannot cease to intervene, or reason is more than a servant of the will. Schopenhauer's theory is not only generally pessimist in respect of life and its many difficulties but also, when it is able to conceive a ray of hope, profoundly elitist and aristocratic. Only geniuses and great artists can escape the rule of the will to reach the truth. For the rest of mortals, mediocrity seems to be the fate.

Lukács has made the point that Schopenhauer introduces such a radical separation between essence and appearance, between phenom-enon and noumenon, that all relation of theory to praxis or human activity must appear as a dishonouring of theory. Proper theory must therefore be pure contemplation.[14] It is in this respect that the ideo-logical character of Schopenhauer's philosophy comes to the fore. Its general pessimism and elitism foster acceptance and resignation; all social activity is regarded as senseless, and therefore there is no point in any effort to change society. As Lukács puts it, pessimism means primarily a philosophical rationale of the absurdity of all political activity.[15] However, it is important to highlight the fact that the ideological mechanism in the philosophy of Schopenhauer is more sophisticated than the usual. He does not simply conceal and deny the contradictions of society; he starts from them, but displaces their meaning. Instead of being a problem which stems from capitalism and which could be overcome by means of political action, such contradic-tions are explained away as the general condition of all existence. The misunderstanding of the contradictions as a natural consequence of life denies the possibility of their resolution.

The Will to Power: Nietzsche

Friedrich Nietzsche was certainly influenced by Schopenhauer in his attack on reason, but he rejected Schopenhauer's view that the intel-lect could reach the truth so long as the will remained passive, a rare but not impossible situation which geniuses could achieve. This meant that for Schopenhauer, although ideology was produced by the intel-lect, the real cause of it was the polluting interference and the impo-sition of the will. For Nietzsche this is an illusion:

> To win back for the man of knowledge the right to great affects! after self-effacement and the cult of objectivity have created a false order of rank in this sphere, too. Error reached its peak when Schopenhauer taught: the only way to the 'true', to knowledge, lies precisely in getting free from affects, from will; the intellect liberated from will cannot but see the true, real essence of things.[16]

There still was in Schopenhauer a thinly disguised critique of the will and of passions and affects as interfering and polluting. There still was an obvious nostalgia for the value of truth which was the proper object of the intellect. For Nietzsche, on the contrary, the problem did not reside in a polluting will, nor did he believe in truth as the main purpose of reason. That is why, with Nietzsche, the sharpness of the irrationalist stand is accentuated, leading to an even more critical concept of ideology. In the first place one finds an extensive critique of knowledge, consciousness, logic, the formal categories of reason, science and truth. For Nietzsche all of them are servants, tools for the preservation of life, which is conceived as will to power. The will to power seeks to control and to dominate for the sake of life; it is not interested in universal truth. To that extent Nietzsche is suspicious of the validity claims of all forms of knowledge and of truth itself, which becomes not a question of reason but a question of power. Nietzsche rejects the categories of 'pure reason', 'absolute spirituality' and 'knowledge in itself', and propounds a conscious relativism. Advancing the concept of perspective which Karl Mannheim will later develop in his 'sociology of knowledge', Nietzsche proposes that 'There is *only* a perspective seeing, *only* a perspective "knowing".'[17]

Knowledge is an instrument, a tool to be used in the enhancement of life. Its origins 'can be traced back to a drive to appropriate and conquer',[18] so truth cannot be its main objective. In terms of maintaining life, a falsity could be as important as or more important than a truth. Nietzsche argues that 'the utility of preservation – not some abstract-theoretical need not to be deceived – stands as the motive behind the development of the organs of knowledge.'[19] In fact, life requires false values which 'cannot be eradicated by reasons'.[20] Nietzsche maintains that 'the falsest opinions . . . are the most indispensable to us . . . the renunciation of false opinions would be a renunciation of life, a negation of life.'[21] On the other hand, some 'truths' can be 'in the highest degree injurious and dangerous' so that 'the strength of a mind might be measured by . . . the extent to which it *required* truth attenuated, veiled, sweetened, damped, and falsified.'[22]

Consciousness, in its turn, is treated as a late development in the evolution of the organic system which emerges out of a communicative necessity within the herd but which is not really a part of the individual human being. As such it is the source of many errors and deceptions which might even lead to death were it not by the fact that other essential human instincts are more powerful.[23] In fact Nietzsche argues that 'the increase in consciousness is a danger'[24] and that the animal functions are 'a million times more important' than consciousness. The latter is a surplus, except when it serves as a tool of the animal functions.[25] The problem is that, 'instead of understanding consciousness as a tool and particular aspect of the total life, we posit it as the standard and the condition of life.'[26] The same can be said of logic and the categories of reason. Nietzsche castigates as an aberration of philosophy the fact that, instead of seeing in them 'means toward the adjustment of the world for utilitarian ends (basically, toward an expedient *falsification*), one believed one possessed in them the criteria of truth and *reality*.'[27] For Nietzsche, 'the illogical is a necessity for mankind' and 'much good proceeds from the illogical.'[28]

As for truth, Nietzsche argues that, on the one hand, it is a kind of inertia, a 'hypothesis that gives rise to contentment'[29] because people normally believe that it is there to be found. Once found, truth is supposed to eliminate ignorance and error, but as a result 'the will to examination, investigation, caution, experiment is paralysed' and the forces that work towards enlightenment and knowledge are cut off.[30] Truth, Nietzsche argues, is 'not something there, that might be found or discovered – but something that must be created'.[31] On the other hand, truth is not the antithesis of error; rather, humanity's truths are ultimately its irrefutable errors.[32] Nietzsche argues that in fact 'our organism is made for the contrary of truth.'[33] Yet he also maintains that 'truth is the kind of error without which a certain species of life could not live.'[34] The need for this particular kind of error stems from the requirements of preserving life and growth. This is not contradictory because it does not mean that 'something *is* true': 'what is needed is that something is held to be true.'[35] The instrumentality of truth for life is thus reaffirmed. And, since life is will to power, the sources of truth must be sought in power. As Nietzsche puts it, 'the methods of truth were not invented from motives of truth, but from motives of power, of wanting to be superior.'[36] This is why truth can also be described as a weapon of war and an instrument of destruction.[37] Consequently the criterion of truth is described by Nietzsche as residing 'in the enhancement of the feeling of power'.[38]

One would be mistaken to believe that for Nietzsche science could be treated differently or that it could be the cure against ascetic and religious ideals: 'No! Don't come to me with science when I ask for the natural antagonist of the ascetic ideal.'[39] Science cannot escape an ideological character similar to that of religion, since it too 'rests upon faith'.[40] Thus Nietzsche can exclaim, 'oh, what does science not conceal today! how much, at any rate, is it *meant* to conceal! . . . Science as a means of self-narcosis: *do you have experience of that*?'[41] For all its opposition to the ascetic ideal, science shares one essential thing with it, namely the belief in and overestimation of truth: 'that which *constrains* these men [of science], however, this unconditional will to truth, is *faith in the ascetic ideal itself*, even if as an unconscious imperative – don't be deceived about that – it is the faith in a *metaphysical* value, the absolute value of *truth*, sanctioned and guaranteed by this ideal alone.'[42] This makes modern science and ascetic ideals necessary allies.

Nietzsche's point is that the belief in truth is still a metaphysical faith, since it 'affirms another world than that of life, nature, and history'.[43] The value of truth requires justification, but most philosophers do not realize this because 'the ascetic ideal has hitherto *dominated* all philosophy, because truth was posited as being, as God, as the highest court of appeal – because truth was not *permitted* to be a problem.'[44] Consequently, 'the will to truth requires a critique . . . the value of truth must for once be experimentally *called into question*.'[45]

There is, then, in Nietzsche a systematic critique of knowledge and reason which points to a critique of ideology. Knowledge and reason are forms of ideological distortion in three senses. First, they conceal the reality of the world, which is 'false, cruel, contradictory, seductive, without meaning'. Second, they conceal the fact that the preservation of life requires falsification, deception, lies, assault and injury. They hide the fact that *'we have need of lies* in order to conquer this reality. . . . That lies are necessary in order to live is itself part of the terrifying and questionable character of existence.'[46] Third, they pretend to be detached and servants of a universal truth. For Nietzsche this is the greatest error that has ever been committed: 'one believed one possessed a criterion of reality in the form of reason – while in fact one possessed them in order to become master of reality, in order to misunderstand reality in a shrewd manner.'[47]

The ideological errors and deceptions of knowledge play a double role. On the one hand they give us strength to continue to live, they seduce us to life. If life did not inspire confidence, if the terrible nature of a cruel and meaningless reality was not concealed, people would not want to live. This is why, although metaphysics, morality, religion and science are various forms of lies, 'with their help one can have *faith* in life.'[48] This is particularly true of morality:

> It was morality that protected life against despair and the leap into nothing, among men and classes who were violated and oppressed by *men*: for it is the experience of being powerless against men, not against nature, that generates the most desperate embitterment against existence . . . if the suffering and oppressed lost the faith that they have the right to despise the will to power, they would enter the phases of hopeless despair.[49]

This role of reason and morality is also shared with art, because for Nietzsche art is 'the great means of making life possible, the great seduction to life, the great stimulant of life'.[50] On the other hand the ideological nature of reason is also a weapon that can be used to dissemble and deceive others, to defend oneself and to conquer. Even the will to truth 'employs every *immoral* means' at the service of the will to power[51] and can be conceived, as we have already seen, as a weapon of war and an instrument of destruction. The higher one goes in the ranking of living creatures, the bigger the increase in dissimulation.[52] Nietzsche argues that 'a higher and more fundamental value for life generally should be assigned to pretence, to the will to delusion, to selfishness, and cupidity',[53] and that 'in great men, the specific qualities of life – injustice, falsehood, exploitation – are at their greatest.'[54]

In so far as these ideas point to a theory of ideology, they are completed by Nietzsche's specific analysis of morality – more precisely, by his comparison between the master morality and the herd (or slave) morality. The former stems 'from a triumphant affirmation of itself', whereas the latter 'from the outset says No to what is outside, what is different, what is "not itself"; and *this* No is its creative deed.'[55] For Nietzsche the slave morality seems to be a form of ideology in that it entails three kinds of falsification: the opponent is falsified as evil; the slave's own weakness is falsified as virtue; and the natural instinct to dominate is falsified as bad.

First, slave morality requires a necessary reference to an oppressing class (the masters) whose image must be falsified. Just in case one could argue that a similar mechanism of falsification may occur in the aristocratic contempt for the lower class, Nietzsche says that, 'even supposing that the effect of contempt, of looking down from a superior height, *falsifies* the image of that which it despises, it will at any rate be a much less serious falsification than that perpetrated on its opponent – *in effigie* of course – by the submerged hatred, the vengefulness of the impotent.'[56] The reason for this is that the noble man derives his morality from the positive affirmation of himself in action: 'they did not need to establish their happiness artificially by examining their enemies, or to persuade themselves, *deceive* themselves, that they were happy (as all men of *ressentiment* are in the habit of doing); and they likewise knew, as rounded men replete with energy and therefore *necessarily* active, that happiness should not be sundered from action.'[57]

The second type of falsification is an attempt to disguise the slave's impotence as if it was a willed and valuable achievement. Slaves are weak, passive and prudent, 'but this prudence of the lower order which even insects possess . . . has, thanks to the counterfeit and self-deception of impotence, clad itself in the ostentatious garb of the virtue of quiet, calm resignation, just as if the weakness of the weak

– that is to say, their *essence*, their effects, their sole ineluctable, irremovable reality – were a voluntary achievement, willed, chosen, a *deed*, a *meritorious* act.'[58] This is why Nietzsche describes the slave's notion of happiness in very similar terms to those in which Marx described the ideological function of religion: 'as essentially narcotic, drug, rest, peace, "Sabbath", slackening of tension and relaxing of limbs, in short *passively*'.[59] The ideological mechanism of the slave morality seeks to compensate in the mind for the inability of the slaves to change their situation in practice. Slaves, says Nietzsche, 'are denied the true reaction, that of deeds, and compensate themselves with an imaginary revenge.'[60]

Third, slave morality conceals the fact that love and hate, gratitude and revenge, good nature and anger belong together, and that 'one could be good only on condition one also knows how to be evil'.[61] This is the nature of life which slave morality masks and denies by demanding 'that man should castrate himself of those instincts with which he can be an enemy, can cause harm, can be angry, can demand revenge.'[62] In one of the few places where the term ideology is used, Nietzsche describes this one-sided consideration of virtue, this rejection of force, self-assertion and life, as 'sickness and ideological unnaturalness', as an 'ideology of good and evil', and maintains that 'there has never before been a more dangerous ideology'.[63] It is so dangerous because it constitutes 'an opposition movement against the efforts of nature to achieve a higher type. Its effect is: mistrust of life in general . . . hostility towards the senses . . . degeneration and self-destruction of "higher natures", because it is precisely in them that the conflict becomes conscious.'[64]

While for Marx ideology clearly served the interest of the ruling class and helped in the domination of the subjected classes, for Nietzsche ideology, this 'false valuation' present in slave morality, seems to be against the higher types and aimed at the interests of the subjected, of the herd. First, because it protects life against despair: 'if the suffering and oppressed lost the faith that they have the right to despise the will to power, they would enter the phases of hopeless despair.'[65] Second, because it helps 'to deny the most splendid and best-constituted men' and aids 'the subjected to their rights against their conquerors'.[66] This is why Nietzsche opposes it as a sickness which brings about 'universal dishonesty', as a cancer that denies life and can corrode even the best men. In fact, against Darwin's optimistic view that natural selection works in favour of the stronger types, Nietzsche maintains that even 'the strongest and most fortunate are weak when opposed by organized herd instincts' and that the values of the herd have had the upper hand.[67] However, Nietzsche is far too clever not to realize that on the other hand.

> a doctrine and religion of 'love', of *suppression* of self-affirmation, of patience, endurance, helpfulness, of co-operation in word and deed, can be of the highest value within such classes, even from the point of view of the rulers: for it suppresses feelings of rivalry, of *ressentiment*, of envy – the all too natural feelings of the underprivileged – it even deifies a life of slavery, subjection, poverty, sickness, and inferiority for them under the ideal of humility and obedience. This explains why the ruling classes (or races) and individuals have at all times upheld the cult of selflessness, the gospel of the lowly, the 'God on the cross'.[68]

Slave morality as ideology is not only a distortion, a falsification in the three senses already shown, it is also a form of 'bad conscience'. That is to say, from the moment man entered society, when he could no longer freely prowl, attack, conquer and destroy as his drives urged him, then he was reduced to consciousness, since 'all instincts that do not discharge themselves outwardly *turn inward*. . . . Hostility, cruelty, joy in persecuting, in attacking, in change, in destruction – all this turned against the possessors of such instincts: *that* is the origin of the "bad conscience".'[69] One can see the impact of this position on Freud's theories a few years later. Nietzsche even speaks of 'the gravest and uncanniest illness, from which humanity has not yet recovered, man's suffering *of man, of himself* – the result of a forcible sundering from his animal past.'[70]

Slave morality has also its own propagating agents, just as for Marx the bourgeoisie had its own ideologists who perfected the illusions of the class. The ideologists of the herd are the ascetic priests who defend the herd against the beasts of prey. But their defence is not active or revolutionary; rather it consists in altering 'the direction of *ressentiment*', in suggesting means to deaden the pain, in providing relief.[71] To the complaint of the member of the herd that 'I suffer: someone must be to blame for it', the ascetic priest replies: 'quite so, my sheep! someone must be to blame for it; but you yourself are this someone, you alone are to blame for it . . . this is brazen and false enough: but one thing at least is achieved by it, the direction of *ressentiment* is *altered*.'[72] That is to say, *ressentiment* is directed back on the sufferer and by that procedure it renders 'the sick to a certain degree harmless' and safeguards 'the more healthily constituted'.[73] Just as Marx criticized Feuerbach and other left Hegelians because they thought that religion was the problem of humankind and that one could be liberated from it by criticism alone, so does Nietzsche say that the ascetic priest 'combats only the suffering itself, the discomfiture of the sufferer, *not* its cause, *not* the real sickness'.[74]

Nietzsche describes several strategies followed by the ascetic priest which involve an ideological mechanism orientated to combating the feeling of displeasure in the member of the herd: to reduce the feeling of life to its lowest point (abstinence, indifference); mechanical activity, to induce some petty pleasure, for instance, by giving pleasure or doing good or by uniting with others; but the most interesting means of fighting displeasure is 'some kind of an *orgy of feeling* – employed as the most effective means of deadening dull, paralysing, protracted pain'.[75] This orgy of feeling is mainly the feeling of guilt and remorse: 'the invalid has been transformed into "the sinner".' The sinner 'must understand his suffering as a *punishment*.' What the ascetic priest achieves is 'the reinterpretation of suffering as feelings of guilt, fear and punishment'.[76]

So, although for Nietzsche ideology is a sickness that must be combated because it serves the cause of the losers, of the slaves, and is thus against life, the recently quoted passages show a different picture, where the role of ideology differs very little from Marx's assessment of it. Thus Nietzsche seems to be hopelessly trapped in an unresolvable contradiction: on the one hand he must strive to destroy slave morality, to get rid of the sickness of this 'dangerous ideology' in order to liberate life, but on the other, that very morality, that ideology, by redirecting *ressentiment* back on the sufferer, helps secure the triumph of the strong, which is also in accordance with life. Nietzsche oscillates between these two extremes without ever solving the problem or even seeing the paradox. The ambiguity pervades the whole analysis. Slave morality appears as useful for the ruling class because it values the humility and passivity of the slaves, yet at the same time it appears to dissolve the will to power of the ruling class. Nietzsche seeks to liberate life as such from the deceptions of morality, but life itself must mean the triumph of the will to power of the superior races, and deception seems a good instrument for them to prevail. So it seems that Nietzsche is critical of ideology only in so far as it deceives the rulers, but appreciates its value when it deceives the ruled. In this Nietzsche's theory shows both its own ideological character and its inherent ambiguity. Nietzsche proposes a concept of ideology which in practice could serve the interests of both the masters and the slaves, and yet his theory of ideology wants to be useful only to the masters.[77]

This points to a more central problem in Nietzsche's conception. On the one hand Nietzsche denounces the conceptions of morality, reason and science as falsities and errors, but, on the other, in denouncing them and criticizing them as ideological errors, he presupposes the existence of some truth, of some measure which allows him to detect the falsities of their propositions. And yet he denies the validity of all claims to truth in so far as they are governed by the will to power. In other words, he seems to be forced to posit for his own approach a validity that he denies to every other form of knowledge. Reason and science cannot discriminate between truth and error, but Nietzsche's philosophy can. Assuming that this is possible and that there is a difference between Nietzsche and everybody else, how can one reconcile these newly discovered Nietzschean 'truths' with the incessantly reiterated principle that life is much more about falsehoods, deceptions and lies than about truths? It seems as if life is about deceptions but also about Nietzschean truths! Or, in other words, neither all philosophies are errors nor is life only about deceptions! On the other hand, Nietzsche's reduction of the criterion of truth to the usefulness for the survival of the individual, to a matter of power, can only lead to pragmatism and total relativism.

Nietzsche proposes that there is no universal knowledge but 'perspective' knowledges, and various 'truths' governed by the biological interest to prevail. But, if this is so, one can then doubt that the principles of his own philosophy are universally applicable or acceptable. Nietzsche could retort that for him truth is not already made, given, there to be found or discovered, but that it has to be created, made. Ultimately, truth is what powerful men or the master race say it is, what is convenient to their rule, in so far as they have the force to impose it on others. The irony is that Nietzsche himself acknowledges the penetration and the invading expansion of the truth imposed by the herd. The best expression is the advance of democracy in Europe which he sees with dismay. How can one reconcile the fact that the truth ought to be imposed by the master race and yet, in practice, it has been imposed by the herd? In fighting against the decadence and mediocrity of the herd morality in Europe, is he not implicitly having recourse to a higher notion of truth that has not yet been created but must be created by the superman, by the superior types still to come? Before that happens how can he justify it? On what basis can he proclaim the superiority of the master morality if in practice the slave morality has gained the upper hand, much to his regret? Once more Nietzsche shows his reluctance to justify his own presuppositions while attacking everybody else's. In this sense Nietzsche's aristocratic theory of ideology is self-defeating, because its very principles must invalidate his own position.

Is Nietzsche's master morality racist? This is a difficult question to answer. On the one hand Nietzsche repeatedly condemns anti-Semitism and nationalism, and one can see the point of his defenders that at least he should be given the benefit of the doubt. The problem is that, on the other hand, the principles of his philosophy, being based upon an aristocratic conception underpinned by biological factors, seem to involve a kind of implicit and unavoidable racism. In effect, the difference between the lower types and the master race is biological in so far as the latter cannot be formed by 'aristocrats of the spirit', 'a favourite term among ambitious Jews. For spirit alone does not make noble; rather, there must be something to ennoble the spirit. – What then is required? Blood.'[78] Nietzsche even toys with the thought of consciously and artificially breeding a superior type.[79] His theory assumes the right of the master race to create values ('it is the peculiar *right of masters* to create values'[80]) and to label the lower classes as bad and contemptible. More than that, the master race can trample on the lower types and this is justified as life itself. Consider the import of the following passages: 'life itself is *essentially* appropriation, injury, conquest of the strange and weak, suppression, severity, obtrusion of peculiar forms, incorporation and at the least, putting it mildest, exploitation.'[81] 'To speak of just or unjust *in itself* is quite senseless; *in itself*, of course, no injury, assault, exploitation, destruction can be "unjust", since life operates *essentially*, that is in its basic functions, through injury, assault, exploitation, destruction and simply cannot be thought of at all without this character.'[82]

It is inevitable, then, that somebody must be at the receiving end of life. In the creation and rearing of a new master race for Europe, the slaves, the weaklings, strangers, lower individuals – all those at the bottom of the scale in every society – are the natural prey for the 'blonde beast'. Indeed, any progress or advance in history 'can even be measured by the mass of things that had to be sacrificed to it; mankind in the mass sacrificed to the prosperity of a single *stronger* species of man – that *would* be and advance.'[83] People of different races are also, but not the only, members of the mass that have to be sacrificed. One can say that in so far as ethnic minorities form part of the 'other', of the repressed and exploited, they are also despised, they have no rights, and they are, justifiably, the natural objects of cruelty and contempt. Indeed they are described as sick and dangerous: 'The *sick* are man's greatest danger; *not* the evil, *not* the "beasts of prey". Those who are failures from the start, downtrodden, crushed – it is they, the *weakest*, who must undermine life among men, who call into question and poison most dangerously our trust in life.'[84]

If one asks why, Nietzsche will elaborate that it is among them that 'the worms of vengefulness and rancour swarm; here the air stinks of secrets and concealment; here the web of the most malicious of all conspiracies is being spun constantly – the conspiracy of the suffering against the well-constituted and victorious.'[85] What is then to be done? Well, Nietzsche propounds the idea 'that the sick should *not* make the healthy sick' and that, therefore, 'the healthy should be *segregated* from the sick, guarded even from the sight of the sick.'[86] How can one avoid construing this vision as racist, as introducing a kind of social apartheid?

Still, the so-called lower races or ethnic groups are certainly not the only ones to suffer, by necessity, this fate. Nietzsche is much more clear about women. He identifies the increasing respect for women with the same democratic tendency he despises, and which responds to the morality of the herd. For Nietzsche the woman

> is unlearning to *fear* man: but the woman who 'unlearns to fear' sacri-
> fices her most womanly instincts.
>   . . . the 'emancipation of woman', in so far as it is desired and
> demanded by women themselves (and not only by masculine shallow-
> pates) thus proves to be a remarkable symptom of the increased weak-
> ening and deadening of the most womanly instincts. There is *stupidity*
> in this movement.
>   . . . here and there they (some idiotic men) wish even to make women
> into free spirits and literary workers: as though a woman without piety
> would not be something perfectly obnoxious or ludicrous to a profound
> and godless man.
>   . . . she is daily being made more hysterical and more incapable of
> fulfilling her first and last function, that of bearing robust children.[87]

For someone so critical of Catholicism, this coincidence with the Catholic assessment of women's role is quite striking. For Nietzsche women also seem to play an important role in the entertainment of noble men. A noble man is someone who among other things takes his

> delight in women, as in a perhaps smaller but more delicate and ethe-
> real kind of creature. What joy to encounter creatures who have only
> dancing, foolishness, and finery in their heads! They have been the delight
> of every tense and profound male soul whose life was weighed down
> with great responsibilities.[88]

Nietzsche's theory therefore achieves the remarkable feat of being itself profoundly ideological in practically all the dimensions which were mentioned in the first chapter. It not only justifies the domination of the lower classes by affirming the superior right of the masters to rule, it not only seeks to convince the downtrodden that superior right is inherent in life itself and therefore natural; it also manages to follow a similar logic in the case of women and ethnic minorities. In Nietzsche's theory three forms of oppression, class, gender and race, are not only justified but also presented as necessary for life enhancement. Like Schopenhauer, Nietzsche does not deny the existence of problems and contradictions. But he does not just accept them as a sad part of human existence; he salutes them as a requirement of life. The ideological effect of concealment, though, is the same. One can hardly find in Nietzsche any concrete references to the capitalist system as a contradictory system that could be changed.

Residues and Derivations: Pareto

Many elements of the Nietzschean approach are further developed by Vilfredo Pareto in his sociological treatise. The most important principle of Pareto's approach is that irrational behaviour or 'non-logical actions' are more important in society than rational behaviour. Despite this fact, most modern writers like Condorcet, J. S. Mill, Auguste Comte, Herbert Spencer and especially the eighteenth-century philosophers of the French Enlightenment have tended to exaggerate the role of reason and logical actions in society. They did not realize that 'the worship of "Reason", "Truth", "Progress", and other similar entities is, like all cults, to be classed with non-logical actions.'[89] In fact only people influenced by sentiment would only classify theories into true and false.[90] Unlike Nietzsche, though, Pareto considers himself to be a scientist who is not guided by sentiment, who argues strictly on the basis of facts and things, and who offers proofs strictly taken from experience and observation.[91] These two positions obviously need to be reconciled because otherwise he could be accused of blatantly contradicting himself: according to Pareto, truth seems to be a myth, but he claims it for his theory.

In fact Pareto's position is more consistent than it appears at first sight and flows from his very principle that non-logical actions have primacy in society. By necessity, then, truth must have very little space in society. But what about the truth he claims for his own theory? Here Pareto boldly adds three principles that confirm the narrowness of even his own truthful observations and which separate truth from social utility, acceptability and impartiality. The first principle denies that honest and intelligent human beings must accept true propositions. The second rejects the idea that what is true is also socially beneficial. The third principle is that a true theory can be beneficial to certain social classes and detrimental to others.[92] In other words, although Pareto argues that he can make truthful propositions, it does not follow that his theory is good for society or other theories opposed to his are bad for society; it does not follow either that honest, intelligent human beings must accept his theory, or that his theory benefits all classes in society. In this way Pareto can both maintain the truth of his theory and relativize its importance for society in the same way as Hobbes criticized religion as being the product of fear and ignorance but recognized its importance in keeping the commonwealth united.

Side by side with the great extension of non-logical actions in society Pareto detects a systematic effort by most human beings and writers to rationalize them, to present them as rational developments. There are two main reasons for this. First, when it is assumed that human conduct is logical rather than non-logical it is easier to construct a theory about it. Second, many theorists are not only concerned with explaining what is but want also to establish what ought to be, and in this latter field 'logic reigns supreme'.[93] Here is where the critical notion of ideology appears, even though Pareto does not use the term. Ideology would be those efforts to ignore, explain away or conceal non-logical actions. In fighting against those efforts Pareto wants his own theory to become a critique of ideology, an attempt 'to tear off the masks non-logical conduct is made to wear and lay bare the things they hide from view'.[94] In that process Pareto discovers the various ways in which ideology performs its function – for instance, totally disregarding non-logical actions, regarding them as prejudices, regarding them as tricks used by individuals to deceive, and so on.[95] In this way Pareto's theory becomes as well a critique of the critical conceptions of ideology already developed by de Tracy, Holbach, Helvetius and other Enlightenment philosophers who attributed the unhappiness of humankind to religious preconceptions and prejudices, and to the priestly conspiracy which tried to keep the people in ignorance.

The general differentiation between logical and non-logical actions leads Pareto to a more specific distinction between residues and derivations. Residues are 'the manifestations of sentiments and instincts'[96] which in the main are responsible for persuading people to act in a certain way. They are constants in human behaviour which characterize individuals, groups and societies. He mentions six generic types: combinations, persistence of aggregates, the need to express sentiments in external acts, sociality, integrity of the individual, and sex. But combinations and the persistence of aggregates are the really important residues in Pareto's theory. The former denote an ability to innovate, experiment and take risks, whereas the latter denote the ability to do things in fixed and traditional ways. Among the residues of combination Pareto lists the 'hunger for logical developments' which 'explains the need people feel for covering their non-logical conduct with a varnish of logic'.[97] This means that derivations, which are precisely the theories or arguments which try to account in a logical manner for non-logical behaviour, derive their force from sentiments rather than from scientific method. Derivations are always found 'whenever we centre our attention on the ways in which people try to dissemble, change, explain, the real character of this or that mode of conduct'.[98]

According to Pareto, derivations arise out of human hunger for thinking and are to be found in the whole range of actions which exist in between purely instinctive behaviour and experimental science. He distinguishes several types of derivation: assertion, authority, accord with sentiments or principles, and verbal proofs.[99] As a form of ideology, derivations must be avoided by the scientist: 'they are objects for his study, never tools of persuasion.'[100] However, this does not mean that science is more persuasive than derivations. The logician may find the fallacy in an argument, but it is the role of the sociologist to discover why that fallacy is widely accepted. It is a mistake to believe that only logical behaviour is good, worthy and beneficial and that non-logical arguments are bad and harmful. As Pareto puts it, 'we are in no sense intending, in company with a certain materialist metaphysics, to exalt logic and experience to a greater power and majesty than dogmas accepted by sentiment.'[101]

All derivations have a common characteristic: 'the arbitrary use of certain non-experimental entities',[102] that is to say, they are not true in the sense of corresponding to social facts. But their social utility is a different matter and does not depend on their experimental truth. For Pareto the very notion of truth may also be a derivation with multiple meanings. As someone who wants to be a scientist in the 'experimental' sense, he adheres to the classical definition of truth as the correspondence between ideas and facts. But he accepts that truth also signifies 'accord with certain sentiments which carries with it the assent of the believer'[103] and that between this meaning and the former there are many other intermediate meanings. Pareto acknowledges that in spite of being false in the experimental sense some derivations may have a 'higher' truth and social significance than experimental truths. But even if this is so he wants to take the point of view of experimental truth and keep it distinct from any other truths, however, superior they may be.[104]

Just as the concept of truth may be a derivation, there is also a common derivation concerning the relationship between derivations and practice which Pareto describes almost in the same way as Marx described in *The German Ideology* the German philosophers' inversion of the relationship between ideas and practice. The error, Pareto avers, 'lies not only in an inversion of terms in the relationship between derivations and human conduct – the derivation being taken, in general, as the cause of the conduct, whereas really, the conduct is the cause of the derivation – but also in ascribing *objective existence* to derivations proper'.[105]

An interesting consequence of Pareto's theory is that in society the distribution of residues and derivations is not equal between strata.[106] This means that society has a heterogeneous character. From the point of view of the social equilibrium two main groups or classes must be distinguished. On the one hand there is the elite, which in every society is that 'class of people who have the highest indices in their branch of activity' and can be divided into the governing elite and the non-governing elite.[107] On the other hand there is the non-elite, which is a lower stratum made of individuals who score low in their activities. Each class has characteristically distinct combinations of residues and derivations. However, some individuals move from one group to the other, taking with them the sentiments and attitudes of the group from which they came. Most aristocracies tend to decline both numerically and in quality 'in the sense that they lose their vigour, that there is a decline in the proportion of residues which enabled them to win their power and hold it'.[108] Their members are thus replaced by individuals coming from the lower classes who bring new vigour and the right combination of residues. There is then a permanent class circulation, or circulation of elites. If this circulation ceases, then violent revolution erupts.

Most governments will use force to keep themselves in power, but will conceal its use by means of derivations – for instance, the idea that they are based on reason, universal suffrage or any such 'democratic' expedient. These derivations normally express the sentiments and interests of the ruling class. But they are confronted by the derivations which justify the use of force by the governed and condemn the use of force by the authority. Pareto finds revolutions beneficial when the ruling class has become too humanitarian and its group-persistence residues have become so weak that even the independence of the country is put at risk.[109] However, the vigour of the ruling classes does not necessarily consist in their always using the residues of group-persistence which command the use of force. In order to prevent rebellion, ruling classes often resort to persuasion, diplomacy, fraud and corruption, that is to say, the residues of combination are enhanced, whereas the residues of group-persistence are debilitated. The assimilation into the ruling class of talented individuals from the dominated class deprives the latter of its potential leaders and so helps to debilitate its residues of combination. But otherwise it is no use for any government to try to change the sentiments of the people. On the contrary, 'the art of government lies in finding ways to take advantage of such sentiments, not in wasting one's energies in futile efforts to destroy them.'[110]

From here a double assessment of ideology emerges. Whereas the scientist must avoid it at all costs and must use logic, not derivations, to convince, the politician must instead use derivations and not logic in order to convince:

> When the engineer has found the best machine, he has little difficulty in selling it, and even without dispensing with derivations altogether, he can for the most part utilize arguments that are logico-experimental. Not so the statesman. For him the situation is precisely reversed. His main resort must be derivations, oftentimes absurd ones.[111]

It is not that Pareto does not recognize the uses of 'scientific arguments' in politics. Science had already in his time become sufficiently influential for him to realize how useful it could become as a political tool; but, unlike Marcuse or Habermas, Pareto is not talking of science as ideology or the necessary source of ideology. He is talking rather of a derivation, of a non-logical reverential faith in science, not of science itself. This is why he can say that 'progress in the logico-experimental sciences has bred a sentiment of reverence for them, and that sentiment has to be satisfied. But that is not a very difficult task, for the plain man is satisfied if his derivation has a remote, indeed a very remote, semblance of being "scientific".'[112] In this way, Pareto's theory of ideology manages to keep the idea of reason in the field of science, but totally suppresses it in the field of politics. Between these two spheres a dichotomy is thus introduced whereby scientific instrumental reason displaces objective reason from the sphere of politics; and this will become the precise centre of the Frankfurt School's critique of reason. Pareto's theory is itself ideological both in that it naturalizes and conceals the capitalist class system by dissolving it into the theory of elites which are supposed to be necessary in all societies, and in that it justifies the purposeful political deception of the masses by the governing elite.

The Problems of Instrumental Reason: Critical Theory

Nietzsche's critique of reason and morality as ideology became quite an influence on the two main representatives of the Frankfurt School, Theodor W. Adorno and Max Horkheimer. Their approach – 'Critical Theory' – started with a critical vision of the Enlightenment as a totalitarian phenomenon which, in its drive to master nature and liberate human beings from myth, ended up subjecting human beings themselves to the impersonal rule of reified relations. Every success in the demythologization of the world was paid for by a new kind of submission to impersonal forces, by the re-creation of new myths. This new kind of alienation was brought about by instrumental reason, which has permeated science and which reduces everything to technical utility and self-interest. Science thus becomes above all an auxiliary means of economic production and confines its activity to the field of manipulation and reification. The philosophers of the Enlightenment attacked religion and metaphysics in the name of reason but ended up destroying reason itself. Horkheimer describes how reason has been subjectivized and has become concerned only with the manipulation of means, unable to decide whether ends are reasonable. Reason has thus ceased to be autonomous and tends to conform to anything. As he puts it:

> When subjective reason becomes dominant, self-interest becomes paramount, all the principles such as equality, freedom, tolerance, etc. which were founded on principles of objective reason lose their intellectual root and justification. One cannot verify by means of subjective reason (by means of science) that freedom is better than unfreedom. Once the philosophical foundation has disappeared, a group can maintain that freedom is good for them but not for others, that democracy is good as long as it benefits the ruling class but dictatorship is better if it protects those interests in a better way; and there is no possibility of opposing an objection founded on reason.[113]

Marx's critique of capitalism had unmasked new forms of domination which were buttressed by the impersonal and reified appearances of market forces, but he had not blamed reason for them. The bourgeois class system and the exploitative capitalist mode of production, which were the necessary but historical causes of alienation, did not exhaust historical reason. Critical Theory, however, accuses Marx of uncritically accepting the bourgeois reduction of reason to instrumental reason. Horkheimer and Adorno no longer trust Marx's ideology

critique because its very foundation, the belief in an alternative solution to capitalist contradictions achieved by means of an ineluctable
expansion of productive forces, that is to say, by means of an expansion of instrumental reason, is impossible. If it is true that the growth
of economic production generates the conditions for a more just world,
on the other hand, individuals are nullified in the face of reified economic forces.[114] Yet implicit in their assault on Marx's ideology critique there is an attempt at ideology critique, an attempt at unmasking
not just bourgeois reifications but also the illusions of the Marxian
critique of ideology. As Jürgen Habermas has put it:

> Horkheimer and Adorno regard the foundations of ideology critique as
> shattered – and yet they would still like to hold on to the basic figure
> on enlightenment. So what enlightenment has perpetrated on myth, they
> apply to the process of enlightenment as a whole. . . . The suspicion of
> ideology becomes *total*, but without any change of direction. It is turned
> not only against the irrational function of bourgeois ideals, but against
> the rational potential of bourgeois culture itself. . . . But the goal remains
> that of producing an effect of unmasking.[115]

Despite their critique of Marx's concept of ideology, Adorno and
Horkheimer share with it not only its critical orientation towards
unmasking but also the methodological principle that the process of
unmasking must be carried out by means of immanent criticism. In
this sense they oppose the Mannheimian reduction of the limitations
of ideology to the fact of its being 'existentially determined'. Thus
Adorno argues that 'the concept of ideology makes sense only in relation to the truth or untruth of what it refers to' and that it is no good
substituting the social function for the truth content of philosophy.[116]
Horkheimer in his turn argues that 'insight into the historically conditioned [nature of a proposition or general perspective] is never
identical with the proof that it is ideological. Rather, for this there
is needed . . . [understanding] of its societal function.'[117] Although there
seems to be a contradiction between the two authors in relation to
the expression 'social function', I believe they are using it in a different
sense. Whereas Adorno is simply referring to the interests which condition philosophy, Horkheimer refers to the fact that recognizing those
interests is not enough and that the ideological nature of a proposition
requires an understanding of its social function in the sense of whether
or not it distorts social reality. This latter sense of social function is
present in Marx: ideas are ideological not because they are socially
determined but because in particular historical contexts they distort
and conceal contradictions in the interest of the ruling class.

The Frankfurt School philosophers use the negative concept of ideology in order to analyse and criticize the emergence of an increasingly reified mass culture which controls individual consciousness and promotes obedience and submission. This mass culture does not arise spontaneously but is manipulated by what they call the 'culture industry', an expression at the level of culture of the logic of industrial production.[118] Art and cultural forms become increasingly standardized and commodified as a result of the rise of the leisure and entertainment industries. The free time of individuals becomes instrumentalized to serve the system. The entertainment fostered by the culture industry is aimed at passive and uncritical individuals. Film, television and radio do not challenge individuals' fantasies or intelligence; they count on, presuppose and foster the lack of imagination and spontaneity of the passive spectator, and they induce conformity. The culture industry is suspicious of the new and does not want to experiment, but needs to present its products as if they were new. The culture industry converts individuals into consumers, and its systematic message is that they cannot conceive of themselves in any other way. As Adorno put it, 'it impedes the development of autonomous, independent individuals who judge and decide consciously for themselves.'[119]

All of this is a result of the processes unleashed by the Enlightenment. As we have seen, according to Adorno and Horkheimer the Enlightenment and technology brought about a new form of subjection to reified relations. In the attempt to dominate nature, reason became subjectivized, manipulative and purely instrumental. But this was paid for by the internalization of domination,[120] 'by the obedient subjection of reason to what is directly given'.[121] Hence the reification of what is given and of the power which controls technology is the new content of ideology.[122] However, this new form of ideology differs from the classical Marxist version of false consciousness. The critique of ideology could confront ideology with its own truth only in so far as ideology contained a rational element, as liberalism did.[123] Contemporary forms of ideology lack that rational element and should be understood not so much as 'the autonomous spirit, blind to its own social implications', as 'the totality of what is cooked up in order to ensnare the masses as consumers and, if possible, to mould and constrain their state of consciousness'.[124]

The new forms of ideology, ever since Nazism, have lost their theoretical status and have become a 'manipulative contrivance'. As Adorno put it, 'during the bourgeois era, the prevailing theory was the ideology and the opposing *praxis* was in direct contradiction. Today, theory hardly exists any longer and the ideology drones, as it were, from the gears of an irresistible *praxis*.'[125] For Critical Theory, ideology has ceased to be a veil – it has become 'a face of the world'; it converges with reality, or, rather, reality has become its own ideology.[126] This is the idea which Herbert Marcuse later expands and develops in his critique of the consumer society: ideology has become absorbed into reality, it has become an unassailable force which stems from the very process of production. Ideology may still be a form of false consciousness, but it has become immune against its falsehood.[127] Reason and domination have ceased to be contradictory forces. By taking to its logical conclusion Adorno and Horkheimer's critique of instrumental rationality, Marcuse argues that 'Today, domination perpetuates and extends itself not only through technology but *as* technology, and the latter provides the great legitimation of the expanding political power, which absorbs all spheres of culture.'[128] Further, 'the very concept of technical reason is perhaps ideological. Not only the application of technology but technology itself is domination (of nature and men) – methodic, scientific, calculated, calculating control.'[129]

Habermas has rightly criticized Adorno and Horkheimer for oversimplifying the image of modernity and not doing justice to the rational content of cultural modernity. They are unable to see that the sciences in their self-reflection go 'beyond merely engendering technically useful knowledge' and that by announcing the destruction of critical reason and verifying everywhere the reduction of reason to instrumental reason they undermine the very basis on which they can make their own critique.[130] In a similar manner Habermas argues that Marcuse went too far in his reduction of technological rationality to ideology and domination, and wants to show that 'neither the model of the original sin of scientific technical progress nor that of its innocence do it justice.'[131] It may be true that ideology in advanced capitalism is a form of technocratic consciousness, but this does not mean that society can do without scientific rationality, nor can contemporary technology be renounced in favour of a qualitatively different one.[132] Adorno, Horkheimer and Marcuse fail to do justice to the achievements of modernity and end up fusing reason with power and domination.

It is, of course, worthwhile to uncover the reifying and alienating consequences of the culture industry as Adorno and Horkheimer do, but the suggestion that through its operation individuals are necessarily induced to conform is mistaken and pessimistic. For a start, as Habermas reminds us, their very critique shows that not everybody loses his or her autonomy and critical ability and that those who criticize draw their critical weapons from the very Enlightenment they criticize. Just as in Althusser there is a danger of overestimating the integrating power of ideology, so there is in Adorno and Horkheimer an overestimation of the powers of the culture industry to alienate individuals. But, beyond that, there is also what J. B. Thompson has called the 'fallacy of internalism', that is to say, a tendency to 'read off the consequences of cultural products from the products themselves', thus neglecting a complex process of interpretation and assimilation.[133] The error is to assume that the products of the culture industry have a particular effect without studying in practice what their impact on individuals really is. This is the ideological aspect of Adorno and Horkheimer's theory: its persistent pessimism demobilizes and paralyses political transformatory activity.

3

Structuralism and the Dissolution of Althusserianism

Introduction

Structuralism represented one of the most forceful contemporary critiques of historicism, Marxist humanism and, therefore, implicitly, of Critical Theory. It became influential in many intellectual domains including anthropology, semiology, cultural studies and Marxism. Its most important contribution was the consideration of language as a crucial phenomenon for understanding culture and social life. Its main problem, which was to lead to poststructuralism and postmodernism, was the neglect of history and a tendency to dissolve social life into discourse. Structuralism was from the beginning closely related to the idea that the study of culture and society needs a more rigorous scientific approach than that provided by historicism. The desire to achieve scientific status is already present in Ferdinand de Saussure's study of *langue* as the explanatory structure of *parole* and in the Prague Circle's idea of a phonological system as the underlying structure of phonemes. The idea that cultural phenomena should be explained on the basis of structural and synchronic laws rather than upon the basis of historical and diachronic laws is taken from these principles. Claude Lévi-Strauss applied them to the study of myth, whereas Louis Althusser applied them to the analysis of ideology.

The idea of a new scientific departure was particularly noticeable in the work of Althusser and his followers and signalled a return to trust in reason which had been lost in the historicist and Critical Theory démarche. But this return to reason was not a particularly critical one, since it refused to justify itself. Dominique Lecourt has approvingly traced Althusser's position to the Spinozian idea of *veritas norma sui et falsi* ('truth is the norm of itself and of what is false') and to Gaston Bachelard's notion that 'the truth of a scientific truth *"imposes itself" by itself.'*[1] Truth is its own measure and automatically devalues all that is external to itself. Hence, the history of science appears as an irreversible form of progress which defeats irrationalism. Science is of itself a critique of ideology which needs not justify itself. Neither Bachelard nor Althusser thinks it necessary to prove the validity of science; they only take cognizance of it. This refusal to use reason to justify the primacy of reason is, paradoxically, one of the many points of contact between Althusserianism and the postmodernist positions which, contrary to the former, criticize reason, but also refuse to account for their own position.

It is my contention that the work of Althusserians, especially on ideology, and the subsequent dissolution of Althusserianism are of particular importance in understanding the emergence of poststructuralism and postmodernism. I shall therefore dwell on Althusserianism and its evolution in this chapter in order to establish its many branches and to track down the elements in them which lead to the dissolution of both Marxism and structuralism into poststructuralist and postmodernist positions. However, I shall start with Althusser himself, since it can be argued that, to a certain extent, the evolution of Althusserianism is foreshadowed by the very evolution of Althusser himself.

The Antinomies of Louis Althusser

From the beginning Louis Althusser posed himself a difficult problem for, as a Marxist, he wanted to explain the role of ideology from within the economic base–superstructure paradigm but, at the same time, he wanted to avoid economic reductionism. He resolved the first part of the equation by arguing that the question of the base and the superstructure should be posed from the point of view of reproduction. He thus introduced his main discussion of ideology by raising the question about the reproduction of the relations of production and the reproduction of labour power both in its skills and its submission to the established rules. His conclusion was that, in addition to state power, they were mainly reproduced by ideology.[2] Ideology works by reproducing the conditions of production and achieves this through interpellating individuals and constituting them as subjects obedient to the system. It is in the nature of the interpellation process that the newly constituted subjects will represent their conditions of existence in an imaginary form, that is to say, they will tend to see their submission as freely chosen.[3] Ideology, therefore, cannot produce true knowledge. Science, on the contrary, is 'always completely distinct from' and is able to 'criticize ideology in all its guises'.[4]

How was this reconciled with Althusser's non-reductionist and non-determinist intention? The solution was based upon a distinction between the dominant and the determining instances of society which allowed each instance or 'floor' of the superstructure a 'relative autonomy' and its own index of effectivity.[5] This means that for Althusser the social totality was understood as a complex structure which was constructed through genuinely different and relatively autonomous instances and which was not reducible to the simplicity of one inner essence which either externally produces or manifests itself in all social phenomena. This is why Althusser rejected the notions of mechanical and expressive causality and proposed a new 'structural' or 'metonymic' form of causality in order to explain his conception of the social 'whole'.[6]

Althusser was critical of all positions which conceived of ideology as having an eminently subjective character, that is to say, as a form of consciousness produced by individual subjects. For such conceptions, ideology is made up of ideas, and has a spiritual form of existence, only in the minds of individuals. This conceptualization, according to Althusser and his followers,[7] can be derived from some of Marx's formulas in *The German Ideology*, where Marx says that in ideology the world appears upside-down 'as in *camera obscura*', or 'as the inversion of objects on the retina', as 'phantoms formed in the human brain'. Ideology would accordingly originate in the thinkers of the ruling class, the conceptive ideologists, those 'who make the perfecting of the illusion of the class about itself, their chief source of livelihood'.[8] Ideology would thus seem to be presented as an illusion, as an inversion of reality, which is produced either by a faulty cognitive process in the human mind or by self-deception induced by class interests. Ideology would be a misperception, a misrecognition of a reality which, standing the right way up, is otherwise perfectly intelligible. As Althusser puts it, Marx's formulas in *The German Ideology* conceive of ideology 'as a pure illusion, a pure dream, i.e. as nothingness. All its reality is external to it.'[9]

This would also be the problem with Lukács's conception of ideology, which is presented by Althusser and his followers as the epitome of an idealist and historicist account that misrepresents the role of the subject and constitutes an assault on the autonomy of science. Nicos

Poulantzas, for instance, accuses Lukács of conceiving the relationship between the class subject and its ideology in genetic terms so that ideologies are seen 'as number-plates carried on the backs of class-subjects'.[10] Gareth Stedman Jones in his turn accuses Lukács of identifying socialist ideology with class consciousness, thus collapsing science into the consciousness of the class, and of failing to consider the institutional apparatuses which sustain bourgeois ideological domination.[11]

In contrast with the subjectivist position, which is assimilated to historicist and humanist deviations, Althusser and his followers propound a radically different conception which they find expressed in Marx's *Capital* and other writings of his maturity. This conception amounts to a new scientific problematic which is hidden, even from Marx himself, and which must be extracted by means of a symptomatic reading. According to this version, ideology has a material existence in apparatuses, rituals and practices; it is not spiritual or ideal, it is not subjective, but material and external; it is an objective level of society, an instance of the social totality, a structured discourse, which is not produced by any subject but which shapes and constitutes the subject. For Althusser ideology is a system of representations, 'but in the majority of cases these representations have nothing to do with "consciousness": they are usually images and occasionally concepts, but it is above all as structures that they impose on the vast majority of men, not via their "consciousness".'[12]

Althusser does not deny that ideology is a misrecognition of reality (or rather a representation of the imaginary relationship of individuals to their real conditions of existence), but he maintains that such misrecognition or representation of the imaginary is neither a product of the subject nor an illusion or false consciousness that inverts reality. As he puts it:

> the distortion of ideology is socially necessary as a function of the very nature of the social totality, more precisely, as a function of its determination by its structure, which is made, like all the social, opaque for individuals who occupy a place determined by this structure. The opacity of social structure necessarily makes mythical the representation of the world, necessary for social cohesion.[13]

In addition to this, Althusser introduces a distinction between a theory of 'ideology in general' and a theory of 'particular ideologies'.[14] The function of ideology in general is primarily to reproduce the relations of production and to secure the cohesion of the social totality by interpellating individuals in order to constitute them as subjects which perceive themselves as freely submitting to the existing order. Ideology allows the subjects to carry out their assigned tasks and helps them bear their situation. In this sense ideology is eternal and omnihistorical.[15] But this essential function of ideology in general is overdetermined in the concrete historical situation of class societies and their particular ideologies by the function of securing the domination of the ruling class by making the exploited accept their condition. In so far as ideology exists in class societies it divides itself into various ideological tendencies, namely dominant and dominated ideologies.[16]

Dominated ideologies may, under certain circumstances, give expression to the protest of exploited classes, but such ideologies are subordinate to, and spontaneously formulate their grievances in the language and the logic of, the dominant class. This is why the working class cannot liberate itself from bourgeois ideology but needs the external aid of science. As Althusser puts it: 'in order for the spontaneous working-class ideology to be transformed to the point of liberation from bourgeois ideology, it is necessary that it receives from without the help of science, and that it transforms itself under the influence of a new element, radically different from ideology: precisely science.'[17]

It is interesting to observe that with this account Althusser has performed the feat of reconciling the Leninist radical distinction between Marxism and the spontaneous consciousness of the working class with a negative concept of ideology. This is achieved by moving the concept of ideology from the domain of science, where Lenin put it, to the terrain of spontaneous consciousness. Marxism continues to be separated in origin and structure from the spontaneous consciousness of the working class, but now it is no longer an ideology, it is science. The ideology of the working class is its spontaneous consciousness, which is naturally subordinate to bourgeois ideology. All ideology is, therefore, a deformed and mystified system of representations, including working-class ideology.

But, of course, this reconciliation between a negative concept of ideology and Lenin's distinction between two kinds of consciousness is achieved at a cost. Two crucial antinomies can be detected. First, how is it possible to conceive of ideology as a comprehensive instance of society and at the same time as the opposite of science? Second, if ideology reproduces the conditions of production by constituting subjects who 'freely' submit to the established order, how can anybody become radically critical of that order? It is almost impossible to conceive how any individual could escape ideology. There is, of course, the Althusserian recourse to science; but then the question arises: where does science come from? To paraphrase Marx, the recourse to science forgets that the educators and scientists must themselves be educated. How can they escape ideology?

It seems, then, that Althusser's theory of ideology is faced with an awkward choice. Either it must divide society into two groups, one of which is assumed to be superior because it possesses science and must save the other, just as the philosophers of the French Enlightenment (criticized by Marx in the third thesis on Feuerbach) believed that they were the natural possessors of reason who alone could enlighten the ignorant and passive masses of the people. Or it has to be construed as a theory of the necessary domination of the ruling ideology in so far as ideology is supposed to be simply realized in certain apparatuses and imposed upon society even against the will, and precisely by means of the unwitting efforts, of dissenters. This could be the reason why Althusser apologizes to progressive teachers who 'do not even begin to suspect the work the system forces them to do . . . so little do they suspect it that their own devotion contributes to the maintenance and nourishment of this ideological representation of the school'.[18]

In December 1976, after having been heavily criticized for these problems and after a half-hearted attempt at self-criticism which was not very convincing,[19] Althusser altered his conception and seemed definitely to abandon the negative concept of ideology. He kept from his earlier conception the notion of interpellation as the basic mechanism of ideology, but he separated it from the notion of a necessary subjection to the ruling ideology. Hence he can speak of a proletarian ideology, upon which the Communist Party constitutes itself, which interpellates individuals as militant subjects against the system.[20] Althusser now argues that the proletarian ideology is not purely based on the spontaneous activity of the working class, but is informed by objective knowledge provided by Marxism. It is, therefore, a very particular ideology: 'it functions at the level of the masses like all ideology (by interpellating individuals as subjects) but it is soaked in historical experiences and enlightened by principles of scientific analysis.'[21] The negative concept of ideology and the opposition between science and ideology have disappeared; Althusser has finally come back to the Leninist fold.

Yet this time he goes further and addresses the problem of the gap between science and spontaneous working-class consciousness by resorting to Gramsci. This is significant because it indicates an important change of perspective. Antonio Gramsci had endeavoured to show

the double current of determinations which bridged the divide between science and spontaneous common sense. Marxism was created
by intellectuals, but there could not be an absolute distinction between
intellectuals and non-intellectuals. Marxism did not substitute for an
irretrievably deficient consciousness, but recognized and expressed a
collective will, a historical orientation which was already present in
the class as a common sense which deserved to be made more critical.[22] It is from this Gramscian perspective that Althusser now affirms
that

> Marxist theory has been, of course, conceived by intellectuals possess-
> ing a vast culture, but they have done so *from within the working-class
> movement*. . . . An intellectual who is not born from the people must *become
> people* . . . by sharing in the struggles of that people. . . . This is what Marx
> did: *he became an organic intellectual of the proletariat* (Gramsci). . . . The false
> problem of the *importation* of Marxist theory from without is thus trans-
> formed into the problem of the *diffusion within the working-class move-
> ment of a theory conceived within the working-class movement*.[23]

In spite of this shift, which resolves a crucial antinomy, Althusser's
theory still conceives of ideology as a discourse confronting subjects
from without. In this perspective subjects are nothing but *supports*. They
are the *bearers* of, and have been constructed for, certain ideological
meanings. Indeed, for Althusser social totality and history are conceived as processes without a subject. In order to deny that subjects
are the producers of ideas and of the processes constituting the social
totality, Althusserians argue that subjects are, rather, produced and
constituted for certain representations; they are conceived as the place
of crystallization of certain objective social practices. But by practice is
meant here not a conscious human activity which constructs social
reality, but rather a hollow objective form rather like the concept of
role in the structural-functionalist tradition, a given system of role-
expectations separated from and shaping the subject from without.
The onslaught on the subject and the emphasis on the primacy of
discourse anticipate what will later become basic premises of poststructuralism and postmodernism.

Althusser's understanding of the unity of social totality not on the
basis of a logic of identity, but on the basis of a logic of difference, was
also pregnant with consequences, for, although Althusser himself
retained the idea of totality and the ultimately determining role of the
economic structure, some of his followers took the logic of difference
to its extreme and ended up abandoning the very ideas of structure
and totality. What in Althusser was the articulation of many relatively

autonomous instances will become in the poststructuralists a necessary non-correspondence and heterogeneity among absolutely autonomous spheres. The ideological instance conceived as discourse will not only be no longer ultimately determined by the economy, but will become itself constitutive of all aspects of social life.

Althusser's theory of ideology started as a complex attempt to combine a search for a more rigorous and non-reductionist Marxism with an attack on humanist and historicist interpretations of Marx. Most of the ambiguities and antinomies of Althusser's theory stemmed from this matrix. In trying to combine the relative autonomy of ideology with the seemingly absolute autonomy of science, the underrating of the subject with the negative concept of ideology, the theory of ideology in general with the theory of ideology in particular historical situations, the closure of discourse with the ultimate determination by the economy, Althusser was sowing the seeds of very difficult problems which would eventually lead to the dissolution of the theory itself.

The Division and Dissolution of the Althusserian School

The extent and depth of Althusser's dramatic about-turn of 1976 remained largely unknown to the English-speaking world,[24] and in any case it came about when Althusser's influence had already begun to wane. It is not surprising, therefore, that the widespread impact of Althusserianism should have drawn mainly on his earlier approach. Besides, two other factors should be borne in mind. On the one hand, the originality and distinctiveness of Althusser's contribution were partly lost when he abandoned the strong opposition between ideology and science. On the other hand, part of the appeal of Althusser's first theory of ideology was due to its obvious connections with structuralist themes which were very fashionable in the late 1960s and the early 1970s. However, it is also true that some authors influenced by the 'young' Althusser became critical of his theoretical shortcomings at an early stage and elaborated ideas which somehow anticipated Althusser's own future change of perspective.

Despite my critical stance in respect of the early Althusser, it has to be said that the number and variety of authors drawn from many disciplines who have been influenced by different aspects of Althusser's first elaborations, and the ability of some of these elaborations to inspire some fruitful lines of empirical research, bear witness to the formidable intellectual power of Althusser's original theory. A brief survey of research areas shows the extent of Althusser's influence which practically covers the whole gamut of the social sciences. An impressive number of academics and intellectuals working in anthropology, philosophy, sociology, political science, linguistics, semiology, semantics, cultural studies, literary criticism, criminology and psychology have been affected by Althusser in one way or another.

In anthropology one can see definite traces of Althusser's approach in the work of Maurice Godelier,[25] Emmanuel Terray,[26] Georges Dupré[27] and Pierre-Philippe Rey.[28] John Taylor[29] bases his entire approach to the sociology of development on the Althusserian conceptions of science and mode of production. In political science, Nicos Poulantzas,[30] Ernesto Laclau[31] and Chantal Mouffe[32] start from Althusserian premises in all that has to do with the concept of ideology. Equally, Stuart Hall[33] develops his approach to cultural studies, ideology and race in systematic dialogue with Althusserian structuralism. Literary criticism shows the impact of Althusser's conception of ideology in the work of Pierre Macherey[34] and to a lesser extent in the early writings of Terry Eagleton.[35] Colin Sumner's research on law and ideology[36] is also heavily indebted to Althusser's conception.

In philosophy and the theory of social sciences the work of John Mepham,[37] Barry Hindess and Paul Hirst[38] has been almost entirely based upon a critique and expansion of the logic of Althusser's theory. In semiology and psychology Julia Kristeva,[39] Jean-Louis Baudry,[40] Philippe Sollers[41] and other French intellectuals gathered around the journal *Tel Quel* have sought to bring together linguistics, psychoanalysis and Althusserian Marxism. Their work has been echoed in Great Britain by the contributions of Rosalind Coward and John Ellis,[42] Diane Adlam and many others grouped around the journal *Ideology and Consciousness*,[43] who have focused their analyses on ideology and the constitution of the subject. Similarly, in the field of semantics, Michel Pêcheux[44] has tried to combine a methodology for the analysis of discourse with the Althusserian conception of ideology.

It is beyond the scope, let alone the permissible length, of this chapter to discuss all these authors and their contributions. Therefore I propose to concentrate on those theories and authors which are more directly related to the elaboration and discussion of the concept of ideology. I want to argue that in this field Althusser's influence is strikingly ambiguous. It has generated some conceptions which retain a negative concept of ideology and others which adopt a neutral perspective. It has been used to support a strong opposition between science and ideology and to support its abolition. It has led to thoughtful and useful Marxist analyses of ideology in many research areas, but it has also resulted in a dogmatic and abstract style of theorizing which has frequently led to self-contradiction and the complete abandonment of Marxism.

In accordance with this basic ambiguity I wish to argue that in general terms one can distinguish three broad strands among Althusserians. First, there is a trend which manages to keep both a negative concept of ideology and some fundamental Marxist premises related to the class determination of ideas and political processes. The Althusserian opposition between science and ideology continues to be one of its most important features. Second, there is an intermediate trend, of Gramscian origins, which abandons the negative concept of ideology and its opposition to science and mainly focuses on ideology as interpellation. This position seeks to redefine the basic Marxist premises about determination by introducing the concept of articulation so as to both keep the crucial role of classes and class conflict and simultaneously exclude class reductionism. Finally, there is a trend which not only challenges the negative concept of ideology but also, in its stead, establishes discourse as the constitutive principle of all social and political life, thus abandoning all idea of social determination based on the economic structure and class analysis. This position ends up attacking Marxism as a form of essentialism, economism and reductionism and merges into poststructuralism.

The Althusserian Orthodox Line

In the first group one can place authors like Poulantzas, Godelier, Mepham and Pêcheux who take, and have maintained throughout their careers, a more or less consistent Marxist line of analysis. They all share some basic Althusserian premises, but they have also studied and know Marx in depth so that they are able both to advance their own independent interpretations of his writings and to develop upon that basis substantial theoretical contributions. Poulantzas contributes a theory of classes and of the state, and, more generally, a theory of the political and ideological spheres of contemporary advanced capitalist societies. Godelier develops a theory of ideology and culture in primitive societies which draws on Marx's elaborations about commodity fetishism and on Lévi-Strauss's ideas about the role of kinship relations in primitive societies. Mepham elaborates an interpretation of the Marxist theory of ideology which draws on *Capital* to the exclusion of *The German Ideology*. Pêcheux explores the relationships between discourse analysis and historical materialism.

In so far as the concept of ideology is concerned they all share Althusser's critique of false consciousness and start from the premise that it is not the subject that produces ideology as ideas, but it is ideology, conceived as a material instance of practices and rituals, that constitutes the subject. Yet in spite of their opposition to the notion of false consciousness, and in line, at least formally, with Marx's theory, they all maintain the negative conception of ideology present in the early Althusser. They emphasize the idea of ideology as an 'imaginary transposition', its opposition to science, and the fact that it interpellates individuals as subjects in a fundamental misrecognition which helps reproduce the domination system. Of course, there are important differences between Marx's concept of ideology and the conceptions advanced by these authors. Yet there are also some striking similarities which stem from the fact that they share with Marx a negative conception and some of the functions attributed to ideology.

Nicos Poulantzas starts with a critique of the historicist conception of ideology. This tradition within Marxism is supposedly initiated by the young Marx himself and continued by Lukács, Gramsci, Marcuse, Adorno and Lucien Goldmann. According to Poulantzas such a conception is centred upon the subject and the idea of false consciousness, and it tends to identify ideology with alienation. Hence ideology is over-politicized and cannot have any autonomy. Because of its emphasis on ideology being the world-view of a class subject, it is not possible to conceive of the ruling ideology possessing ideological elements originating in other classes, nor can the working-class ideology be contaminated by the ruling ideology.

Following Althusser very closely, Poulantzas conceives of ideology as an objective level of society which is not only a conceptual system but also, and mainly, a 'lived experience' inasmuch as it determines the way in which individuals live their relationships with their conditions of existence. Yet, in spite of his rejection of the problematic centred on alienation and false consciousness, Poulantzas maintains that ideology is 'necessarily falsified' and that it 'has the precise function of hiding the real contradictions and of reconstituting on an imaginary level a relatively coherent discourse which serves as the horizon of agents' experience'.[45] This quotation is perfectly compatible with Marx's conception.

John Mepham, in his turn, shares Althusser's critique of *The German Ideology* but elaborates his attack in greater detail and proposes to replace its allegedly mistaken approach by three theses which he draws from *Capital*. First, ideology is structured discourse. Second, the relation between ideology and reality is the cognitive relation. Third, ideology arises from the opacity of reality. The traditional Althusserian concerns are shown in these theses, and ideology continues to be a mystification based on a 'misrecognition'. By having recourse to Marx's distinction in *Capital* between 'real relations' and 'phenomenal forms', Mepham argues that reality presents itself to human beings under some appearances which conceal the real relations. Hence the origin of ideological illusions is in the phenomenal forms of reality itself and 'the function of ideology is to keep hidden the real social relations.'[46] This is, again, compatible with Marx's conception, despite many other aspects in which Mepham differs from Marx.

Maurice Godelier too starts from the Marxian distinction between essence and appearance found in *Capital*. According to his interpretation, it is not the subject that misperceives reality, but reality itself that misleads the subject.[47] For Godelier this is the necessary consequence of commodity fetishism and shows that the basis of ideology is objective and not subjective. Noticing that in explaining commodity fetishism Marx resorts to comparisons with the world of religion and mythology, Godelier puts forward the idea that in pre-capitalist societies there exists a religious and mythical variety of fetishes which also results in illusory and mystified representations. The origin of these religious ideological forms is not commodity production but the poverty and backwardness of productive forces. Nature is represented by primitive peoples as a mysterious reality by analogy with the human world, that is to say, the invisible forces of nature, which are not properly understood, are represented as subjects endowed with consciousness and will and capable of communicating with human beings. For primitive humankind, nature and society spontaneously assume mystified and fantastic forms.

Here Godelier finds that the Marxian theory of ideology meets Lévi-Strauss's analysis of myth. For the latter, kinship relationships underpin mythology, but, at the same time, Godelier observes, kinship relationships function in primitive societies as the structure of the social relations of production. So the predominance of kinship relations discovered by contemporary anthropology in traditional societies is at the same time the pre-eminence of the economic structure as Marxism propounds. In this way Godelier extends the Althusserian concept of ideology, as the domain of the illusory representations of the real, to primitive societies, and conceives of a possible general theory of ideology which would cover both class and classless societies.[48]

This suggestive analysis tends to dissolve myth into ideology in a manner which probably Marx would not have accepted. In commodity fetishism the products of human labour acquire life, whereas in the mystified world of mythology it is nature which is invested with subjective characters. For Marx, ideology could only exist in class societies where there is an antagonistic structure of production relations. Myth, on the contrary, exists predominantly in classless societies. Yet in spite of these differences there is a formal analogy between myth and ideology in so far as both mask contradictions: the former conceals the inability to control nature, the latter explains away class domination.

Michel Pêcheux tries to combine the Althusserian theory of ideology with a critical exploration of linguistic science. He starts from a basic distinction between language and discourse which he substitutes for the traditional structuralist distinction between *langue* and *parole*. Thus Pêcheux maintains that

> the system of *langue* is indeed the same for the materialist and the idealist, for the revolutionary and the reactionary, for someone who possesses a given knowledge and for someone who does not. This does not mean, however, that these diverse characters have got the same discourse: *langue* appears as the common *base* of differentiated discursive *processes*.[49]

Discursive processes cannot be considered as individual contingent uses of language, as *parole*, but they are inscribed in class ideological relations. Althusser's central thesis that ideology interpellates individuals as subjects is considered by Pêcheux to be the key to a materialist theory of discourse in so far as it rejects the idea of subjectivity as the source or origin of discourse. A non-subjectivist theory of the subject is in fact a theory of the ideological conditions of reproduction and transformation of relations of production. This presupposes the contradictory character of all modes of production which in the case of the ideological region means that class struggle passes through ideological state apparatuses.

By adopting Althusser's notion of ideological state apparatuses, but in the context of class struggle, Pêcheux wants to emphasize the following points. First, ideology is not reproduced as the 'spirit of an epoch' for the whole of society. Second, it is impossible to attribute an ideology to each class as if classes could exist before class struggle. Third, ideological state apparatuses are not an expression of the ruling ideology but the place and means of realization of the ruling ideology. Fourth, ideological state apparatuses are not therefore simple instruments of the ruling class.[50]

The fact that the materiality of ideology is given by various ideological state apparatuses means that ideology exists in the form of 'ideological formations' which have a regional character and entail class positions. Within these ideological formations 'discursive formations' determine what can and must be said. The complex whole of discursive formations is called 'interdiscourse'. Pêcheux advances two central theses in this respect. First, words, expressions, propositions, etc., have not got sense by themselves but receive their sense from the discursive formations within which they are produced. The sense of words is therefore determined by the ideological positions of those who use them. Thus Pêcheux affirms that 'individuals are "interpellated" as speaking subjects (as subjects of *their* discourse) by the discursive formations which represent "within language" the ideological formations which correspond to them.'[51] In other words, ideology constitutes both subjects and meanings, that is to say, both subjects and meanings are presented as primary unquestionable evidence.

Second, this evidence which tells us that we are subjects and that words have obvious meanings is an ideological effect. All discursive formation conceals, by the seeming transparency of the sense it has constituted, the contradictory material objectivity of interdiscourse, its ultimate dependence upon ideological formations. In other terms, all discursive processes are based on class ideological relations and are intrinsically affected by the class struggle which traverses the ideological state apparatuses, but these contradictory foundations are masked by the apparent obviousness of the meaning constituted by ideology. A clear negative concept of ideology emerges from these remarks. However, Pêcheux goes beyond Althusser by emphasizing that the ideological state apparatuses, in so far as they are the terrain of class struggle, contribute not only to the reproduction of the relations of production but also to their transformation.

Whatever the differences between Marx and the writers discussed in this section, they have remained true to some fundamental Marxist principles. They tend to be concerned with upholding the relative autonomy of the ideological spheres and with giving ideology a greater role and efficacy than classical Marxism ever did. But they still maintain the determination in the last instance by the structure of the social relations of production. They conceive of ideology as a discourse which constitutes individuals as subjects, but they do not erect language and discourse as the last independent instance of social life. They may criticize class reductionism and a conception of ideology as 'number-plates' carried on the back of social classes, but they still give pride of place of class analysis and to the central role of class struggle. They may believe in class alliances as a necessary condition for the pursuit of socialism, but they also accept that without the crucial role of the working class socialism cannot be constructed.

Politics as Articulation and Ideology as Interpellation

There are two main contributions in this strand. First and foremost is the early work of Ernesto Laclau, which is best represented by the publication of his seminal *Politics and Ideology in Marxist Theory*. Second is the prolific work of Stuart Hall, which spans from an interesting theoretical synthesis of Althusser, Laclau and Gramsci to revealing concrete studies of ideology in the media and other cultural expressions. Both these authors start from Althusserian premises but, unlike the group of writers discussed in the previous section, are unambiguously critical of Althusser's shortcomings and selectively synthetic in trying theoretically to fuse what was best in his approach with a Gramscian perspective.

Laclau and Hall know Marx very well and want to develop their theories within Marxism, but do not hesitate in abandoning both the original Marxian negative concept of ideology and Althusser's early negative version. In a way, they anticipate Althusser's own change towards a Gramscian neutral concept of ideology. The idea of a theory of ideology 'in general', the exclusive functional role of ideology as reproducing production relations and the opposition between science and ideology are discarded, and class struggle is reinserted at the centre of the problematic of ideology. Yet this reinsertion is carried out in a way which entails a renewed attempt to depart from essentialism and class reductionism. The principles of this attempt are, first, that difference cannot be reduced to identity, and therefore social totality cannot be conceived as constituted by a basic contradiction which manifests or expresses itself at all levels but must be thought of as 'a unity which is constructed through the *differences* between, rather than the homology of, practices';[52] and, second, that although not every contradiction in society can be reduced to a class contradiction 'every contradiction is overdetermined by class struggle.'[53]

Laclau starts by establishing against Althusser that ideology cannot be simultaneously a level of any social formation and the opposite of science. So he decides to abandon the negative connotation of the concept.[54] Hall underlines this point by defining ideology as 'those images, concepts and premises which provide the frameworks through which we represent, interpret, understand and "make sense" of some aspect of social existence'.[55] Three aspects of this conception are high-lighted. 'First, ideologies do not consist of isolated and separate con-cepts, but in the articulation of different elements into a distinctive set or chain of meanings.' 'Second, ideological statements are made by individuals; but ideologies are not the product of individual con-sciousness or intention. Rather we formulate our intentions *within ideology*.' Third, ideologies 'work by constructing for their Subjects (individuals and collective) positions of identification and knowledge which allow them to "utter" ideological truths as if they were their authentic authors'.[56]

Both Laclau and Hall take Althusser's idea that ideology interpellates individuals as subjects as the basic explanation of how ideology works. Ideologies are not really produced by individual consciousness; rather, individuals formulate their beliefs, within positions already fixed by ideology, as if they were their true producers. However, individuals are not necessarily recruited and constituted as subjects obedient to the ruling class, since the same mechanism of interpellation operates when individuals are recruited by revolutionary ideologies. Laclau's key insight is that ideologies are made of elements and concepts which have no necessary class belongingness and that these constituent units of ideologies can be articulated to a variety of ideological discourses which represent different classes. The class character of a concept is not given by its content but by its articulation into a class ideological discourse. Hence, there are no 'pure' ideologies which necessarily correspond to certain class interests. Every ideological discourse arti-culates several interpellations, not all of which are class interpellations. In fact Laclau identifies two possible kinds of antagonism which gen-erate two types of interpellations. At the level of the mode of produc-tion there exist class contradictions and class interpellations. At the level of the social formation there are popular-democratic contra-dictions and interpellations, that is to say, ideological elements which interpellate individuals as 'the people', as the underdog. The idea is that class interpellations work by trying to articulate popular-democratic interpellations to the class ideological discourse:

> *The popular-democratic interpellation not only has no precise class content, but it is the domain of ideological class struggle par excellence.* Every class struggles at the ideological level *simultaneously* as class and as the people, or rather, tries to give coherence to its ideological discourse by presenting its class objectives as the consummation of popular objectives.[57]

Examples of successful ideological articulations between popular-democratic interpellations and ruling-class interpellations are, for instance, the effective way in which the fascist ideology integrated nationalist and anti-plutocratic popular traditions with racism, or the way in which the Thatcherite brand of neo-liberal ideology articulated British popular opposition to wage controls and high taxation with the idea that wages should be determined by the free operation of market forces and with the idea that the progressiveness of the tax system should be rolled back in favour of those who earn more. This shows that ideologies work by disarticulating ideological elements from other ideological discourses and re-articulating them into a new discourse, so that, in acquiring a new meaning within a new totality, they help to reconstitute subjects for different political objectives and actions. It is because the German working class did not understand this that it foolishly pursued a policy of ideological purity and sep-aration from other classes which resulted in the triumph of Nazism.

Because classes articulate to their ideological discourses a multi-plicity of interpellations and many elements which are not their own creation, it is not possible abstractly to reduce working-class ideology to Marxism-Leninism or bourgeois ideology to liberalism. As Laclau puts it, 'the class character of an ideology is given by its *form* and not by its *content*.'[58] For example, nationalism, of itself, is not a feudal, bourgeois or proletarian ideology, but it can be articulated to any of these. Thus the bourgeoisie can articulate nationalism against the re-gionalism of feudalism but the proletariat can also articulate national-ism against imperialism. Liberalism was the ideology of the European bourgeoisie, but it was also the ideology of semi-feudal landowners in Latin America.

Whereas Laclau never attempts to ascertain Marx's concept of ideo-logy, and the starting point of his own construction is a critique and elaboration of Althusser, Hall is explicitly aware of Marx's contribu-tion and seeks to assess it. The first problem he confronts is the nature of the 'distortion' it apparently entails. But even before he addresses that problem he has already established his own definition (quoted above) which totally leaves out the idea of distortion. This does not present a problem for Hall because (1) there is no fully developed theory of ideology in Marx; (2) there are severe fluctuations in Marx's use of the term; (3) we *now* use the term 'to refer to *all* organized forms of social thinking'; and (4) 'Marx did, on many occasions, use the term ideology, practically, in this way.'[59] However, to his credit, Hall rec-ognizes that most of the time Marx used the term as a critical weapon against other religious, philosophical and economic theories and acknowledges 'the fact . . . that Marx most often used "ideology" to refer specifically to the manifestations of bourgeois thought; and above all to its negative and distorted features.'[60] Having said this, Hall critically examines the theoretical bases of the classical version: (1) ideas arise from and reflect the material conditions; (2) ideas are effects of the economic level; and (3) ruling ideas are the ideas of the ruling class. In spite of showing the insufficiency and problematic nature of these propositions, Hall proposes to be constructive, especially in relation to the issue of distortion, and discovers, for instance, that the way in which Marx deals with the question of truth and falsehood in relation to classical political economy is far more complex than the critics would have us believe. Distortion in this context would amount to eternalization and naturalization of social relations. Equally, Marx's analysis of the operation of the market and its deceptive appearances provides another source of sophisticated insights into the problem of distortion, this time as 'one-sidedness', 'obscuring' or 'concealment'.[61]

Ultimately Hall's effort to interpret Marx's notion of distortion aims at bypassing the distinction true/false, that is to say, at excluding from the definition of distortion the connotation of falsehood in the sense of illusion or unreality. In second place he aims to show that the 'economic relations themselves cannot prescribe a single, fixed and unalterable way of conceptualizing' reality, but that reality 'can be "expressed" within different ideological discourses'.[62] With both of these objectives I can agree except in his calling all discourses 'ideological'. This in itself is symptomatic of a theoretical decision which Hall has legitimately taken from the beginning but which one can easily lose sight of at this point – namely, the fact that his discussion and partial rescue of the notion of 'distortion' has not been done with a view to adopting Marx's critical concept of ideology. In fact Hall continues to uphold the definition he started with, a definition which leaves out the problem of distortion as inherent in the ideological phenomenon. Nevertheless, his effort to understand and accept the best senses in which Marx spoke of distortion gives one the impression that for Hall, at this stage, Marx's critical notion of ideology has a place, and that it could be partially rescued from the critics, even if it is not the way in which Hall himself proposes to deal with or use the concept.

There are many valuable elements in Laclau's and Hall's approach which have been profitably used to study fascism, to examine the ideological construction of black people in England and to explain the successful Thatcherite appeal to the British working class. The richness of the Gramscian inspiration is obvious and makes their concept of ideology all the more worthwhile. Of course, there are also some problems. First, Laclau's distinction between two kinds of contradictions, namely, class contradictions and people/power bloc contradictions, is problematic. A contradiction is by definition an antagonism between two poles which are constituted by their opposition and reproduce one another. So the people/power bloc opposition, which does not inclusively constitute its two sides, cannot be a contradiction. What can be affirmed instead is that not all conflicts and struggles in society are a direct expression or manifestation of the basic class contradiction, but all conflicts are necessarily overdetermined by it.

Second, although Laclau is right in asserting that ideological elements cannot be reduced to one class only and can be found articulated to other class discourses, it is a mistake to assume that there are non-class contents which are freely articulable to just any class discourse. As Mouzelis has argued, 'if there is no one-to-one correspondence between classes and ideological themes, neither is there a completely arbitrary relationship between the two', and when classes are theorized in a historically specific manner and not abstractly 'then it becomes obvious that there are strict limits to the types of content that their ideological discourse can have.'[63] So the process of ideological articulation does not integrate totally neutral contents into a class discourse but disarticulates and re-articulates certain (not just any) class-produced contents which are more easily detachable from the original discourse. Third, Laclau's critique of the class reductionism and the economism of the German working class which facilitated the success of Nazism is very interesting and plausible, but, paradoxically, instead of finally disposing of Marx's negative concept of ideology, it may presuppose it. For ultimately the question is why the German working class and its representative party interpreted the contradictions of pre-war German society within such a narrow economism. One possible answer is that they were deceived by an ideology which distorted and concealed the true nature of these contradictions.

After having initially found a place for Marx's negative concept of ideology, Hall has subsequently made a determined effort to argue that the ideological analysis of certain phenomena is incompatible with Marx's concept of ideology. In effect, Hall argues that Thatcherism, as an ideological phenomenon, cannot be explained by the so-called classic variant of the theory of ideology derived from *The German Ideology*. Hall presents four main arguments. First, the basic correspondence between ruling ideas and ruling class postulated by Marx overlooks ideological differences within the dominant classes and the fact that certain ideological formations, like Thatcherism, must vigorously fight against traditional conservative ideas in order to become 'the normative-normalized structure of conceptions through which a class "spontaneously" and authentically thinks or lives its relations to the world'. For Hall, 'the conventional approach suggests that the dominant ideas are ascribed by and inscribed in the position a class holds in the structure of social relations . . . it is not assumed that these ideas should have to win ascendancy . . . through a specific and contingent . . . process of ideological struggle.'[64] The critique which Poulantzas and Laclau make of classical Marxist theory for conceiving of ideology as the 'number-plates' on the back of social classes, and for arguing that each ideological element or concept has a necessary class belongingness,[65] expresses similar concerns.

Second, Hall argues, 'in the classical perspective, Thatcherism would be understood as in no significant way different from traditional conservative ruling ideas.' But Thatcherism for Hall is 'a quite distinct, specific and novel combination of ideological elements',[66] and, although it integrates some elements of traditional Toryism, it does so in a radically new way. Third, the classical theory of ideology can only explain the penetration and success of the ruling ideas within the working class by the recourse to false consciousness. The popular classes are duped by the dominant classes, temporarily ensnared against their material interests by a false structure of illusions, which would be dispelled as real material factors reassert themselves. But this has failed during Thatcherism because 'mass unemployment has taken a much longer time than predicted to percolate mass consciousness.' 'The unemployed . . . are still by no means automatic mass converts to labourism, let alone socialism.'[67] False consciousness 'assumes an empiricist relation of the subject to knowledge, namely that the real world indelibly imprints its meanings and interests directly into our consciousness. We have only to look to discover its truths. And if we cannot see them, then it must be because there is a cloud of unknowing that obscures the unilateral truth of the real.'[68] In contrast to this view, Hall argues that 'the first thing to ask about an "organic ideology" that, however unexpectedly, succeeds in organizing substantial sections of the masses and mobilizing them for political action, is not what is *false* about it but what about it is *true*. By "true" I do not mean universally correct as a law of the universe but "makes good sense".'[69] Fourth, Hall argues:

> it is a highly unstable theory about the world which has to assume that vast numbers of ordinary people, mentally equipped in much the same way as you or I, can simply be thoroughly and systematically duped into misrecognizing entirely where their real interests lie. Even less acceptable is the position that, whereas they, the masses, are the dupes of history, we – the privileged – are somehow without a trace of illusion and can see right through into the truth, the essence, of a situation.[70]

What can one say about these arguments? First of all, one must recognize that they are not at all new and that Hall has already expressed them in other contexts, even within the article where he dealt at length with Marx's notion of distortion.[71] However, the celebrationary context of that article and the careful scrutiny of Marx's texts allowed a far more balanced outcome. In the new version,[72] elaborated before the tribunal of Thatcherism, the criticisms take over completely and very little of Marx's theory seems to be worth saving. Further, Hall's arguments against the classical variant show some confusion in that a flawed neutral concept of Leninist origin seems to be conflated with Marx's negative concept. Moreover, although Hall is careful to state that his criticisms are no reason to throw over some of the insights of the classical Marxist explanation, his account of such insights is insufficient and rather partial (only a couple of paragraphs), whereas the accent is overwhelmingly placed on the fact that Thatcherism has positively confirmed Althusser's key insights. In examining Hall's arguments I shall try to show three main points. First, that Hall's approach to ideology is important and necessary to the analysis of Thatcherism and indeed of any 'ideology' which succeeds in attracting widespread support. Second, that, important and necessary as that analysis may be, it is still partial and limited, and must be complemented by a critical approach. Third, that Marx's theory of ideology is also indispensable to the analysis of Thatcherism, although from a different point of view.

One can agree with Hall's first argument that the ideological unity of classes is non-existent and that Thatcherism had to fight to gain ideological ascendancy within the ruling classes, let alone the dominated ones. But this assertion presupposes a concept of ideology which is different from Marx's. For Marx, ideology was not equivalent to 'the ruling ideas', nor, for that matter, to 'those images, concepts and premises which provide the frameworks through which we represent, understand and make sense of some aspects of social existence', as Hall prefers to put it. Marx did not speak of class ideologies or 'ideological discourses' in the sense Hall does. It seems to me that there are three problems with the way in which Hall argues. First, he chooses to ignore in this particular context the negative character of Marx's concept of ideology. Second, he imputes to Marx, and particularly to *The German Ideology*, a neutral concept, albeit a flawed one. Third, in so far as the ruling class is concerned, he identifies Marx's supposedly neutral concept of ideology with the dominant ideas.

Let us clarify these issues. In general, negative or critical conceptions of ideology (like Marx's) refer to a kind of distorted thought, whatever the way in which we choose to understand such distortion.

Neutral conceptions (like Lenin's) refer to political ideas, discourses and world-views which are articulated around some principles related to the interests of some social group, party or class. A negative concept of ideology is inherently capable of discriminating between adequate and inadequate ideas; it passes epistemological judgement on thought, whatever its class origin or the expressed intention of its supporters. An ideological idea is a distorted idea. The neutral concept of ideology does not of itself discriminate between adequate and inadequate ideas; it does not pass epistemological judgement on them, but emphasizes that through them human beings acquire consciousness of social reality and links those ideas to some class interests or to some articulating political principle. Thus one can speak of bourgeois ideology and proletarian ideology, liberal ideology and nationalist ideology without necessarily wanting to establish or prejudge their adequacy or truth.

Within the neutral conception of ideology, critical judgement can be passed on ideologies, but always from the perspective of a different ideology. Thus when Marxists in the Leninist tradition criticize bourgeois ideology they do it from the point of view of proletarian ideology, and what they criticize is its bourgeois character, not its ideological character, which their own Marxist doctrine shares. In this conception, ideology of itself does not entail any necessary distortion. For the neutral version the 'ideological' is the quality of any thought or idea that serves or articulates group or class interests, whatever they may be. For the negative version, on the contrary, the 'ideological' is the attribute of any thought or idea which distorts or inverts reality.

So, when Laclau, Poulantzas and Hall criticize classical Marxist theory for conceiving of ideology as the 'number-plates' on the back of social classes and for overlooking ideological differences within the dominant classes, they are not criticizing Marx's concept but a version of Lenin's, and are proposing an alternative which, admittedly, improves on certain interpretations of Lenin's conception. However, by conflating Marx and Lenin on this issue, they fail to make a crucial distinction between two different traditions within Marxism and they do not seem to be aware of any difference between Marx and Lenin in relation to the concept of ideology.

Hall's second argument that with Marx's theory of ideology Thatcherism would be understood as in no significant way different from traditional conservative ruling ideas misses the crucial point, again, that for Marx ideology and ruling ideas are not the same. By definition, Marx's theory of ideology did not and could not address the question of competing political outlooks within a ruling party.

Hall's argument is right against an interpretation of the Leninist concept of ideology which rigidly imputes an ideology to a particular class position, but not right against Marx's conception. However, even addressing a neutral Leninist definition of ideology, the charge must be made with caution. True, Thatcherism and traditional conservatism are different forms of political thought corresponding to different stages of accumulation in the capitalist system. But one must not forget that there is also an element of continuity. Both ideological forms are concerned with the protection and expansion of the capitalist system under a different form. Margaret Thatcher did not preside over any change in the mode of production; she propped up and defended the same capitalist system at a different stage of development. The novelty of her position should not therefore be exaggerated.

Third, Hall criticizes Marx's alleged recourse to false consciousness in order to explain the success of ruling ideas, and its implicit empiricist connotations. First of all, it must be clarified that Marx never defined ideology simply as false consciousness or even used such an expression. It was Engels who used this expression, and only once.[73] It is not that I am trying to deny that ideology for Marx and Engels involved a form of false consciousness. It certainly did, but it was not false consciousness in general, nor was it conceived as an illusion; it was a very specific form of distortion. The notion of false consciousness on its own is problematic and quite different from Marx's concept of ideology. In this I agree with Hall and other critics. It is certainly an equivocal expression for it can convey both the idea of a distortion and the idea that such distortion is an invention or a delusion of individual consciousness, a mirage without any base in reality. I contend that Marx's concept of ideology entails the former but not the latter idea. I underline the fact that the problem here is ambiguity and not that false consciousness, of itself and necessarily, entails the connotation of deception by individual subjects.

If there are any remaining doubts about this issue, Marx dispels them in *Capital*. It is not the ruling class directly that dupes the working class; the very reality of market relations creates a world of appearances which deceive people. Contrary to Hall's version, Marx never thought that the material reality of capitalism would directly dispel the illusions of the workers. It was material reality itself that deceived them. However, as Hall well realizes, neither deception nor liberation from deception is directly prescribed by economic relations. According to Marx, the operation of the market was 'a very Eden of the innate rights of man. There alone rule Freedom, Equality, Property and Bentham.'[74]

These four principles were for Marx the basis of bourgeois political ideology. As in all ideology, these principles concealed what went on beneath the surface where 'this apparent individual equality and liberty disappear' and 'prove to be inequality and unfreedom'. This is why unemployment and/or low wages by and of themselves do not necessarily transform the beliefs of people. There is no 'cloud of unknowing' for Marx that obscures an easily seen reality. Such a view can perhaps be attributed to Bacon and his theory of idols or to Holbach and Helvetius and their theory of prejudices, but not to Marx. This is why for Marx what can dispel ideological forms are not critical ideas or science, but political practices of transformation.

As for the rest of the ruling ideas, is not true either that Marx explained their success and penetration within the working class by a recourse to false consciousness. His explanation in *The German Ideology* is quite different. If the ideas of the ruling class are the ruling ideas it is because 'the class which is the ruling *material* force of society is at the same time its ruling *intellectual* force. The class which has the means of material production at its disposal, consequently also controls the means of mental production, so that the ideas of those who lack the means of mental production are on the whole subject to it.'[75] Hall seems to believe that for Marx 'the control over the means of mental production' is the reason why the masses have been duped. In fact Marx in this passage is not talking about ideology at all, but about the ruling ideas, which are two different things. Yet Hall does otherwise understand exceedingly well the point of this quotation when he describes some of the 'insights of the classical Marxist explanation':

> The social distribution of knowledge *is* skewed . . . the circle of dominant ideas *does* accumulate the symbolic power to map or classify the world for others . . . it becomes the horizon of the taken-for-granted. Ruling ideas may dominate other conceptions of the social world by setting the limit to what will appear as rational, reasonable, credible . . . the monopoly of the means of intellectual production . . . is not, of course, irrelevant to this acquisition over time of symbolic dominance . . .[76]

For Marx, neither ideologically distorted ideas nor correct ideas can be explained as emerging from an empiricist relation whereby the real world indelibly imprints its meanings, be they distorted or sound, directly into our consciousness. This assumes that the real world is simple and transparent and that the subjects are rather passive recipients. For Marx, on the contrary, the real world of capitalism is not transparent; phenomenal forms created by the market conceal the real relations at the level of production. But subjects are not passive either, bound to be deceived or bound to scientifically understand reality;

they are actively engaged in practices which, in so far as they are limited and merely reproductive, enhance the appearances of the market, and, in so far as they are transformatory or revolutionary, facilitate the apprehension of real relations.

When Hall says that the first thing to ask about an ideology which succeeds in organizing a substantial section of the masses is not what is false about it but what is true about it, he overlooks two things. First, in talking about an ideology which succeeds in organizing masses, he is clearly using a neutral concept of ideology in the Gramscian tradition. Marx worked with a different, negative concept, and therefore to criticize him for not putting the problem of ideology in terms of political ideas which become popular does not make good sense. Second, even if one accepts Hall's Gramscian definition of ideology as useful, as I do, he does not seem to see the different but complementary contribution which Marx's concept of ideology could make to it. For why should we restrict ourselves to finding out what makes good sense in an ideology? Is it not also quite necessary to find out what is wrong and expose it? Assuming that Nazism and fascism are ideologies in the Gramscian sense, which however unexpectedly succeeded in organizing important sections of the German and Italian masses, is it not important to find out not only what was true about them, which seduced people into accepting them as good sense, but also to find out and expose what was false about them and did not make good sense?

Finally, Hall castigates Marx's theory for assuming that vast numbers of ordinary people can be duped into misrecognizing where their real interests lie, whereas a few privileged theoreticians can see right through into the truth. But this is a misunderstanding, for misrecognition, in Marx's terms, has nothing to do with the mental equipment or intelligence of people. The concept of ideology is not a device to label a part of the community as stupid or less intelligent. According to Marx, capitalists themselves, just as much as the workers, as the bearers and agents of the capitalist system, are deceived by the very operation of the market.

Laclau's and Hall's analyses in the Gramscian tradition make a very important contribution to the understanding of how political discourses and currents of thought are formed or transformed, and how social groups seek to articulate their interests with those of other groups. The critical concept of ideology, in the Marxian tradition, is certainly inadequate to account for the formation, articulation and transformation of discourses, currents of thought, political ideas, in short, ideologies in the neutral sense. But then it was not produced to perform that task, but to criticize certain distortions. What is to be lamented is the fact that these two aspects, which are different and must be complementary, should dispute the same concept of ideology. In fact they operate with totally different logics. Ideally, the concept of ideology should be restricted to only one of them, to avoid confusion. But what is behind the alternative concept must be maintained.

This is ultimately the reason why both the negative and the neutral concept of ideology have persisted within the Marxist tradition; they both perform necessary tasks within social science: one seeks to pass critical judgement on the attempted justifications and concealment of undesirable and contradictory social situations; the other seeks to provide an account of how certain political discourses in search of hegemony are constructed and reconstructed, expand or contract, gain ascendancy or lose it. I defend the importance of Marx's negative concept but I can see the value of the neutral concept, especially in its Gramscian variety. The contributions of the early Laclau and Hall to our understanding of Thatcherism have been absolutely crucial. Unfortunately many authors using the neutral concept do not accept that there could be two different concepts in the Marxist tradition which perform different tasks.[77]

It seems to me that the early Laclau and Hall have made an important contribution to the Marxist study of ideology. Although they depart from Marx's concept, their theory is a creative development of the Leninist and Gramscian neutral understanding of ideology. In spite of the fact that in his 1988 article Hall shows a rather unjustified intolerance of the heuristic possibilities of Marx's negative concept of ideology, throughout his writings he maintains a more consistent Gramscian approach and shows a greater degree of awareness about the pitfalls which surround an excessive emphasis on difference. Laclau, on the contrary, is driven more directly by the structuralist logic of discourse, and, although at an early stage he manages more or less successfully to integrate it with a Marxist class perspective, he will eventually succumb to the logic of absolute non-correspondence and radical difference which not only disposes of Marxism but also makes it very difficult for capitalist social formations and socialism to be adequately thought. It can be argued that the subsequent evolution of Laclau from class-articulated ideology to the absolute autonomy of discourse embodies the transition from Althusserianism to poststructuralism.

Althusserians and the Dissolution of Marxism

A third strand of Althusserians started from the original intention of making Marxism a more rigorous science by purging it of humanist, historicist and subjectivist deviations, but ended up turning their systematic criticism upon Marxism itself and, as a consequence, have dismissed it almost entirely as an untenable form of essentialism, reductionism and determinism. Their central premise is that discourse is the essential constitutive element of all social and political life. This leads them to a radical scepticism about the possibility of any form of determination or correspondence between various social practices. Thus politics and ideology become autonomous and irreducible fields which are not determined by economic or class positions.

An important difference between the orthodox Althusserians and these authors is that the latter rarely start from or refer to Marx's writings when elaborating their conceptions of ideology. They start from Althusser's concept of ideology which they all too easily assume to be the correct interpretation of Marx. In general, they are inclined to see Marx only through Althusserian spectacles. So in criticizing Althusser they tend to believe, with rare exceptions, that they are necessarily criticizing Marx or Marxism in general.

Three main lines of development can be distinguished within this perspective. First, a semiological and psychological line, represented by Rosalind Coward, John Ellis and Diane Adlam, which loosely follows the theoretical analyses of the French group *Tel Quel*. Second, a philosophical line developed by Paul Hirst and Barry Hindess which leads to a radical attack on epistemology. Third, a political line which is elaborated by the later work of Ernesto Laclau and Chantal Mouffe, who, although different from other authors in this strand because of their substantial early contribution to Marxism, end up severing all necessary connections between socialism and the working class and substituting discourse analysis for ideology critique. In this chapter I shall only discuss the first line, since the last two are more fully involved with the poststructuralist problematic, which will be explored in next chapter.

Ideology, Semiology and Psychoanalysis

This particular trend seeks to integrate Freud and Marx by means of an interpretation of ideology which almost exclusively privileges the production and constitution of human subjects. Starting from a very selective but possible reading of Althusser, Adlam, Coward and Ellis put an enormous emphasis upon the ideological mechanism of interpellation of individuals as subjects, and neglect the class basis of ideology which Althusser tried, belatedly, to reintroduce in a post-script to his famous article on 'Ideology and the Ideological State

Apparatuses'. Coward and Ellis begin by identifying Marxism in general with a 'crude' conception of ideology as a 'system of ideas' or 'false consciousness', which they dismiss as totally inadequate because it is unable to deal with the notion of ideological practice. In a typical passage they affirm:

> The (dialectical materialist) idea that the production of representations necessarily entails the production of subjects for these representations has only been developed occasionally by such writers as Brecht, Mao and Althusser. . . . It is therefore the aim of this chapter to elaborate the idea of ideological practice, and to show how in Marxist thought it has not been extended to provide an adequate explanation of the social formation of the individual. . . . we assert that it is only psychoanalysis which has gone any way to analysing the formation of the subject which receives its specific subjectivity in the work of ideology.[78]

Diane Adlam and colleagues, in their turn, go further than any Althusserian trained in the 'epistemological break' doctrine would have gone, by arguing that the origin of the mistaken Marxist concept of false consciousness is not only in *The German Ideology*, but also in some epistemological premises found in *Capital*, specifically in the distinction between phenomenal forms and real relations with which Marx analyses commodity fetishism. Whereas Mepham and other orthodox Althusserians hail this distinction as the basis of a new and sounder theory of ideology which supersedes the problematic assertions of *The German Ideology*, Adlam and colleagues maintain that 'the formulations used by Marx to address the problem of ideology, both in *Capital* and elsewhere in his theoretical writings, are grounded in an epistemology which is, to say the least, questionable from the point of view of materialism.'[79] They argue that the distinction between essence and appearance does not apply to the real object of knowledge (capitalist circulation of commodities) but belongs to the process of knowledge. Hence Marx's theory of commodity fetishism which distinguishes the appearances from the real relations in reality itself is accused of being idealist! What is then the true materialism which Marx failed to grasp? To answer this question they try to paraphrase Althusser as if he had said that ideology has a material existence because it is made of representations.[80] However, Althusser too is criticized because of his insistence that the place and function of ideology are assigned by the economic: 'either the ideological has no independent effectivity in this model . . . or else it is always the dominant instance.'[81]

Equally, for Rosalind Coward and John Ellis, although Althusser's theory goes some way towards clarifying the role of ideology, his elaborations are still inadequate, mainly for two reasons. First, Althusser is right in asserting the materiality of ideology, but, in affirming that this is because ideology exists in material apparatuses, he has a distorted and empiricist view of it. Ideology is material chiefly because it is 'a force which operates to produce a certain subject within a certain meaning'.[82] Second, although Althusser asserts the constitution of the subject by ideology, he 'closes off the possibility of the human subject being constructed in contradiction'.[83]

On the one hand, ideology for Coward and Ellis is conceived as 'the way in which a subject is produced in language to represent his/ herself and therefore able to act in the social totality, the fixity of those representations being the function of ideology'.[84] Ideology fixes the subjects in certain positions of discourse; it constitutes the subject for a certain meaning. But on the other hand the subject is never constructed as a perfect unity; his/her identity is in crisis, his/her very self is divided; and, just as in society a dialectical process of struggle occurs, the subject too is in conflict with him/herself. This is why only a combination of Lacanian psychoanalysis, which incorporates linguistics, with a Leninist dialectical materialism, which incorporates the idea of contradiction, is able to analyse the subjective processes of the construction of the subject.

One of the main concerns of this psychological current of thought is to uphold 'genuine materialism'. Yet the way in which materialism is conceived is, to say the least, peculiar. For Adlam and colleagues, ideology seems to be material because it consists of representations. This conception is not only in itself a very inadequate definition of materialism – why should representations be the essence of materialism? – but also, as Hall has pointed out, it cannot be attributed to Althusser either. For Althusser, ideology is material not because it consists of representations but because the representations exist in apparatuses, rituals and material practices.[85]

The notion that Marx's distinction between essence and appearance is questionable from the standpoint of materialism reveals again that these authors operate with a concept of materialism that is at variance with the whole philosophical tradition in this respect. One could expect such a distinction to be criticized for being the foundation of a theory of reflection, that is to say, of a theory of knowledge which is too crudely materialist. I would disagree with that interpretation of the distinction, but I would see the point of the criticism. To attack the distinction as idealist, as Adlam and colleagues do, is simply beyond comprehension.

Similarly, Coward and Ellis's attempt to show that genuine materialism means mainly that the subject is produced for/in fixed relations of predication is flawed. They seem to believe that materialism is about the psychological constitution of individuals as contradictory subjects. Not to see the subject in crisis was Althusser's main weakness. Ideology would be material because it produces the continuity of the ego, because it closes off contradictions, thus giving the subjects the appearance of unity. As only Lacanian psychoanalysis can account for this process and can show how in spite of the role of ideology the subject is constructed in contradiction, it seems to Coward and Ellis, therefore, that psychoanalysis is the only way for Marxism to become materialist. They totally disregard what Marx and Engels saw as the essence of materialism: 'as individuals express their life, so they are. What they are therefore coincides with their production, both with what they produce and with how they produce. The nature of individuals thus depends on the material conditions determining their production.'[86]

This means that, for Marx, individuals are constituted as subjects in/by their material practices, and that their ideas are determined by those practices. By contrast, the conception of ideology as constitutive of the subject inflates the role and autonomy of ideology and obscures its own determinacy. There may be good arguments for proceeding in this way, but it is surely too much to argue that this is the 'genuine materialism'. True, for Marx, representations, ideologies and ideas have a material base. One could even agree with Althusser that they exist in material practices and apparatuses. But this is very different from assimilating representations to their material base, so that they themselves become the determining material force.

Coward and Ellis criticize Engels for having suppressed the dialectic and contrast his failures with Lenin's achievements in formulating dialectical materialism. It is quite extraordinary that they do not see the direct descent of dialectical materialism from Engels's elaborations in *Anti-Dühring* and *Dialectics of Nature*. They do not seem to be aware either of the almost metaphysical character that the concept of contradiction takes within 'dialectical materialism' as the principle of movement of all beings. Besides, it is paradoxical that Coward and Ellis should have recourse to, and fully endorse, dialectical materialism and Leninism as the theoretical underpinnings of an approach that sees individual change through psychoanalysis as the only possibility for revolutionary action. As they put it, 'until Marxism can produce a revolutionary subject, revolutionary change will be impossible.'[87]

One would have thought that for Marx and Engels the change of the subject is not prior to the change of circumstances and that only in a revolution will human beings succeed in overcoming ideology. Equally, one would have thought that for Lenin revolutionary change required the construction of the party and the political activities of the masses, not necessarily the previous psychoanalysis of their members. Coward and Ellis transfer the basis of revolution to the individual. Just as ideology constitutes the subject for a conservative meaning, psychoanalysis constructs the subject for a revolutionary meaning. There is nothing really materialist or Marxist left in this account. This in itself may not be considered to be a big problem, but it shows how Althusserianism begins to lose its identity in different directions. The next two lines of development of Althusserianism will be dealt with in the next chapter, since they signal its final dissolution into poststructuralism.

4

Poststructuralism and Postmodernism

Introduction

I have already argued that in my view some of the roots of post-structuralism and postmodernism can be traced to the dissolution of the structuralist problematic, especially that of Marxist character. Many poststructuralist and postmodernist authors started as Marxists attracted by the apparently anti-determinist and anti-reductionist promises of Althusser's theory and by his critique of orthodox Marxism. But they eventually turned their newly acquired critical tools against Althusser himself and started a process of systematic critique and deconstruction which took them beyond Marxism. This is the reason why, inevitably, the poststructuralist language, themes and inner structure bear the imprint of the Althusserian structuralist problematic and have Marxism as a necessary, if negative, point of reference.

The dividing line between poststructuralism and postmodernism is far from clear. They certainly share a good number of premises and principles – for instance, the centrality of discourse for social life, the relativist distrust of truth, the discursive constitution of the subject, and so on. For some authors, like Boyne and Rattansi, the term post-modernism should in principle be applied only to some contemporary new aesthetic projects which react against some forms of modernism in the arts. However, they accept that it is difficult to restrict the term in this way, given the fact that in practice it has already been extended to cover poststructuralist developments in philosophy, literary theory and the social sciences.[1]

Without denying important overlaps, I would like to suggest that it is useful to keep a distinction between poststructuralism and postmodernism. In my opinion the former label should be applied preferably to those authors like Foucault, Hindess, Hirst, Laclau and Mouffe who do not dissolve social reality into fragmentary images and signs and who still think it possible for a variety of collective subjects to be politically constituted by progressive discourses which resist power or aim at socialism. Postmodernism, on the other hand, is a label which should be applied preferably to those authors like Lyotard and Baudrillard who no longer hope that meaningful change can be attempted and tend to dissolve reality into simulacra. Hence, apart from their general abhorrence of all forms of totalitarianism and all theories of purported universal truth, they do not consider it worthwhile to engage in any form of emancipatory struggle. In fact they suspect all discourses of emancipation, and prefer to accept the chaotic and hyperreal character of society where not even power exists as a reality any more. While for poststructuralism ideology critique is replaced by the articulating discourse which creates ideologically active subject positions, for postmodernism ideology critique is replaced by the end of ideology.

In this chapter I am going to focus first on poststructuralism. I shall start with some remarks on Foucault, who should be considered as the father of this tendency, and then, as announced in the previous chapter, I shall consider two main currents in Britain: a philosophical strand developed by Hindess and Hirst, which leads to a radical attack on epistemology, and the political line of Laclau and Mouffe.

Foucault and Ideology

Michel Foucault too was heavily influenced by structuralism and Marxism in the early 1960s and reacted against them because of their totalizing rationality. As a historian he set out to uncover the necessary links between, on the one hand, disciplines or forms of knowledge and, on the other, oppressive institutions and their practices which subject the individual. As Poster has suggested, there is a good case for considering Foucault's work as a theoretical response to the difficulties of Western Marxism.[2] A comparison of Foucault with Althusser is instructive because it shows that they share certain basic concerns: they both closely connect knowledge with institutional practices, they both tend to reject the centrality of the subject and conceive of it as constituted by discourse, and, more important, they both want to expose various forms of domination. But, of course, the theoretical differences are very substantial. Foucault rejects the categories of totality, base and superstructure and has serious reservations about the very concept of ideology. He refuses to accept the opposition between ideology and science and between knowledge and power, and takes the problematic of power beyond the sphere of class rule and state domination.

Whereas Althusser analysed the mode of production as a totality made up of various social instances articulated according to specific determinations and ultimately determined by the economic structure, Foucault emphasizes discontinuity, dispersion and difference by affirming that the possibility of a total history has begun to disappear as the possibility of a general history emerges: 'a total description draws all phenomena around a single centre – a principle, a meaning, a spirit, a world-view, an overall shape; a general history, on the contrary, would deploy the space of a dispersion.'[3] This is the result of the multifarious deployment of power relations, but it does not mean that history is chaotic:

> The history which bears and determines us has the form of a war rather than that of a language: relations of power, not relations of meaning. History has no 'meaning', though this is not to say that it is absurd or incoherent. On the contrary, it is intelligible and should be susceptible of analysis down to the smallest detail – but this in accordance with the intelligibility of struggles, of strategies and tactics.[4]

While Althusser distinguished state power from state apparatuses, and distinguished the repressive state apparatuses which function by violence from the ideological state apparatuses which function by ideology, Foucault affirms the omnipresence of power and the fact that power is not something that is acquired or seized or which is in a position of exteriority with respect to other types of relations. Power is something that circulates, that is never precisely localized or appropriated as a commodity,[5] 'power is everywhere; not because it embraces everything, but because it comes from everywhere.'[6]

Foucault wants to explore the mechanisms or techniques of power, wants to analyse the 'micro-relations' of power, 'the capillary level of power', that is to say, 'the point where power reaches into the very grain of individuals' rather than providing a universal definition or theory of power at the central political level of society. Since the eighteenth century, power has changed in that its exercise is no longer merely 'from above' but also 'from within' the social body. He accepts that there may be connections between 'the small-scale modes of exercise of power' and more structural societal changes, but he denies 'that the change at the capillary level of power is absolutely tied to institutional changes at the level of the centralized forms of the State'.[7] Foucault does not deny the importance of state power, but is quite clear that very little will change in society if the capillary mechanisms of power are not changed. This is what happened in the USSR: the revolution ran into the ground because it changed state power but kept the everyday mechanisms of power.[8]

In a move influenced by Nietzsche, Foucault goes on to affirm that power cannot be conceived as separate from knowledge. He wants to abandon the humanist idea that knowledge can only be acquired in the absence of power and argues that the exercise of power creates new objects of knowledge and systems of information. Knowledge, in its turn, constantly produces power effects:

> No body of knowledge can be formed without a system of communications, records, accumulation and displacement which is in itself a form of power and which is linked, in its existence and functioning, to the other forms of power. Conversely, no power can be exercised without the extraction, appropriation, distribution or retention of knowledge.[9]

> we should abandon a whole tradition that allows us to imagine that knowledge can exist only where the power relations are suspended and that knowledge can develop only outside its injunctions, its demands and its interests ... we should abandon the belief that power makes mad and that, by the same token, the renunciation of power is one of the conditions of knowledge. We should admit rather that power produces knowledge ... that power and knowledge directly imply one another; that there is no power relation without the correlative constitution of a field of knowledge.[10]

It is not surprising, therefore, that Foucault should have been influenced by a Nietzschean conception of ideology which criticizes the very concepts of knowledge, science and truth. It is possible to find in Foucault's early writings a utilization of the concept of ideology in a negative sense, but with the proviso – against Marx and especially Althusser – that there is no such thing as an opposition between science and ideology:

> Ideology is not exclusive of scientificity. Few discourses have given so much place to ideology as clinical discourse or that of political economy: this is not a sufficiently good reason to treat the totality of their statements as being undermined by error. ... By correcting itself, by rectifying its errors ... discourse does not necessarily undo its relations with ideology. The role of ideology does not diminish as rigour increases and error is dissipated.[11]

The rejection of the science/ideology opposition leads Foucault to underrate questions related to the epistemological validity of discourse. For him discourses are not in themselves true or false, scientific or ideological. Each society has its own regime of truth, its own accepted discourses which function as true, its own mechanisms and proced- ures for deciding what counts as true. Truth is not outside power.[12] Epistemological questions are then replaced by questions related to the constitution of fields of knowledge which have their own 'truth' and which express a form of power. Thus psychiatry, criminology, clinical medicine, pedagogy and other human sciences arose in institutional settings such as asylums, prisons, hospitals, schools, etc., which constituted their own power systems to control and discipline their inmates. But the institutional disciplines achieve subjection not necessarily by means of violence or by aiming at the minds of the inmates in order to deceive and conceal (ideology); what they aim at is the docility of the body. They control by disciplining, extorting the forces and optimizing the capabilities of the body. This is what Foucault calls the political economy of the body[13] or the anatomo-politics of the body.[14] It is not surprising, therefore, that Foucault should have begun to have increasing doubts about the usefulness of the concept of ideology.

In effect, from the 1970s onwards most references to ideology or ideological processes are in contexts where Foucault is arguing against reducing a particular phenomenon or process to ideology. For instance, Foucault points out that the formation of discourses need not be analysed in terms of ideology,[15] that the apparatuses of knowledge, the major mechanisms of power, are not ideological constructs,[16] that the political question about intellectuals and truth is not alienated consciousness or ideology,[17] that power does not impose ideological contents on knowledge,[18] etc. Foucault is particularly critical of Marxism in so far as it gives too much importance to ideology as a vehicle of power: 'what troubles me with these analyses which prioritize ideology is that there is always presupposed a human subject on the lines of the model provided by classical philosophy, endowed with a consciousness which power is then thought to seize on.'[19] What this criticism seems to be arguing is that it is a mistake to think that in- dividuals submit to power because they are either deceived or con- vinced by ideology. Rather than the effects of power on individual consciousness one must study the effects of power on the body. Power does not seize the consciousness of a pre-given subject, but the subject is the product of a relation of power which affects the body of indi- viduals, 'power relations can materially penetrate the body in depth, without depending even on the mediation of the subject's own representations. If power takes hold on the body, this isn't through its having first to be interiorized in people's consciousness.'[20]

Ultimately, Foucault's idea seems to be that the explanatory and heuristic capabilities of the concept of ideology have been greatly overrated, especially within Marxism. In fact he explicitly recognizes that for him it is difficult to make use of the notion of ideology, for three reasons:

> The first is that, like it or not, it always stands in virtual opposition to something else which is supposed to count as truth. . . . The second drawback is that the concept of ideology refers, I think necessarily, to something of the order of a subject. Thirdly, ideology stands in a secondary position relative to something which functions as its infrastructure, as its material, economic determinant, etc. For these three reasons, I think that this is a notion that cannot be used without circumspection.[21]

If at first Foucault argued that science was not exclusive of ideology, now he maintains that the analysis of forms of knowledge or 'discursive formations' cannot be carried out from the point of view of epistemology, that is to say, the question whether discourses are true or false, ideological or scientific, rational or irrational, is no longer relevant. It is in this context that Foucault outlines his ideas about the constitution of objects and subjects which will be so influential among former Althusserian like Hindess, Hirst, Laclau and Mouffe. First he suggests that the objects of discourse have no reality outside discourse. Foucault wants 'to dispense with "things". To "depresentify" them. To substitute for the enigmatic treasure of "things" anterior to discourse, the regular formation of objects that emerge only in discourse.'[22] Second, he argues that subjects are not the producers of discourse but rather 'positions' in discourse which can be occupied by individuals. The subject is 'not the speaking consciousness nor the author of the formulation but a position which may be filled in certain conditions by various individuals'.[23] However, unlike Althusser, Foucault refuses to accept that the subject is constituted by ideology. The subject is, rather, shaped by power through his/her body rather than through his/her consciousness. As he puts it, 'we should try to grasp subjection in its material instance as a constitution of subjects.'[24]

It is nevertheless quite clear to me that Foucault's attacks on the concept of ideology are not entirely consistent with his own practice as an intellectual who is at the centre of important debates where he wants to devalue or cast doubts on other theoretical positions. Thus in a lecture he strongly argues against both the liberal and the Marxist conception of power as sharing a form of economism. The former takes power as a right which one can possess like a commodity; the latter considers class power as stemming from the economic control over the means of production. Foucault criticizes both and argues in favour of a notion of power as a relation of force whose best expression is war.[25] Whether we agree or not with such a conception is immaterial. What really matters is that it seems to point to a kind of ideology critique. Foucault might counter-argue that showing the shortcomings and inadequacies of other positions is not necessarily ideology critique. But then the way in which he goes on to discuss in a second lecture and in *The History of Sexuality* the role of the juridical conception of power based on sovereignty is highly symptomatic. Foucault argues that the new form of disciplinary power which emerges in the eighteenth century cannot be explained in terms of sovereignty, and yet this has

> allowed a system of right to be superimposed upon the mechanisms of discipline in such a way as to conceal its actual procedures, the element of domination inherent in its techniques, and to guarantee to everyone, by virtue of the sovereignty of the State, the exercise of his proper sovereign rights.[26]

> once it became necessary for disciplinary constraints to be exercised through mechanisms of domination and yet at the same time for their effective exercise of power to be disguised, a theory of sovereignty was required to make an appearance at the level of the legal apparatus.[27]

Could there be a clearer endorsement of the importance of the ideological role of the theory of sovereignty? Foucault is arguing that the juridical discourse on power is not only inadequate to explain disciplinary power but also masks and disguises its existence. Is this not very similar to the role Marx gave to the concept of ideology? One can agree that a new form of power has emerged which has no necessary ideological character, but the concealment of its operation by the theory of sovereignty is not unimportant, since Foucault seems to suggest that the masking is a condition of its effective exercise. In *The History of Sexuality* Foucault wonders why the juridical notion of power, being so inadequate, is so readily accepted, and he suggests:

> let me offer a general and tactical reason that seems self-evident: power is tolerable only on condition that it masks a substantial part of itself. Its success is proportional to its ability to hide its own mechanisms. . . . For it, secrecy is not in the nature of an abuse; it is indispensable to its operation.[28]

Foucault finds that, although the contemporary exercise of power is ensured by technique, normalization and control and not by right, law or punishment, most discourses on sexuality still work with the juridical representation of power. The undermining of the new techniques of power seems to require a new theory of power which unmasks its secretive operation. This is why he proposes to 'break free' from the (ideological, one would say) juridical conception in order to 'conceive of sex without the law and power without the king'.[29] Thus ideology critique has acquired a renewed importance, not just as a demystifying form of exercise but also as a precondition for developing an effective resistance to power. At the very least, then, Foucault is here open to the very objection which he has levelled against those who overrate the role of ideology.[30]

Ideology and the End of Epistemology

The trend represented by the work of Paul Hirst and Barry Hindess in Britain forms part of the wider poststructuralist intellectual movement which, having started from Althusserian premises, turned against them and ended up disowning Marxism. The influence of Foucault in this process is quite clear. Althusser had wanted to steer away from a conception of ideology based on the ability to distinguish between true and false representations of reality and asserted the existence of a crucial difference between 'real objects', which are external to thought, and 'objects of knowledge', which are internally constituted in/by discourse. Hindess and Hirst reaffirm this principle by stating that

> the entities referred to in discourse are constituted solely in and through the forms of discourse in which they are specified. Objects of discourse cannot be specified extra-discursively. . . . There is no question here of whether *objects of discourse* exist independently of the discourses which specify them. Objects of discourse do not exist at all in that sense: they are constituted in and through the discourses which refer to them.[31]

But here Hirst uncovers a major inconsistency, for although Althusser denies that ideology is a false representation of reality he still accepts that ideology represents the 'lived relation' of human beings to their conditions of existence and that it involves a misrecognition. That is to say, Althusser's conception of ideology not only 'separates "representation" and the "lived relation" it represents' but also 'restores its classical status as a false representation'.[32] This means that he reintroduces through the back door both the epistemological idea of falsity and the subject/object theory of knowledge which he had previously rejected.

It is in this context that Hirst and Hindess launch a general attack on epistemology which in their view will accomplish, in a more consistent way than Althusser's theory, the destruction of the classic Marxist problematic of ideology and of its twin supporting concepts of representation and determination. The problem of all epistemologies is that they are inherently dogmatic because they postulate a given correspondence between the realm of knowledge and the realm of external objectivity which is guaranteed by means of a privileged form of discourse. Every epistemology assumes that there is a level of discourse which serves as the absolute standard against which all claims to knowledge are evaluated. With this absolute yardstick, epistemology assesses the degree of correspondence between knowledge and objective reality achieved by other discourses. But this privileged form of discourse is not itself rationally demonstrable 'except by means of forms of discourse that are themselves held to be privileged'.[33] A privileged form of discourse which cannot be proved is inherently arbitrary and dogmatic. The Althusserian appeal to science as the ultimate touchstone will not do because it is the very adequacy of scientific discourse in relation to its object which should be justified. This is why all epistemologies must be got rid of.

The only way of escaping epistemology is to reaffirm that each discourse specifies its own objects. It follows that discourses can only be judged in terms of their own internal consistency. If this is so, then no discourse can be said to 'represent' or 'misrepresent' an external reality. Hence both Marx's and Althusser's negative theories of ideology are inevitably flawed. Furthermore, if there is no privileged discourse, neither are there privileged concepts, nor can a discourse be simply derived from such concepts. Applying this to the Marxist conception of society means that from the concept of relations of production (the economy) one cannot derive the concept of political and ideological forms, and hence the concept of determination must be rejected as invalid. Two main consequences are drawn from this. First, 'we must face up to the real autonomy of political and ideological phenomena and their irreducibility to manifestations of interests determined by the structure of the economy.'[34] Second, *'there can be no "knowledge" in political practice.'*[35]

Hindess and Hirst's critique of epistemology inevitably leads to relativism and to an even more entrenched dogmatism than the one they claim to fight against. They refuse to privilege any particular form of discourse, but then, by contrast, they must privilege all discourses. Every discourse becomes a closed world which creates its own objects, its own logic and its own truth. Because discourses cannot be measured against any external yardstick, they cannot be properly compared to one another, nor can they be disproved. Discourses become incommensurable and there cannot be any rational discussion between them.

But this conclusion is in itself contradictory with Hindess and Hirst's very enterprise, for they are inevitably constituting their own discourse as a privileged instance against which all epistemological discourses are assessed and found wanting. If they did not consider their own discourse as privileged, they could not possibly criticize the closure of epistemologies. Hindess and Hirst are trapped in this self-contradiction. They cannot escape epistemology, they cannot avoid laying claims to know (for instance, that 'objects of discourse cannot be specified extra-discursively') which are not fully demonstrated and which seem equally dogmatic.[36]

Politics and the Logic of Discourse

We have already discussed Ernesto Laclau's important contribution to the Marxist theory of ideology developed in his early writings. Subsequent elaborations of his thought, now in collaboration with Chantal Mouffe, progressively move away from Marxism in general and Althusser in particular. One of the noticeable features of Laclau and Mouffe's new approach to Marxism – which is also common to Hindess, Hirst, Coward and Ellis – is the fact that they hardly ever refer to Marx's work directly but adopt the practice of 'interpretation by proxy',[37] that is to say, they quote from Althusser or G. A. Cohen in order to attack Marxism as a form of essentialism and technological determinism. However, Althusser continues to provide some crucial insights, especially in relation to the constitution of the subject by ideology, although the interpretation of this proposition is taken to its logical and most extreme political conclusion.

Under the influence of Foucault, Laclau and Mouffe propound a radical logic of heterogeneity and difference based on the absolute primacy of discourse. According to Laclau and Mouffe, there is no possible distinction between discursive and non-discursive practices. All objects are constituted as objects of discourse and every discourse has a material character.[38] The identity and unity of a discourse is purely relational and does not depend on a founding subject; rather, 'diverse *subject positions* appear dispersed within a discursive formation' but these subject positions can neither be permanently fixed nor enter into permanently fixed relations.[39] This is why subjects cannot be the origin of social relations and why their discursive character cannot specify the type of relations which could exist among them. Because there is no distinction between the discursive and the extra-discursive, everything in society is discursively constructed including social relations and contradictions. Indeed, contradictions can only be conceived as an opposition between two objects of discourse, for there cannot be contradictions between 'real objects'.

In a discourse no relation or identity is necessary or ever fully constituted. There can only be partial fixations of meaning or 'nodal points' which are constructed by a practice of articulation.[40] As subject positions are constructed within discourse, they cannot be totally fixed, nor can they have fixed relations. Hence, articulatory practices are essentially contingent and have no necessary 'articulating subject'. All that is required for a process of hegemonic articulation to take place is 'the presence of antagonistic forces and the instability of the frontiers which separate them'.[41] Marx would have made the mistake of reducing the presence of antagonistic forces to class struggles, whereas 'class opposition is incapable of dividing the totality of the social body into two antagonistic camps, of reproducing itself *automatically* as a line of demarcation in the political sphere.'[42] For Laclau and Mouffe there are no privileged points of rupture, no privileged subjects or privileged struggles. Plurality and indeterminacy are their banners.

Marxism is a form of essentialism from the point of view of both the process and the subject. From the point of view of the process, Marxism reduces difference to identity by introducing a rigid separation between base and superstructure and conceiving of the latter as an 'expression' of the economic base. From the point of view of the subject, Marxism gives the working class a privileged status, 'an essential identity constituted around privileged interests and positions'.[43] Against this essentialism Laclau and Mouffe argue that we should accept the 'irreducible nature of difference' and the 'precarious identity' of all subjects. Politics should be conceived as the process of articulation of these differences and constitution of new subjects.

In advanced industrial societies increasing complexity and differentiation promote new forms of antagonism whereby various social movements (feminist, anti-nuclear, anti-racist, ecological, etc.) question relations of subordination on a plurality of fronts. According to Laclau and Mouffe, these movements constitute moments of a deepening 'democratic revolution' which threatens the post-war hegemonic formation. However, this does not mean that these new struggles are necessarily progressive and left-wing. Feminism, ecologism, anti-racism and other movements can be reactionary or socialist, libertarian or authoritarian, depending upon the way in which the antagonism is discursively constructed. Ronald Reagan and Margaret Thatcher gained popular support because they succeeded in articulating some of these democratic forms of resistance against state bureaucracy with their basically inegalitarian project of dismantling the welfare state and weakening the trade unions.

Laclau and Mouffe argue that the task of the left is therefore to try to articulate in a different political discourse the same forms of democratic resistance but in the direction of a more egalitarian and fully developed democracy. The left has to abandon the temptation to establish *a priori* a privileged agent of social change and democratization. All struggles, including working-class struggles, are partial, can be articulated to opposite political discourses and therefore can be retrieved by the existing dominant order. There is no essential subject, no necessity, no guarantee of success of any struggle. Socialism is, of course, an important dimension of the struggle for a radical and plural democracy, but by no means the only one or the most important. From the fact that socialism may succeed in destroying inegalitarian relations of production it does not follow that it will cure other inequalities. Socialism must cease to be a discourse of the universal.

One of the merits of Laclau's early approach had been his ability to combine a thorough critique of reductionism and economism with class analysis, his ability to reject determinism while proposing a new conception of determination as articulation. In their subsequent development Laclau and Mouffe abandon the search for a better conception of determination and seem to believe that the only alternative to crude reductionism and determinism is total indeterminacy and contingency. There are no subjects which can be specified extra-discursively, no fixed identities, no essential interests, no determining conditions, no necessary contradictions and struggles, no necessary relations. Everything in society is infinitely variable and contingent because it is discursively constructed and, in a discourse, there can only be partial and temporary fixations of meaning. As Meiksins Wood has argued, this 'entails not only the dissolution of social reality into discourse, but a denial of *history* and the logic of historical process',[44] what Anderson has called '*the randomization of history*'.[45]

In effect, by denying the necessary limiting effects of extra-discursive material conditions, Laclau and Mouffe abandon not just a mechanistic and unilineal conception of history but the very possibility of making sense of history. If discourse itself cannot have extra-discursive determinations, then there is no limit to what could have happened in history at any time. What has happened is the result of pure discursive contingency and therefore there cannot be any sense in the direction that history has taken. Laclau and Mouffe have gone further than jettisoning a providentialist conception which thinks of history as a process totally pre-ordained by a superior reason – they have eliminated the very possibility of any rationality in history. I agree that history is not rationally predetermined by a superior logic, but what Laclau and Mouffe do not see is that history becomes rational as it is made by human beings within certain limiting material conditions. There is no absolute necessity in history but neither is there absolute contingency. The radicalization of the discursive logic of non-correspondence and heterogeneity is not only a decisive departure from Marxism but also a renunciation of any rational understanding of society and history.

Although they want to underline complexity and difference, Laclau and Mouffe's highly abstract and formalistic discussion ultimately reduces society to a conjunction of indeterminate antagonisms between various forms of power and resistance to power. However, because they also want to explain in each case the reasons for the emergence of particular struggles against power, they are forced implicitly to reintroduce through the back door the class conditions and extra-discursively specified subjects which they had dismissed from the front. In other words, they find it difficult to avoid all form of essentialism. Towards the end of their book a privileged subject makes its entrance – not a class, not a party, but 'the left' – and tasks are assigned to it: to expand liberal-democratic ideology in order to construct radical democracy or socialism. It seems to me that 'the left' is a poor substitute for a subject of change, and as far as I know it has not been discursively constructed with any rigour. In effect, one wonders how it is possible for Laclau and Mouffe to say that the 'task of the left' is not to 'renounce liberal-democratic ideology',[46] as if 'the left' were an extra-discursive subject which could freely choose its ideology.

For Laclau and Mouffe, the various social antagonisms can be transformed into political struggles only by the appearance of a specific kind of discourse:

> Our thesis is that it is only from the moment when the democratic discourse becomes available to articulate the different forms of resistance to subordination that the conditions will exist to make possible the struggle against different types of inequality. . . . But in order to be mobilized in this way, the democratic principle of liberty and equality first had to impose itself as the new matrix of the social imaginary. . . .

This decisive mutation in the political imaginary of Western societies took place two hundred years ago . . . we shall speak of 'democratic revolution'. With this we shall designate the end of a society of a hierarchical and inegalitarian type, ruled by a theological-political logic in which the social order had its foundation in divine will. . . . The key moment in the beginnings of the democratic revolution can be found in the French Revolution.[47]

There is more than a casual coincidence between this description of 'democratic revolution' and the emergence of capitalism and the struggles of the progressive bourgeoisie against feudalism two hundred years ago. Just as Foucault's radical logic of difference ends up implicitly recognizing the correspondence between the emergence of capitalism and central moments of transition in sexuality, the asylum and the prison, the analysis of this new democratic discourse in terms of a change in the matrix of the social imaginary cannot conceal its implicit correspondence with the rise of a new class and a new mode of production. The new democratic discourse, with all its initial limitations, was not conjured out of thin air by a mysterious process of self-generation; it was the rising bourgeoisie that brought it about. There seems to be a close historical correspondence between the struggles of the rising bourgeoisie and democratic discourse, just as there is a correspondence between the emergence of the working class and socialism. True, this does not mean that democratic discourse is the exclusive privilege of the bourgeoisie any more than socialism is the sole patrimony of the working class. But it is equally mistaken not to see their close historical correspondence.

Laclau and Mouffe argue that there are no privileged points for the unleashing of a socialist political practice. But they never justify their interest in socialism, nor do they accept what to me is the necessary consequence of their theory, namely, that without a structural cause there is no reason for anyone to want socialism. Why should oppressed groups such as women, homosexuals, ethnic minorities, etc., want a socialist political practice? Laclau ends up identifying socialism with radical democracy. But in my view this identification not only loses all that was specific to socialism but also contradicts the autonomy of the spheres of struggle. Laclau wants to have it both ways. On the one hand he emphatically affirms that '*there are not* necessary links between anti-sexism and anti-capitalism', and that 'the unity between the two can only be the result of a hegemonic articulation.' Yet a few lines below he says that 'of course every project for radical democracy implies a socialist dimension, as it is necessary to put an end to capitalist relations of production.'[48] One wonders why, or who will be really interested in the socialist dimension. Laclau and Mouffe fail to recognize that there is more than a purely contingent relationship between socialism and the working class, just as there is a necessary relationship between feminism and women, anti-racism and black people, and so on.

Laclau and Mouffe concede to discourse not only an absolute autonomy but also, inevitably, the central role in social and political life. But as discourses – and the subjects and relations constructed therein – are eminently incommensurable, contingent and variable, a total relativism and indeterminacy seems to be the necessary outcome. It is, of course, valuable to underline complexity and difference as against reductionism and essentialism, but these theories seem to find no alternative short of total contingency, indeterminacy and randomness. Poststructuralism transposes the structuralist attack on the subject into an onslaught on the structures themselves. The cost for social sciences is very high because it ultimately reduces society to a random arrangement of floating antagonisms between various forms of power and resistance to power. Such a position renounces all possibility of rationally explaining these antagonisms by resorting to anything which is beyond their own closed discursive reality. The problem lies not so much in trying to investigate different institutional settings and their specific technologies of power – which is a valuable objective – but in trying to investigate them as totally and necessarily disconnected from the state and the class system.

Postmodernism

I shall be analysing postmodernism from a particular perspective, namely, its complex and ambiguous relationships with the concept of ideology. This perspective is not entirely arbitrary, since it can be argued that ideology critique was at the centre of the most representative theories of modernity. It is therefore no wonder that postmodernism should have explicitly questioned the concept of ideology as part of its global attack against the Enlightenment concepts of reason and truth which characterized modernity. But prior to analysing the postmodernist attack on ideology it is necessary briefly to establish what I shall understand by postmodernism, since there is no easy or obvious answer to this question.

On the one hand postmodernism is related to the development of new aesthetic and artistic forms and also to some of the substantive themes developed by the poststructuralism of Michel Foucault and Jacques Derrida. Emphasis on discourse as a central instance of social life, distrust of all forms of essentialism and reductionism, and scepticism about the autonomy of the subject and about the existence of absolute truth are some of its most immediate antecedents. The pessimism and relativism stemming from the philosophies of Schopenhauer and Nietzsche are its more distant antecedents. On the other hand postmodernism is a cultural phenomenon which goes beyond new artistic and architectural forms of expression or new philosophical principles of social analysis. As Harvey has aptly put it, postmodernism is 'a new structure or mode of feeling',[49] a special manner of experiencing, interpreting and being in the world which has undermined modernist sentiments.

According to this view, postmodernity is a kind of cultural change starting around 1972 which is bound up with some economic and political changes in the development of capitalism and mediated by a new way of experiencing time and space. Postmodernism represents a kind of reaction to modernity. Whereas the latter emphasizes linear progress, technology, positive science and reason, the former privileges indeterminacy, fragmentation, heterogeneity and difference.[50] It distrusts both absolute truths and meta-narratives or totalizing discourses of universal application, especially those which propound human emancipation. For postmodernism the world cannot be coherently represented in its totality, nor does historical development have a universal sense. Individuals themselves are also fragmented and decentred, unable to project themselves in time. If history has no sense, neither has the future of individuals.

Foucault's thought is certainly important for the development of postmodernism, and its influence can be noticed in various ways and degrees in the work of Jean-François Lyotard and Jean Baudrillard. As postmodernism questions our ability to reach a truth which is not relative to a particular discourse, and doubts the existence of fundamental social relations and contradictions, the epistemological judgement implicit in ideology critique becomes impossible. Nevertheless, Lyotard and Baudrillard, just as much as Foucault, began in positions very close to Marxism and were much influenced by Althusser's thought, as could be appreciated in their early work. This is why they were not initially averse to using a critical concept of ideology, but consciously separated themselves from it in their subsequent intellectual evolution.

From Ideology to Totalitarian Meta-narratives: Lyotard

In effect, in one of his first works Jean-François Lyotard accuses Edmund Husserl of wanting to find a third way between idealism and materialism and, by means of that ambiguity, to conceal the 1914 imperialist crisis, which is the main cause of the crisis in philosophy. Lyotard criticizes phenomenology because 'its ahistoricity, its intuitionism, its radical intention, its phenomenism, constitute so many ideological factors seeking to conceal the true sense of the crisis, to avoid drawing ineluctable conclusions.'[51] Later on, in the last of a series of lectures delivered at the Sorbonne in 1964, Lyotard keeps using Marx's concept of ideology when discussing philosophy and action. He considers philosophy as an ideology, a false position, not because its contents are false, but because it tends to get disconnected from the reality it represents.[52] Lyotard finds that Marx's conception of ideology is very close to Freud's position and concludes that 'it is true that there is a truth of ideology which corresponds to a real problematic which is that of its time, but its falsity consists in that the answer to that problematic, the very manner in which it informs and presents the problems of the real man, goes outside the real world and does not lead to their being resolved'.[53] In *Les Dispositifs pulsionnels* (1973) Lyotard still speaks of 'ideological screen'[54] and of 'historicist-dialectic ideology'.[55] But he begins to move away from the concept of ideology. Analysing the social effects of cinema, he avers: 'Let us underline how miserable it is to answer this question in terms of the simple superstructural function of an industry, cinema, whose products, films, would act on the public's consciousness *in order* to dull it by means of ideological infiltrators.'[56]

In a second stage, Lyotard makes a critique of Marx and tries to abandon the concept of ideology. The first problem he faces is that, in order not to contradict himself, he must deny that the point is to criticize Marx or to read his writings as if they were a theory subject to assessment. Hence Lyotard argues:

> it is necessary to consider Marx as if he was a writer, an author full of affections, his text as madness and not as theory. . . . It is not necessary to criticize Marx; even if we criticize him, we understand that this is not a critique: it has been said and repeated that critique is a joke, because it is to remain within the field of the criticized thing and within the paranoiac, dogmatic relation of knowledge.[57]

Lyotard strives to consider Marx's texts as if they were works of art, pulsions of desire, libidinal values. Thus he can say that 'signs can be approached also as . . . signs of intensity, as libidinal values (which are not use or exchange values) as pulsions of desire',[58] and that 'money, more generally all objects in the system of capital, since it is a commodity . . . is not only a convertible value . . . but a charge of libidinal intensity . . . the system of capital is not the place for hiding a pretended use value which would be prior.'[59]

Lyotard even attacks Baudrillard for criticizing Marx in terms of a theory: 'What governs the approach of this brother remains burdened by the mortgage of critique and theory (critique equals imperialism; theory equals racism, I agree with all that). But as beautiful and holy as his rage may be, it still envisages the truth.'[60] One must not allow oneself to be intimidated by a reference to truth, and, addressing a hypothetical theoretical contradictor, he says: 'You know nothing about truth and never will; we know that it is the weapon of paranoia and power . . . the return of terror. Let us thus struggle against the white terror of truth.'[61] The same ideas are expressed in a different form in more recent works. 'There is no reason, only reasons,' Lyotard argues, or, similarly, society is a series of language games, each with its own rules and criteria of truth, each incommensurable with the rest.[62] Hence the lack of unity and totality in society. No game can be privileged. The pretension of one game to be truer or superior to the others must be resisted. 'The grand narrative has lost its credibility' or is 'breaking up'; 'most people have lost their nostalgia for the lost narrative'; 'the social subject itself seems to dissolve in this dissemination of language games';[63] 'there is no subject of history.'[64]

For this conception a critical concept of ideology, which pretends to know what are the social contradictions and how can they really be resolved, shares with other meta-narratives a totalitarian character: they are not only extreme simplifications but also 'terroristic' in that they legitimize the suppression of differences. The plurality of language games must be respected: all attempts on the part of one language game to regulate other language games is terror.[65] This is why Lyotard exclaims: 'Let us wage a war against totality. We have paid a high enough price for the nostalgia of the whole and the one.'[66] This is also the reason why Lyotard is critical of the Marxist and Freudian meta-narratives of emancipation and does not trust Marx's and Freud's attempts at 'unmasking'. As Richard Rorty aptly puts it, Lyotard and other French thinkers start off 'from suspicion of Marx and Freud, suspicion of the masters of suspicion, suspicion of "unmasking".'[67]

From Ideology to Hyperreality: Baudrillard

Jean Baudrillard's thought about ideology also undergoes an evolution in time. In a first stage until 1970, Baudrillard uses the concept of ideology more or less in Marx's critical sense. Thus, for instance, Baudrillard criticizes the ideology of personal fulfilment as 'the triumphant illogicality of drives cleansed of guilt' which is 'nothing more than a tremendous endeavour to materialize the superego'.[68] He also criticizes the ideology of consumption and affirms that 'the isolated consumer is the carefully maintained illusion of the *ideological discourse on consumption*',[69] and that 'the ideology of consumption would have us believe that we have entered a new era' (the age of consumption which would have replaced the age of production). But there is no truth in this, Baudrillard argues: 'Production and Consumption are *one and the same grand logical process in the expanded reproduction of the productive forces and of their control*. This imperative, which belongs to the system, enters in an inverted form into the mentality, ethics, and everyday ideology, and that is its ultimate cunning: in the form of the liberation of needs, of individual fulfilment, of pleasure and of affluence, etc.'[70]

With *For a Critique of the Political Economy of the Sign* (1972) a sort of second stage opens up whereby a critical notion of ideology is still kept (influenced by the structuralism of Louis Althusser and Roland Barthes) but, simultaneously, a critique of Marx's theory of ideology is attempted. Baudrillard starts by criticizing the status of use value within the Marxian approach. Contrary to Marx, he argues that society should be conceived as a system in which the signifiers (exchange values) have pre-eminence over the signified (use values): 'Use values and needs are only an effect of exchange value. Signified (and referent) are only an effect of the signifier.'[71] Baudrillard questions the primacy of use value in Marx's conception: neither needs nor use values are autonomous realities; 'at bottom they are only simulation models, produced by the interplay of exchange value and of signifiers.'[72] This is the reason why 'there is no reality or principle of reality other than that directly produced by the system as its ideal reference . . . the use value and the signified do not constitute an *elsewhere* with respect to the systems of the other two; they are only their alibis, . . . the system of use value is produced by the system of exchange value as its own ideology.'[73] In short, Marx was able to unmask the fetishism of exchange value, but he nevertheless failed to see that there was an even deeper mystery in the fetishism of use value; for it is grounded anthropologically in the self-evidence of naturalness.

A consequence of this discussion about the secondary importance of use values and the primacy of signifiers (exchange value) is the displacement of the ideological phenomenon. Baudrillard shows that he has understood well what ideology was for Marx when he says that 'ideology can no longer be understood as an infrastructural–superstructural relation between a material production (system of relations of production) and a production of signs (culture, etc.), which expresses and masks the contradictions at the "base".'[74] The weakness of Marx's theory of ideology is that it cannot grasp 'the "ideological" function of culture and of signs – except at the level of the signified'. This is the result of the artificial separation between the economic and the ideological, whereas the truth is that ideology is the form that 'traverses both the production of signs and material production'.[75] So the Marxian critique of ideology 'feeds off a magical conception of its object. It does not unravel ideology as form, but as content.'[76]

Baudrillard argues against the traditional dichotomies which are supposed to be at the centre of Marxist theory: subject/object; infra-structure/superstructure; exploitation/alienation. 'Ideology is thus properly situated on neither side of this split. Rather, it is the one and only form that traverses all the fields of social production. Ideology seizes all production, material or symbolic, in the same process of abstraction, reduction, general equivalence and exploitation.'[77] This is why Baudrillard concurs with Roland Barthes's turn-around in *S/Z* on the subject of the denotation/connotation distinction. In this book, Barthes abandons the exclusive distinction between these two terms which he had propounded earlier,[78] and argues that 'denotation is not the first among meanings, but pretends to be so; under this illusion, it is ultimately no more than the *last* of the connotations.'[79] Baudrillard draws the consequence of this for the theory of ideology and affirms that 'ideology is as rife with the denotative as with the connotative process and, in sum, denotation is never really anything more than the most attractive and subtle of connotations.'[80] Denotation appears objective and innocent but in fact, 'far from being the objective term to which connotation is opposed as an ideological term, denotation is thus (since it naturalizes the very process of ideology) *the most ideo-logical term.*'[81]

In a third stage, Baudrillard finally abandons both Marxism and the concept of ideology. At first Marxism is still the object of analysis and is rejected as a reflection or mirror of a productivist capitalism and as too conservative and petty-bourgeois a critique of political economy to be truly revolutionary. The main argument of *The Mirror of Pro-duction* is, in fact, that Marxism depends on the same assumptions as political economy. It criticizes exchange value only to exalt use value, thus still believing in the possibilities of the economy. Baudrillard wants to leave the economy behind and declares that the era of production of objects is over and that it has been replaced by a new era of production of signs. This is why all the fundamental concepts of Marx's analysis (production, mode of production, productive forces, etc.) must be radically questioned.[82]

Soon, though, Marxism ceases to be the object of Baudrillard's analyses and he develops his position into a new theory of simulations, where codes, spectacles, models, images and the interplay of signs become the organizing principles of contemporary life in advanced capitalist societies. One of the main characteristics of these codes and signs is that they no longer refer to anything 'real' beyond themselves. Hence the new world is characterized by hyperreality and simulation 'in the sense that from now on signs will exchange among themselves exclusively, without interacting with the real.'[83] The other main characteristic of the domination of the code is the end of determination: 'determination is dead, indeterminism reigns. . . . Everything becomes undecidable.'[84] All the traditional criteria of value, be they moral, aesthetic or practical, vanish in the system of images:

> Today, the entire system is fluctuating in indeterminacy, all of reality absorbed by the hyperreality of the code and of simulation. It is now a principle of simulation, and not of reality, that regulates social life. The finalities have disappeared; we are now engendered by models.[85]

As reality itself is evacuated of sense and all that survives is its simulation, the critique of ideology loses its foundation. Baudrillard formally announces that 'there is no longer such a thing as ideology; there are only simulacra.'[86] The notion of ideology belongs to a conception of the sign as dissimulating something ('a theology of truth and secrecy'). But in the age of simulation signs only dissimulate that there is nothing behind them; the image 'bears no relation to any reality whatsoever: it is its own pure simulacrum.'[87]

> Ideology only corresponds to a betrayal of reality by signs; simulation corresponds to a short-circuit of reality and its reduplication by signs. It is always the aim of ideological analysis to restore the objective process; it is always a false problem to want to restore the truth beneath the simulacrum. This is ultimately why power is so in accord with ideological discourses and discourses on ideology, for these are all discourses of truth – always good.[88]

Following different but convergent ways, Lyotard and Baudrillard abandon both Marxism as a general theory of history and more specifically the concept of ideology as a tool of analysis adequate to the postmodernist era. For Lyotard the central problem of all ideology critique is the incommensurability of discourses and the absence of an absolute discursive referent which allows the assessment of other discourses. Just as Foucault denies that there is a unique truth and affirms that each discourse establishes its own regime of truth, so Lyotard maintains something similar for language games. For Baudrillard the problem is more complex and resides in the absence of a reality which could be falsified by representations. Everything is pure sign, simulation and hyperreality.

A Critique of Postmodernism on Ideology

A careful reader of Lyotard and Baudrillard cannot but notice the paradoxical fact that, while they try very hard to get rid of the concept of ideology, the very logic of their arguments leads them to reintroduce it through the back door. Yet such a concept, rejected and not assumed but none the less implicitly utilized, can only become even more arbitrary than the notion they criticized. In their onslaught against meta-narratives and theories of universal application, postmodernists nevertheless feel perfectly able to discriminate between the theories that fall within such labels and those that can be saved; and this, of course, with the intention of rejecting the former as erroneous or, one might even say, as somewhat ideological.

In fact Lyotard uses the term 'ideology' in a critical sense, even in his late writings, without noticing the paradox. Thus, for instance, in arguing against a certain way of understanding the libidinal economy, he says: 'otherwise a libidinal economy will be constructed which will resemble a trivial political economy, that is to say, an ideology with a pretension to order, unable to seize the *duplicity* of the movements which are said to be economic.'[89] Similarly, in an interview he affirms that 'there is no reason, only reasons. . . . It is never a question of *one* massive and unique reason – that is nothing but ideology. On the contrary there are *plural* rationalities.'[90] Lyotard does not realize that he can only affirm this upon the basis of a totalizing meta-narrative, and that his concern for preserving the purity and singularity of each language game makes him stumble into the pitfall he wanted to avoid, namely, the affirmation of the primacy of a certain game. As I said above, following Rorty: what Lyotard propounds, without acknowledging it, is the unmasking of the unmasking, the critique of the critique.

John Keane has denied that there is any paradox in Lyotard's approach and argues, on the contrary, that his theory of language games based on relativist premises is the basis for a new, redesigned, 'post-Marxian' concept of ideology 'appropriate for a democratic theory of civil society and the state'.[91] This redesigned concept should replace the old Marxian version of ideology, regarded as a veil-like substance or misrepresentation masking a previously established pre-linguistic reality which serves as the touchstone of truth. Keane proposes that in Lyotard there is a still critical but more humble conception of ideology,

> one that abandons the search for foundations and totalizing truth and instead embraces the logic of particularity . . . ideology would be understood as a grand récit, as a particular type of (potentially) hegemonic language game which functions, not always successfully, to mask the conditions of its own engendering as well as stifle the pluralism of language games within the established socio-political order of which it is an aspect. In other words, the concept of ideology would apply to any and all language games which endeavour to represent and/or secure themselves as a general or universal interest. . . . Ideological language games are those which demand their general adoption and, therefore, the exclusion and/or repression (the 'terrorizing', as Lyotard would say) of every other particular language game.[92]

The main difference between this humble critical concept and Marx's arrogant critical concept, Keane argues, is that the former will accept its limitations as a particular language game whereas the latter considers itself to be privileged. In unmasking a particular language game which poses as universal, the new post-Marxian concept of ideology would consider itself as particular, 'as a specific language game which tolerates other language games just so long as they remain humble and self-limiting, and hence particular'.[93] Ideology must be eliminated because it undermines the plurality of discourses – in other words, it undermines democracy. Clearly, then, Keane believes that cognitive and ethical relativism is a precondition of democracy.

I find Keane's arguments irredeemably flawed in at least three respects. First, I believe they misinterpret Lyotard in trying to derive from his theory a critical concept of ideology which Lyotard has precisely tried to rid himself of. True, my own argument is that implicit in Lyotard's position there is an unconscious reintroduction of the notion of ideology. But my point is that this reintroduction is through the back door, that it is publicly unacknowledged and in contradiction with Lyotard's explicit approach. The implicit notion of ideology cannot be theoretically justified by the very theory which explicitly disowns it. Second, there is a contradiction between the affirmation that a post-Marxian concept of ideology can as a particular language game criticize and seek to exclude another language game simply because it purports to be universally true, and the affirmation that such a concept of ideology can escape from postulating that exclusion as also universally true. Since Lyotard starts from the assumption that excluding other language games is terroristic, how can Keane's ideology critique, which seeks to exclude meta-narratives, avoid being terroristic? Arguments that this humble concept accepts its self-limitations and is tolerant of other language games will not do simply because tolerance seems to evaporate in the face of universalistic discourses. Keane does not realize that one can only exclude a universal discourse or meta-narrative by means of another, equally universal meta-narrative, which is implicit in the very act of exclusion.

Third, the association of cognitive and ethical relativism with democracy shows a misunderstanding of what democracy is about. Keane seems to believe that the only thing that guarantees democracy is the existence of discourses which do not claim to have the truth. But this is manifestly absurd. Democracy is about allowing different positions to argue and posit their claims to truth, not about denying the possibility of truth from the start. Why should claims to truth be necessarily arrogant? Is it not the case that Lyotard and Keane too implicitly lay claims to knowledge? Their position is untenable and at certain points this becomes quite apparent. Keane, for instance, argues that 'if this relativist conclusion is to have any social and political credibility, if it is to avoid sliding into an uncritical deference to contemporary patterns of inequality and unfreedom ... then it must engage in a further questioning of its own tacitly presupposed conditions of possibility.'[94] Unless Keane is going back to the old idea that there is a reality of unfreedom and inequality which is pre-linguistic, one cannot see how he can stop his own language game from passing adverse judgement on the discourses of inequality and unfreedom. This shows once more that he is laying claims to truth and that he is inadvertently treating his own discourse as privileged. He is also mistaken in believing that this is in any way a threat to democracy.

Like Lyotard, Baudrillard cannot avoid reintroducing ideology critique through the back door either. In proposing interpretations of certain phenomena, he implicitly postulates that apparently obvious realities are not real, or that certain particular realities he analyses conceal an excess of that very reality, hyperreality. But implicit in such affirmations there is a contradiction. Callinicos has expressed it well when he asks 'how can Baudrillard – or anyone else trapped within simulation, as presumably we all are – describe its nature, and outline the transition from the real to the hyperreal?'[95] It is also interesting to observe that the mechanism of the critique in Baudrillard has some similarities with Marx's ideology critique, especially the fact that certain phenomena conceal deeper realities. Let us examine some examples.

According to Baudrillard, Disneyland presents itself as an imaginary infantile world in order to conceal the fact that the rest of America is infantile:

> Disneyland is there to conceal the fact that it is the 'real' country, all of 'real' America, which is Disneyland (just as prisons are there to conceal the fact that it is the social in its entirety, in its banal omnipresence, which is carceral). Disneyland is presented as imaginary in order to make us believe that the rest is real, when in fact all of Los Angeles and the America surrounding it are no longer real, but of the order of the hyperreal and of simulation. It is no longer a question of a false representation of reality (ideology), but of concealing the fact that the real is no longer real, and thus of saving the reality principle.[96]

Even if we agree with Baudrillard's suggestion that Disneyland is not a distorted representation of America in the traditional sense of ideology, he is still claiming that it masks the fact that Los Angeles is no longer real but hyperreal. In other words, in so far as Disneyland plays a concealing role, it uses a similar mechanism to that of ideology, except that instead of masking a reality it masks an absence, or the fact that what is beyond Disneyland is also simulation and hyperreality. Why should this not be a kind of ideology critique? What is this simulation or hyperreality if not the new transposed being of Los Angeles which is concealed by Disneyland and absolutely affirmed by Baudrillard as a fact?

Another example analysed by Baudrillard is the Watergate affair. It was presented by the media as the denunciation of a scandal whose aim was to revive public morality. In fact, Baudrillard argues, the presentation of Watergate as a scandal conceals, first, the fact that 'there is no difference between the facts and their denunciation', since identical methods were employed by the CIA and the *Washington Post* journalists,[97] and, second, the fact that Watergate was not a scandal.[98] Again, Baudrillard argues that, if we had resorted to the concept of ideology, its role would have been to dissimulate the scandal, whereas in reality the mass media dissimulated the fact that there was no scandal, no principle at stake, no difference between those in government and those denouncing the scandal. But why can we not say, then, that in Baudrillard's opinion the ideological function of the media coverage of the Watergate affair was to conceal or mask the fact that the government and its denouncers were the same and that ultimately capitalism and the system of government themselves are fundamentally corrupt and unprincipled? When Baudrillard describes the Watergate mechanism as a question 'of proving the real by the imaginary; proving truth by scandal; proving the law by transgression . . . proving the system by crisis'; when he argues that 'everything is metamorphosed into its inverse in order to be perpetuated in its purged form'[99] – is he not really describing, without acknowledging it, the new role of ideology?

The same happens when Baudrillard comments on a conference about 'the end of the world' which took place in New York in 1985. For him such a discussion makes no sense because New York is already the end of the world. But the discussion about the idea of the end of the world masks this fact. For Baudrillard 'the scenario is strikingly inferior to its model.'[100] However, intellectuals seem unable to recognize this fact and fall into an error similar to the one Marx criticized in the German ideology: namely, their discussion is an attempt 'to save *the idea* of the end of the world from the real event – this is the habitual work of intellectuals.'[101] Another remarkable example is Baudrillard's analysis of Zinoviev's idea that the Third World War would have as a consequence the establishment of universal communism as the mode of organization of the survivors. For Baudrillard, communist states had already proceeded with the extermination of their own societies and the West had done likewise by other means. This means that the Third World War has already happened and it is useless to fear it because it is among us. In other words the discussion about a Third World War in the future conceals the fact that such a war is already happening.[102]

In all these examples Baudrillard is outwardly using, without recognizing it, a critical concept of ideology which operates with a mechanism similar to Marx's. But, of course, for Baudrillard what is concealed is not an inner, twisted, inverted reality (the real contradictions in Marx's terms); what is concealed is the fact that that which is presented as real is not longer real but hyperreal, a mere reproduction of a model, subordinate to representation. What is masked is the fact that reality itself has been dissolved. For Baudrillard the boundary between representation and reality implodes, and society is now governed by signs and codes. As Kellner puts it, 'we live in a "hyperreality" of simulation in which images, spectacles and the play of signs replace the logic of production and class conflict.'[103] Reality as Marx knew it no longer exists, or it has become subordinate to the new reality of the sign produced by the media.

'New York is already the end of the world'; 'the social is carceral'; 'the real country is Disneyland'; 'Watergate is not a scandal'; 'there is no difference between the facts and their denunciation'; 'the Third World War has already occurred': these are the realities which ideology conceals, the realities which surpass their representations – namely, the conference in New York, prisons, Disneyland, Watergate, Zinoviev's forecast. These events are presented as the real but are really hyperreal in the sense that their reality goes beyond themselves. Whereas for Marx the appearances fixed in ideology were the reverse of the concealed inner relations, for Baudrillard the elements present in the events he analyses reflect in miniature a wider reality which is concealed in the process. What is concealed is not the reverse but an excess of that very reality, hyperreality. Marx's theory of ideology is typical of modernity in that it wanted to penetrate social appearances in order to find a hidden meaning lying behind them. For Baudrillard, on the contrary, what is typical of postmodernity is the fact that meaning itself has been destroyed: 'in postmodern society . . . everything is visible, explicit, transparent, obscene.'[104] Nevertheless, it is impossible not to see that in the cases analysed by Baudrillard certain appearances are also operating. True, they do not invert real relations as in Marx, but at least they reduce a certain reality to the particular, thus concealing its universality.

The same logic of these examples is followed by Baudrillard in his critique of other theories. Let us take Marxism, for example. When Baudrillard unwittingly invites us to 'unmask everything hidden behind the concepts of production, mode of production, productive forces . . . etc.', and accuses Marxism of assisting the 'cunning of capital' by convincing people 'that they are alienated by the sale of their labour power, thus censoring the much more radical hypothesis that they might be alienated as labour power',[105] is he not implicitly alluding to a masked reality which he can discover by means of ideology critique? Equally, in the case of Foucault, Baudrillard argues that his analyses of power and sexuality are obsolete because there is something that Foucault does not see. In the case of power Baudrillard asks himself 'what if Foucault spoke so well to us concerning power . . . only because power is dead . . . dissolved purely and simply?'[106] The micro-analysis of power in a multiplicity of places and social instances does not constitute evidence, as Foucault believes, of the omnipresence of power, but rather conceals the fact that power itself has disappeared. Instead of being omnipresent, power has been hyperrealized into simulation. Hyperreality is finally the dissolution of reality. This is why Baudrillard affirms that 'the secret of great politicians was to know that power *does not exist*. That it is nothing but a perspective space of simulation . . . and that if power seduces, it is because it is a simulacrum.'[107] The same kind of argument is repeated in relation to Foucault's analysis of sexuality: 'what if Foucault spoke to us so well of sexuality . . . only because this figure of sexuality . . . was, like that of power, in the process of disappearing?'[108]

In his critique of the left, Baudrillard resorts to a more Machiavellian-Nietzschean concept of ideology, but all the same critical. The left, he says, believes in solidarity, the common good, honesty, public virtue, and so on. It does not see that those are only masks because politics is about private vices, base instincts and distortions:

> The recognition of a dimension of illusion, of irony, of perversion . . . is excluded in the perspective of the edification of the social.
> . . . To make use and take advantage of evil, vice, the interests, the passions, to count on evil, that is to say on the intelligence of the secret detour of things and not to ever count on good, that is to say upon their rectitude, was the only possible way of existing for the political.[109]

Paradoxically, therefore, the aggressive position of postmodernism in relation to the concept of ideology fails fully to eradicate – and implicitly postulates – the totalizing perspective it sought to abolish, and therefore ends up contradicting itself. It rejects the critique of ideology but introduces a sort of ideology critique in its attack against meta-narratives and in its analyses of diverse social phenomena which seem to conceal a deeper reality. However, this ideology critique is, in Habermas's words, 'totalized and self-consuming';[110] that is to say, it 'attacks its own foundations', because, although it is profoundly sceptical and wants to escape from the belief in truth, it has to presuppose its own validity. This is the fate of all sceptical theories which deny the sense or even the possibility of truth: either they implicitly claim it for themselves, thus running into a flagrant contradiction, or they end up condemning their own validity claims, in which case they cease to be credible.

As Harvey has put it, 'obsessed with deconstructing and delegitimating every form of argument', they end up doubting their own legitimacy to the point where no solid basis remains for rational action.[111] Postmodernist conceptions want to take leave of modernity but do not want to account for their own position; they so undermine the differences between Enlightenment and manipulation, truth and ideology, reason and domination that they themselves could not survive their own critique. Thus they become very one-sided and insensitive theories unable to see the positive aspects of modernity, unable to understand how those positive aspects are articulated with, and coexist in opposition to, the repressive and alienating features they absolutize.

Ultimately postmodernist conceptions are themselves ideological in that they help to mask the real contradictions of the global capitalist system and objectively seek to deflect people's attention away from them into the rarefied world of simulacra and hyperreality. They are ideological also in the sense that, by unilaterally emphasizing pluralism and difference, they tend to conceal the elements of humanity common to different cultures and races. In openly attacking the concept of ideology but secretly using it to unilaterally criticize the theories (meta-narratives) which propose critical concepts of ideology, postmodernism not only contradicts itself but also becomes a convenient ideology of the status quo. Postmodern relativism and distrust of reason make it impossible for anyone to believe in a better future or in the possible resolution of major societal problems. Consciously sought change and politics in general seem to lose all sense. In the end reality and agency themselves have been dissolved. In times of accelerated technological change, political and economic crises in the ex-communist world, and deep economic problems in the capitalist West including the Third World, no other ideological form seems to be better suited than postmodernism to defend the system as a whole, because it makes chaos, bewildering change and endless fragmentation the normal and natural state of society.

This is why, paradoxically, postmodernism seems to co-exist so well with neo-liberalism: market forces left on their own tend to produce chaotic change and revolutionize all spheres of life and are even able to penetrate and commodify art and cultural production. The brave new hyperreal world in which postmodernism revels is in fact the result of market forces set free. True, neo-liberalism and postmodernity seem to come from totally opposite philosophical premises in that the former is universalistic, believes in reason and generally draws on the Enlightenment idea of progress, whereas the latter attacks reason, does not believe in progress and emphasizes locality and particularity. Yet what is not usually acknowledged is that, in propounding the free play of market forces as the cornerstone of its theory, neo-liberalism is upholding and supporting both the individual rationality of the private producer and the overall irrationality of the system or total outcome. Postmodernism connects with this latter aspect, not so much with the rationality of the entrepreneur as with the irrationality of the market results. Thus it could be said that postmodernism has become the philosophical logic of neo-liberalism just as neo-liberalism has become the economic logic of postmodernity.

Habermas and the New Concept of Reason

Introduction

There are two stages in the development of Jürgen Habermas's conception of ideology. The first stage goes up to 1981 and emphasizes two main elements: (1) the shift from the nineteenth-century type of ideology and the impact of science and technology on the emergence of a technocratic ideology; (2) the replacement of the theory of consciousness by a theory of communicative competence as the main theoretical underpinning of the concept of ideology. The second stage, which is marked by the publication of *The Theory of Communicative Action* in 1981, signals a new approach where the concept of ideology seems to lose importance in the face of a new kind of 'fragmented consciousness', in spite of the fact that many of its analyses reiterate and clarify the principles developed in the first stage. The concept of ideology and the critique of ideology are first elaborated as key elements of any critical social science. In the second stage, however, ideology no longer performs a central role within Critical Theory, although the actual critique of certain neo-conservative conceptions, especially those which absolutize their attack on modernity, is accentuated.

Habermas starts his approach to ideology within the theoretical tradition of Marxism and Critical Theory. From Marx he takes the notion of ideology as a critical concept which makes a reference to the legitimation of forms of domination in society. From Critical Theory he takes the critique of the instrumental reason brought about by modernity and the new ideological role of science and technology, especially in its Marcusean version. But he introduces a new element, without which the critique of instrumental reason is self-defeating and the role of science is unilaterally downgraded: namely, the role of communication in the conceptualization of reason and in the supersession of the philosophy of consciousness. This new element separates him from Marx, Adorno and Horkheimer.

Habermas commences by maintaining that in contemporary developed societies ideology is no longer based upon the market economy and the principle of just exchange, which were the hallmarks of liberalism in the nineteenth century. The change from early capitalism to a situation where the state intervened to regulate the economic process and provide general welfare invalidated in practice the ideology of equal exchange and called for a new form of legitimation for political power. This was found in a kind of technocratic consciousness which depoliticizes practical issues, thus justifying the exercise of power as if it were merely a problem of technical decisions best left to technicians. It is a form of depoliticized consciousness which blurs the difference between communicative interaction and purposive-rational action. This new kind of ideology stems from technology and science, which have become fused and increasingly manipulative.[1]

In this respect Habermas wants to steer a middle course between Marx and Marcuse. Contrary to Marx, he argues that productive forces

> do not appear, as Marx supposed, *under all circumstances* to be a potential for liberation and to set off emancipatory movements – at least not once the continual growth of the productive forces has become dependent on scientific-technical progress that has *also* taken on functions of *legitimating political power*.[2]

On the other hand Habermas argues that Marcuse could not properly reconcile the ideological nature of technological rationality with the fact that it is also a progressive productive force. Habermas wants to affirm that technological rationality is both progressive in so far as its continuous growth threatens the institutional framework, and ideological in so far as it 'sets the standard of legitimation for the production relations that restrict this potential'.[3] Science functions as ideology inasmuch as it is connected with instrumental interests which in late capitalism have become predominant and have reduced the sphere of practical or communicative interests. But at the same time science and technology facilitate the control of nature by means of the logic of instrumental action, and, to that extent, Habermas finds it impossible to accept Marcuse's suggestion of a totally different technology and science:

The idea of a New Science will not stand up to logical scrutiny any more than that of a New Technology, if indeed science is to retain the meaning of modern science inherently oriented to possible technical control. For this function, as for scientific-technical progress in general, there is no more 'humane' substitute.[4]

Kunneman has made the interesting point that, in spite of appearances, Habermas views science and technology as politically neutral 'because the logic of their development mirrors the logic of instrumental action as such'.[5] In other words, it is not science and technology themselves which are criticized as ideological but the extension of their logic to the sphere of symbolic interaction. Kunneman suggests that Habermas did not make a crucial distinction between the basic orientation of modern science and technology as such and the specific way in which this inherent orientation is actualized, incorporated into and deformed by the process of capitalist accumulation.[6] The suggestion is, of course, that in respect of the second aspect Marcuse was right, and science can be unmasked as ideology. Curiously enough, one can find in Marx the elements of such a distinction. On the one hand 'science realized *in the machine* appears as *capital* in relation to the labourers. And in fact all these applications of science . . . appear as *means for the exploitation* of labour.'[7] But on the other hand 'it does not follow that therefore subsumption under the social relations of capital is the most appropriate and ultimate social relation of production for the application of machinery.'[8] It is to Habermas's credit that he accepts Kunneman's criticism in his reply at the 1990 Utrecht symposium on Habermas.[9]

The Concept of Ideology

For Habermas the problem of ideology arises in the context of the relationship between knowledge and human interests. He distinguishes three types of interests: the technical or instrumental type, which corresponds with empirical sciences; the practical or communicative, which governs historical sciences; and the emancipatory, which is related to Critical Theory. Habermas criticizes Marxism for having neglected the distinction between instrumental and communicative interests and for having reduced the latter to the former in its account of historical evolution. He also criticizes Adorno and Horkheimer because in their critique of modernity they too ended up identifying reason in general with instrumental reason. Whether instrumental reason was made to play a positive role in history (as in the case of Marxism) or a negative one (as in the case of Critical Theory), the conclusion is the same: both are forms of a reductionism which stems from the traditional philosophy of the subject. This can be described as 'the relation of a solitary subject to something in the objective world that can be represented and manipulated'.[10] Such a conception can only conceive of the objective world as a means for the subject, and of reason as an instrument to dominate it. It neglects the fact that subjects do not relate to the objective world as individuals but only collectively, which entails some prior communicative action oriented to agreeing a form of understanding and co-ordination. This is the base of a new conception of reason conceived as the process of reaching understanding. In Habermas's words, it is necessary to

> give up the paradigm of the philosophy of consciousness – namely, a subject that represents objects and toils with them – in favour of the paradigm of linguistic philosophy – namely, that of intersubjective understanding or communication – and put the cognitive-instrumental aspect of reason in its proper place as part of a more encompassing *communicative rationality*.[11]

The process of reaching understanding is normally achieved through language and speech acts, and this is why Habermas wants to analyse communication from the perspective of a 'universal pragmatics' which would enable him to discover general norms that apply to all speech situations, as against an 'empirical pragmatics' which analyses the contextual and extralinguistic conditions of communication. In other words, Habermas's goal is to reconstruct 'the universal validity basis of speech'.[12] He suggests that in every exchange of speech acts there implicitly exists the idea of a genuine consensus:

> a communicatively achieved agreement has a rational basis; it cannot be imposed by either party.... The speech act of a person succeeds only if the other accepts the offer contained in it by taking (however implicitly) a 'yes' or 'no' position on a validity claim that is in principle criticizable.[13]

For Habermas, understanding entails the mutual acceptance of 'redeemable validity claims', and 'consensus can arise only through appropriately interpreted, *generalizable* interests, by which I mean needs *that can be communicatively shared.*'[14] Although this may not happen always, all speech acts implicitly posit it as their necessary horizon. Every speech act has as its goal the aspiration of uncoerced consensus: 'in taking up a practical discourse, we unavoidably suppose an ideal speech situation that, on the strength of its formal properties, allows consensus only through generalizable interests.'[15] The 'ideal speech situation' is the realm of pure intersubjectivity, where no barriers obstruct free communication, and hence rational, constraint-free consensus is achieved.[16] This rational, uncoerced consensus therefore constitutes a norm against which all validity claims have to be measured, and it becomes the only yardstick by which to judge situations where, because of coercion, communication has been distorted.

According to Habermas, the phenomena of domination and ideology just as much as the phenomena of liberation and critique of ideology take place in the sphere of communicative action. Ideology, in particular, makes reference to a situation where, because of violence, censorship or repression, no genuine consensus can emerge. Ideology is thus understood as 'systematically distorted communication' and arises out of a communicative framework which puts obstacles in the way of discursively achieved and constraint-free consensus. Two important consequences flow from this. First, not only is the new technocratic ideology linked to the interests of particular classes, but it basically affects the emancipatory interests of humankind:

> today's dominant, rather glassy background ideology, which makes a fetish of science, is more irresistible and farther-reaching than ideologies of the old type. For with the veiling of practical problems it not only justifies a *particular class's* interest in domination and represses *another class's* partial need for emancipation, but affects the human race's emancipatory interests as such.[17]

Second, the problem of ideology is very similar to Freud's problematic of rationalization:

> From everyday experience we know that ideas serve often enough to furnish our actions with justifying motives in place of the real ones. What is called rationalization at this level is called ideology at the level of collective action. In both cases the manifest content of statements is falsified by consciousness' unreflected tie to interests, despite its illusion of autonomy.[18]

The main feature of the ideological phenomenon is the fact that its operation cannot be easily recognized by the participants, just as the neurotic patient cannot easily discover the real problem behind his/her disturbance. As Habermas puts it:

The barriers to communication which make a fiction precisely of the reciprocal imputation of accountability, support at the same time the belief in legitimacy which sustains the fiction and prevents its being found out. That is the paradoxical achievement of ideologies, whose individual prototype is the neurotic disturbance.[19]

This is why Habermas's model for a critique of ideology is psychoanalysis. Just as the neurotic patient is not aware of the repression which is causing the neurotic symptoms, so people in society participate in situations of pseudo-communication in which the false assumption of consensus makes it impossible for them to recognize any communication disturbance. Just as the psychoanalyst is required at the individual level in order to explain through language analysis the meaning of symptomatic manifestations,[20] the Critical Theorist is needed at the social level to help uncover through a process of self-reflection the real causes of pseudo-communication. In both cases, the psychoanalyst and the Critical Theorist have a preconception of non-distorted communication, a counterfactual ideal situation which is implicitly postulated. In so far as all discursive validity claims must be measured against this ideal norm, the critique of ideology can only find and pass judgement on situations of systematically distorted communication by comparing historical situations with the ideal speech situation, or, in Habermas's words, by comparing 'normative structures existing at a given time with the hypothetical state of a system of norms formed, *ceteris paribus*, discursively'.[21]

This hypothetical state in which uncoerced, rational consensus is achieved not only provides a criterion of truth against which all claims to validity have to be measured, but also provides a model of society which is implicitly postulated in every speech act: the kind of social organization that may allow a discursively achieved consensus. This is how truth comes to be connected with freedom and justice: 'the utopian perspective of reconciliation and freedom is ingrained in the conditions for the communicative sociation of individuals; it is built into the linguistic mechanism of the reproduction of the species.'[22] In so far as the critique of ideology makes necessary reference to such an ideal state anticipated in every speech act, its normative foundation is to be found in the very structure of language. Habermas's ideal speech situation works in a fashion similar to Lukács's concept of 'ascribed consciousness', which operates by relating consciousness to the whole of society so that 'it becomes possible to infer the thoughts and feelings which men would have in a particular situation if they were *able* to assess both it and the interests arising from it in their impact on immediate action and on the whole structure of society.'[23] Similarly, for Habermas, the ideal speech situation makes reference to the following question:

> how would the members of a social system, at a given stage in the development of productive forces, have collectively and bindingly interpreted their needs (and which norms would they have accepted as justified) if they could and would have decided on organization of social intercourse through discursive will-formation, with adequate knowledge of the limiting conditions and functional imperatives of their society?[24]

The similarity between Lukács and Habermas is, in this respect, striking. The comparison of existing structures with those that hypothetically would exist if human beings possessed adequate knowledge allows Lukács to determine the ideological shortcomings of psychological class consciousness and allows Habermas to measure the degree of ideology in a given society.

Some Critical Points

One of the problems with the foregoing account is that the reconstruction of a hypothetical state of perfect rationality seems totally disconnected from historical practice. Just as Lukács's 'imputed consciousness' is inscribed in the very structure of the class being, Habermas's free and just society necessary for a rational consensus is implicit in the very structure of language. Ideology, therefore, is not criticized in terms of a possible better society which human beings can practically construct by following those tendencies which are objectively present in contemporary society; it is, rather, criticized in terms of an abstract, unhistorical and ascribed 'ought-to-be'. The scope of emancipation is no longer dependent upon a conscious transformative practice which responds to the analysis of real historical tendencies. It is, rather, the ideal model as anticipated in basic structures of language that normatively and counterfactually fixes the scope of emancipation. The problem is that this regulative model is too abstract to be able to provide concrete criteria which can be used when passing judgement on specific theories and political programmes. For, as David Held has pointed out, even if

> we have opted for argument, and discourse has begun, the old questions re-emerge: Does the symmetry requirement (the requirement that there should be symmetrical distribution in chances to select and

employ speech acts) set bounds on the kind of theoretical and practical positions that can be established? How do we judge the force of the better argument? What kind of evidence can legitimately be employed? How do we solve disputes between competing positions claiming to establish objective moral and political stances?[25]

The very attempt to construct such a hypothetical state begs the question because it presupposes the previous existence of criteria which it is itself supposed to provide. To this extent the practical construction of an unimpeachable model is an impossible task. Terry Eagleton has very generously praised Habermas, as against other older members of the Frankfurt School who parachuted solutions 'from some ontological outer space', for 'securing an internal bond between present and future' by means of his idea of communicative rationality. Just as Marx did, Eagleton argues, 'a degraded present must be patiently scanned for those tendencies which are at once indissolubly bound up with it, yet which – interpreted in a certain way – may be seen to point beyond it.'[26] I cannot understand how Eagleton sees that Habermas has done this. I accept that in the very structure of speech acts there is a foundation for an immanent critique, but, unlike Eagleton, I believe that this is not exactly the same as Marx's immanent critique. The reason is simple. Marx's immanent critique is historical; it is derived from historical analyses. Habermas's immanent critique is totally abstract, unhistorical and derived from a universal and invariable structure.

Although the analogy between the critique of ideology and psychoanalysis is suggestive, the difficulties of a transposition from the individual plane of neurosis to the social plane of class power and domination have been noted by many authors, especially in respect of the problem of positing individual psychoanalytic treatment as a model for political action.[27] Habermas answers such objections by distinguishing the level of the processes of enlightenment, where the objective is the initiation of a process of group reflection and the model of action is the therapeutic discourse, from the political level, where the objective is the making of prudent decisions on the appropriate strategies and where there is no single model of action. Psychoanalysis is thus not intended as a model for political action.[28] However, Habermas's analogy does entail that the analyst–patient relationship be a model for the process of enlightenment which the Critical Theorist must initiate within the oppressed group. The difficulty with this comparison is that at the social level classes stand in a relationship of domination and possibly conflict, whereas at the individual level the interaction between the analyst and the patient entails conscious co-operation. The neurotic patient is aware of his/her problem and is willing to submit to the therapeutic process, whereas the oppressed social group may not be aware of its problem and may not be prepared to listen to the self-appointed Critical Theorist. As Paul Ricoeur puts it, 'in ideology-critique no one identifies himself or herself as the ill, as the patient, and no one is entitled to be the physician.'[29]

In order to conceive of neurosis as the prototype of ideology, Habermas must focus on the most abstract and formal aspects that they share, namely that both are cases of distorted communication, but the cost of such general analogy is that both neurosis and ideology are deprived of their specific contents. As Held has argued,

> by seeing both ideology and neurosis through a communication paradigm, Habermas risks deflecting attention from the specificity of each; that is, from the link of neurosis with the dynamic of desire and the necessity of repression in the achievement of self-identity, on the one hand, and on the other, the connection of ideology with the clash of material interests.[30]

From a different point of view, perhaps the most important problem of Habermas's conception is the fact that it does not make any explicit reference to the material interests and class antagonisms which are at the basis of ideology. True, for Habermas the notion of systematically distorted communication entails the existence of discursive barriers to constraint-free consensus which in a vague and general manner refer to situations of repression, violence and censorship. But he hardly ever makes a specific reference to the class material inequalities, power asymmetries and antagonisms of interests which divide contemporary society. This, of course, is the result of his belief in 'the pacification of class conflict and the long-term success of reformism in European countries since World War II'.[31] Class antagonism is still built into the capitalist economic system, but it has been rendered 'innocuous' by 'welfare-state mass democracy' buttressed by sustained economic growth.[32] Instead, Habermas tends to present systematically distorted communication itself as the problem of society, or, as Anthony Giddens has put it, the very idea of domination is made equivalent to distorted communication.[33]

This means that the real problem of capitalist societies is assumed to be a problem of communications rather than of economic and material asymmetries. Domination is no longer mainly sustained by material inequalities and class oppression; it has become a pure ideological problem situated at the level of the communicative framework which puts obstacles to discursively achieved and constraint-free consensus. It is not that the antagonisms produced by the private ownership of the means of production have totally disappeared. They remain constitutive for the structure of the economic system; but they no longer shape 'the life-world of social groups'.[34] This is why the particular emancipatory interests of the oppressed class are no longer important and have been replaced by the universal emancipatory interests of the human species. Just as the German ideologists criticized by Marx thought that religious ideas were the true problems of humankind, Habermas considers systematically distorted communication and the barriers to genuine discursive consensus as the real chains of humankind. Marx's scathing comment on the German ideologists seems somehow to fit Habermas: 'They forget, however, that to these phrases they are only opposing other phrases, and that they are in no way combating the real existing world.'[35]

Habermas not only maintains that the influence of class antagonisms on people's consciousness is waning, which is a plausible proposition, at least in developed countries, but also minimizes the role of bourgeois liberal ideology based on free and equivalent exchange in the market, which is more doubtful. Given the increasing global importance of neo-liberalism, with its emphasis on free market forces and its continuous appeal to the values of equality, freedom, property and self-interest, it seems as if the quintessential nineteenth-century bourgeois ideology which Marx knew and criticized has far from disappeared. This does not mean that technological and depoliticized forms of consciousness have not become increasingly important within advanced capitalist societies, but to argue that they have replaced the ideology based on just exchange is, in my view, certainly not the case. Habermas has yet to take on board the attacks on the interventionist, high-tax and welfare state and the extolling of the virtues of the free market forces which successfully led in the 1980s to the repeated electoral triumphs of neo-liberal political forces in the United Kingdom, the United States, Germany and several other less developed countries.

The End of Ideology?

In Habermas's monumental work, *The Theory of Communicative Action*, the concept of ideology loses the centrality it had in his early writings. As we have seen, although Habermas detected an important change in the predominant form of legitimating ideology in advanced societies from liberalism to technological rationality, in either case he believed in the importance of a critique of ideology carried out by

Critical Theory and governed by emancipatory interests. In *The Theory of Communicative Action*, on the contrary, Habermas seems to maintain that the very notion of ideology should be restricted to the totalizing systems of the nineteenth century. This means that in contemporary advanced industrial societies ideology has finally disappeared and has been replaced by a 'functional equivalent' which prevents the formation of totalizing forms of consciousness and which fragments everyday consciousness: 'in place of "false consciousness" we today have a *"fragmented* consciousness" that blocks enlightenment by the mechanism of reification.'[36] Hence Critical Theory should no longer be conceived as a critique of ideology but instead has to 'explain the cultural impoverishment and fragmentation of everyday consciousness'.[37]

On a superficial level this might be interpreted as a belated rapprochement between Habermas and the 'end of ideology' thesis. This is unlikely in so far as fragmented consciousness seems to perform the same role as ideology and Habermas is far from arguing that oppression and conflict no longer exist in contemporary society. He accepts that class conflict continues to be constitutive for the structure of the economic system, but he doubts its ability to produce the same effects as before: as we saw above, in highly developed societies class antagonism no longer shapes the consciousness of social groups, and therefore the theory of ideology has lost its necessary referent. This does not mean that everything is now clear and that people can see through the instrumentalization of the life-world for what it is. They are still prevented from doing so in late capitalism by a functional alternative to ideology: the fragmentation of daily consciousness. Whereas ideology works by explaining away and masking, fragmentation works by impeding consciousness to reach an articulated synthesis. One wonders why Habermas does not see the connection between ideology and fragmented consciousness. No doubt he will eventually clarify his position. In any case, as J. B. Thompson rightly argues, it is 'quite mistaken to maintain that fragmentation is an equivalent, "functional" or otherwise, for ideology and that these two equivalents operate *in exclusion* of one another.'[38]

The fact that since *The Theory of Communicative Action* in 1981 the critique of ideology has faded into the background of Habermas's work, in the sense that he does not refer to the problem in an explicit manner any more, must nevertheless be qualified if one takes into account Habermas's critical engagements. Whenever and wherever Habermas confronts neo-conservative contemporary theories, elements of ideology critique come to the surface, even though possibly in an unacknowledged way. This is very clear in Habermas's staunch

defence of modernity and his critical analysis of French postmodernism.[39] Douglas Kellner complains that many of Habermas's attacks on
the discourses of postmodernity assume a guilt by association (with
Nietzsche, Heidegger and fascism),[40] but the truth is that they go further than that to castigate the untenable performative contradictions
and the self-defeating abandonment of reason. Of course Habermas
recognizes in postmodernism the elements of a powerful critique of
instrumental reason grounded in subjectivity, whose ancestors were
Weber, Nietzsche, Adorno and Horkheimer; but, as Thomas McCarthy
has put it, 'it is the "totalization" of critique that he objects to, the
transformation of the critique of reason by reason – which from Kant
to Marx had taken on the sociohistorical form of a critique of ideology
– into a critique of reason tout court.'[41]

Habermas's discussion of postmodernist totalizing theories of ideology goes beyond the mere apportioning of guilt by association with
Nietzsche. What Habermas perceptibly objects to in Nietzsche's
'totalized and self-consuming' critique of ideology is the fact that it
'attacks its own foundations',[42] the fact that, being profoundly sceptical and wanting to escape from the belief in truth, it has to presuppose
its own validity. This can be easily and accurately extended to most
postmodern conceptions: they savage modernity but fail to provide
the foundation for their own position.[43] By reducing Enlightenment
to manipulation and reason to domination, they are bound both to
undermine their own critique and to become insensitive to the positive sides of modernity. Their unilaterality makes them unable to
understand the articulation of repressive and alienating features with
the liberating aspects of modernity, thus forcing them to absolutize
the former.

It may be argued that in taking these instances of Habermas's
critique of postmodernism and its ancestors I am unduly identifying
critique with ideology critique. Why should Habermas's critique of a
performative contradiction in postmodernism be considered a form of
ideology critique? Well, I do not really know whether Habermas himself considers his critique to be a form of ideology critique. In fact he
never says so in his twelve famous lectures on the subject. Yet from
my vantage point the answer should be that the character of ideology
critique is given more by the nature of the problems which such
critique detects than by the author's intention. If the problems were
only of a logical nature, one could accept the case for a mere neutral
critique. But in the case of postmodernism's onslaught on reason the
problems analysed by Habermas are not purely logical. The attack on
reason, because of its supposed intrinsic connection with power and

domination, apart from undermining its own foundation (only a reason already compromised by domination can arrive at such conclusion)
is also a way of dissolving the idea of political domination or, at least,
a way of downgrading the priority given to the idea that domination
must be contested at a general societal level. The localization of
regimes of truth also localizes forms of power and forms of resistance.
None can claim any political priority; hence societal class domination
disappears from the horizon or at least loses its importance. Is this not
the quintessence of ideology?

Towards a New Concept of Reason and Rationalization

A frequent critique of reason is based on its reduction to instrumental
reason. This is what Nietzsche, Adorno, Horkheimer, Marcuse and the
postmodernists do in various ways. Reason is identified with manipulation and domination and therefore rejected as ideological. Habermas
has counter-attacked by arguing that if reason has become fused with
domination how is it possible for these critics of reason to become
critical? How do they validate their positions without appealing to
reason? As this cannot be done, Habermas accuses, they end up presupposing their own validity. The problems of reason are not resolved
by reducing reason to instrumental reason and dismissing it as ideological; they can only be solved by accepting that instrumental reason
is merely a part of a wider conception of reason.

One of Habermas's most important contributions is the idea of a
communicative rationality which goes beyond instrumental reason.
We have already seen that for Habermas the reduction of reason to
instrumental reason is derived from the limitations of the philosophy
of consciousness, according to which a solitary subject relates to something in the objective world that can be represented and manipulated.
Reason, then, is conceived in the monologic relationship of an individual and his/her object. Such a relationship necessarily involves
an instrumental conception of rationality: an external world made of
objects is presented to the subject as a means to his/her own ends.
Reason is therefore constituted within the framework of a means–end
relationship shaped by the subjects' need to dominate an environment
that is essentially alien and external to them.

The problem is that human beings need to control and dominate
nature in order to survive and that this entails what seems to be a
purely manipulative conception of reason. Habermas proposes that a

way out of this reductionism is possible by giving up the paradigm of the philosophy of consciousness and replacing it with the paradigm of linguistic philosophy:

> Subject-centered reason finds its criteria in standards of truth and success that govern the relationship of knowing and purposively acting subjects to the world of possible objects or states of affairs. By contrast, as soon as we conceive of knowledge as communicatively mediated, rationality is assessed in terms of the capacity of responsible participants in interaction to orient themselves in relation to validity claims geared to intersubjective recognition.[44]

Hence it is a question not of abandoning instrumental reason but of subsuming it under the more comprehensive concept of communicative reason which is dialogical and more fundamental. Instrumental reason is only a part, a subordinate moment, of communicative reason. In order to define this new concept of reason Habermas starts by distinguishing between purposive-rational action and communicative action, which he thinks Marx had elided. According to Habermas, Marx had reduced his concept of practice to labour, that is to say to purposive-rational action, thus neglecting communicative interaction. The analysis of these two dimensions contains further distinctions and is carried out by Habermas at a number of different levels and contexts, where the use of terms is not always consistent. In general, though, purposive-rational action or 'action oriented to success', instrumental, strategic action, is that in which the individual subject pursues his or her goals in relation to an external object; communicative action, on the contrary, is that where 'the actions of the agents involved are co-ordinated not through egocentric calculations of success but through acts of reaching understanding.' Reaching understanding is the inherent end of human speech, and consists in 'a process of reaching agreement among seeking and acting subjects'.[45]

   This distinction seems to me to miss the point that even instrumental, strategic action orientated to success is hardly ever an individual egocentric enterprise. Behind most actions in the area of science and technology there is a co-ordination which entails agreement between several individuals, consensual norms, expectations, and so on. The orientation towards reaching understanding does not stand in opposition to egocentric calculations between several individuals. This is why McCarthy has suggested that the distinction should be a matter of degree, whereby in purposive-rational actions 'the calculated pursuit of individual interests predominates over considerations of reciprocity' whereas in communicative interaction 'the orientation to reciprocity based on mutual understanding is decisive.'[46]

The new conception of rationality allows Habermas to avoid a uni-lateral understanding of the process of rationalization as the continuous and unstoppable progress and dominance of instrumental reason. Rationalization in the dimension of communicative interaction means the expansion of communication free from domination. Weber, Adorno and Horkheimer only focused on the expansion of instrumental reason and failed even to consider the situation in the area of communicative reason, thus giving the impression that the latter had been totally crushed by instrumental reason. Habermas, on the contrary, provides a more balanced account: 'the communicative potential of reason has been simultaneously developed and distorted in the course of capitalist modernization.'[47] If it is true that only certain aspects of rationality, understood broadly and in terms of communicative action, have been embodied in modernity, then one cannot only focus on the overwhelming expansion of instrumental reason; one must also focus on the incompleteness of communicative reason: contrary to the pessimism of Nietzsche, Weber and Adorno, modernity suffers not from an 'excess but from a deficit of rationality', that is to say from a deficit of communicative rationality.

Although instrumental reason is indispensable for society to meet its needs (by controlling and using nature), it also has the unfortunate tendency to penetrate and invade other areas of social life where communicative reason should predominate. This is what Habermas calls the colonization of the life-world: 'cognitive-instrumental rationality surges beyond the bounds of the economy and the state into other, communicatively structured areas of life and achieves dominance there at the expense of moral-political and aesthetic-practical rationality.'[48] This process of colonization of the life-world is responsible not just for the pathologies of advanced capitalist countries but also for Western logocentrism.

In effect, Habermas differentiates between three cultural spheres or domains – science and technology; morality and law; and art and eroticism – to which three orders of rationality correspond: cognitive-instrumental, moral-practical and aesthetic-practical. Western logocentrism, Habermas argues, 'means neglecting the complexity of reason effectively operating in the life-world, and restricting reason to its cognitive-instrumental dimension (a dimension . . . that has been noticeably privileged and selectively utilized in processes of capitalist modernization).'[49] A selective pattern of rationalization takes place when one of the three dimensions is not systematically developed, or when it is not sufficiently institutionalized, or when it 'predominates to such an extent that it subjects life-orders to a form of rationality which is alien to them'.[50] Thus, for instance, the Western pattern of rationalization, excessively based on the instrumental logic of capitalist production, encroached upon the moral and aesthetic dimensions of communicative rationality. The problem of modernity, therefore, was not rationalization as such, as Weber perceived it, but the lack of a harmonic development of communicative rationality.

In arguing that the process of rationalization in the area of communicative interaction consists in the expansion of communication free from domination, Habermas is linking rationalization to the overcoming of ideology. If communicative rationalization means the elimination of power relations which are concealed in the very structures of communication and which prevent real conflicts from becoming conscious and regulated by genuine consensus, then rationalization in this area means the overcoming of systematically distorted communication, the defeat of ideology.[51]

The question of selectivity in the pattern of rationalization has been crucial to the processes of capitalist modernization in the developed West, but has also been important to the pattern of modernization in Latin America, where the state has played a preponderant role since independence. Habermas has argued that in advanced societies instrumental rationality has invaded the life-world – for instance, by means of a technocratic consciousness which depoliticizes practical issues and promotes the exercise of power as equivalent to the taking of technical decisions. I would add that the penetration of instrumental rationality in advanced capitalist societies is also shown by the generalization of the process of commodification of life, the penetration of the market rationality into art, religion and morality. In many Third World countries, where the markets and consumption patterns are not as universally developed or sophisticated, the invasion of instrumental rationality into other orders of life is frequently mediated through the state.

One of the most striking facts encountered in the analysis of underdeveloped societies is the lack of autonomy and the general weakness of their civil societies, especially when compared with the enormous strength, extension and importance of the state. In these societies the state subordinates and instrumentalizes the rest of civil society to a greater extent than in developed countries. This is particularly true of cultural institutions, which tend to be highly dependent on the state. The connection between university and institutional politics is a good example: most political parties and the state use universities as recruiting fields for their most important cadres and also as handy refuges for the functionaries and politicians which have been, or are about to be, displaced from government. Recruitment of academic staff is therefore *ad hoc* and based on political allegiance.

The lack of autonomy of cultural institutions such as universities, and the extraordinary importance of the state in their organization and running, leads to the field of culture being feudalized or divided in a series of fiefdoms which are controlled by certain political parties. As there is no objective competitive system for gaining access to university teaching posts, appointments are made on the basis of political and ideological patronage. Sectarian appointments and ideological tutelage are usual. No one who 'does not belong' can become a member. The state uses its patronage quite openly according to the colour of the government in power and the economic leverage that can be exercised. Universities are not always of the same political persuasion as the government in power, and sometimes they become the refuge of opposition parties. However, at the end of the day it is assumed that deans, heads and many other central administrators should respond to the political or ideological colour which is predominant in the particular university.

Communicative Rationality, Consensus and Truth

In the everyday practices of communication which affect morality and law, art and eroticism, Habermas maintains that an implicit rationality, communicative rationality, is also operating. This means that whatever I say to others on these topics involves validity claims which could be made explicit: intelligibility (that what I say is intelligible); propositional truth (that the propositional content of what I say is true); subjective truthfulness or authenticity (that I am justified in saying it, and that I speak sincerely, without intent to deceive). All these claims are contingent or fallible and can be criticized or grounded by the offering of reasons in a process of argumentation. According to Habermas it is this fallibility of our claims (a touch of Popper, Giddens would argue[52]) which avoids transcendentalism. Totalizing theories are foundationalist and essentialist; they admit no fallibility.

Albrecht Wellmer has explored the issues around rationality and intersubjectivity by resorting to Kant's normative conception of rationality. According to Wellmer, for Kant rationality means: (1) to think autonomously; (2) to think by putting ourselves in the place of everybody else; (3) to think coherently, in accordance with oneself.[53] The second principle, to think from the perspective of everyone else, means to think in such a way that what we think can be accepted by others, that we take into account arguments which the others can put against our affirmation. To think from the point of view of all the rest is a way of securing the intersubjective validity of our judgements, and this can be achieved only in the sphere of communication and intersubjective discourse. To put it in a different way, Habermas is quite correct to believe that a conception of what it is to be rational is involved in the orientations that language-users take up towards each other. But is it right to believe, as Habermas does, that from intersubjectivity one can derive fundamental criteria of truth?

Wellmer has argued that the communicative concept of rationality seems very reasonable so long as the intersubjective agreement does not become, of itself, the criterion of truth. The problem with Habermas's conception of communicative rationality is that it ends up claiming that intersubjective agreement is the criterion of truth. As Alex Callinicos has put it, a speech act or sentence may be agreed on in terms of the current state of knowledge, or in terms of a consensus arising from discussion in an ideal speech situation uncontaminated by inequalities of power, and still be false.[54] For Wellmer, to speak and to argue with others, to try to understand them and to make ourselves understood, is the only way of testing our claims to truth. But this is different from Habermas's claim that truth is a rational consensus or the content of a rational consensus, a rational consensus which can only be reached in an ideal speech situation. It is not the consensus that may convince us of the validity of a claim to truth. It may confirm our convictions, but it cannot guarantee the truth. It is not a criterion of truth.[55]

Although only language opens up a space of meaning and truth which is basically intersubjective, the notion of truth, Wellmer argues, cannot be separated from those of belief and judgement, which always belong to individual speakers. It is only together that we can confirm that we understand each other, that we speak a common language, that our claims to truth are intersubjectively acceptable, but we can never be sure that in the future new objections or problems may not arise.[56] I would go beyond Wellmer and say with Callinicos that, although intersubjectivity and communication are the only spheres where claims to truth can be made good and accepted by others, truth itself does not depend on that agreement, or on the individual belief, as Wellmer puts it, but partly on the state of the world.[57] When Wellmer says that one cannot be sure that 'in the future new problems or objections can arise', he is making an implicit reference to 'the state of the world' which may be different from what the participants in rational communication agree on.

To the criticism that truth is a normative concept which cannot be tied to the *de facto* achievement of consensus (how do we know that consensus has been achieved rationally?), Habermas answers that the only consensus that applies is one that is rationally motivated, that is to say a consensus achieved solely through the force of the better argument.[58] As McCarthy puts it, 'If the agreement achieved in critical discussion is to provide a warrant for truth claims, there must be some way of distinguishing a rational consensus from a merely de facto consensus, for the claim to truth requires a stronger justification than our matter-of-fact agreement; it requires that we attach to our agreement the normative sense of being well grounded.'[59] The criterion of truth, Habermas argues, is 'not the fact that some consensus has been reached, but rather that at all times and all places, if only we enter into a discourse, a consensus can be arrived at under conditions which show the consensus to be grounded'.[60] This means that only a consensus based on the force of rational arguments and not merely on other contingent factors can claim the truth. However, even if consensus is rationally motivated and reached upon the basis of the better argument, it is still possible that the state of the world may be at variance with such rational consensus.

So the close relationship between rationality, intersubjectivity and truth which the theory of consensus explains cannot provide a definitive criterion of truth or rationality. However, the lack of a criterion of truth or rationality does not entail, as Rorty claims, that reason and truth cannot have a claim to universality, beyond any particular language game. Wellmer correctly argues against Rorty, Karl-Otto Apel and Habermas that they make the mistake of believing that the fate of reason depends on the existence or inexistence of a fundamental criterion of rationality. Rorty maintains that there are no such criteria; Apel and Habermas try to show that such criteria exist in the procedures. Both arguments are mistaken: reason can exist without fundamental criteria of rationality and truth. Wellmer accuses these theories of fundamentalism, and fundamentalism is closely related to a procedural conception of rationality: the search for an Archimedean point, the search for a fundamental level of rules or premises which, if they are adhered to, guarantee reaching the truth.[61]

The second objection which Wellmer makes to Habermas is that there is no simple connection between moral truths and scientific truths. The nature of affirmations of moral truth cannot be explained by referring only to the requirement of intersubjective validity. On the one hand Wellmer agrees with Habermas that we cannot understand rationality in its various manifestations if we do not understand how the claims of moral or aesthetic truth are related to the affirmations of truth of a cognitive-instrumental type. But on the other hand the meaning of affirmations of moral or aesthetic truth have to be explained upon a different base. Wellmer suggests that perhaps we can speak of different styles of rationality which are characteristic of the different dimensions of the truth.[62]

Ethnocentrism, Relativism and Cultural Identity

We have seen that Habermas is critical of the transcendentalism, foundationalism and essentialism of totalizing theories which admit no fallibility. But he thinks historicism is also wrong in that it is bound to be self-referential and cannot be consistent. It is true that forms of life always emerge in the plural. Individuals, groups and nations have drifted apart in their background and socio-cultural experience.[63] This explains the pluralization of diverging universes of discourse. But these differences, Habermas argues, do not automatically result in their incompatibility. Besides, it is typical of modernity to tolerate dissent and 'to put controversial validity claims to one side for "the time being", hoping for a future resolution.[64] Still, Habermas wants to maintain against Rorty that there is a difference between valid and socially accepted views, between good arguments and those which are successful for a particular audience. As he puts it, 'the question of which beliefs are justified is a question of which beliefs are based on good reasons; it is not a function of life-habits that enjoy social currency in some places and not in others.'[65]

Habermas's discussion of logocentrism and the reduction of the complexity of reason in the Western developed world provides a good basis for understanding ethnocentrism. Because the technical dimension of reason has been privileged in the West, there is a tendency to assess other cultures only in terms of their effective use of such a cognitive-instrumental dimension. The relative backwardness of some underdeveloped societies in this respect may easily serve as a basis for a negative assessment of their cultural achievements. Recognizing the communicative dimensions of reason is very important because communicative rationality has built into its very conception a dialogical reference to the other, a relationship of mutual recognition between different individuals which in itself contains the need to reach an understanding of the other's arguments. This does not mean, as

Habermas says, that because some ideas are successful and widely accepted within a culture they are necessarily as valid as their opposite, but at least communicative reason demands from the Western individual both the effort to try to understand and not to dismiss out of hand the other's arguments, even if those ideas do not fit the cognitive-instrumental dimension of reason, and the assumption 'that the rationalization of worldviews takes place through learning processes'.[66]

This means that Habermas's arguments against ethnocentrism follow a universalist rather than a relativist pattern. The attractions of relativism in this respect are well known. Peter Winch has argued that the idea of universal standards illegitimately assumes that the researcher's culture is the paradigm of rationality and therefore inevitably fosters the judgement that the culture of primitive peoples is inferior. For Winch each culture is a language game with its own rules and rationality standards. So the researcher has no right to judge any aspect of the cultural life of primitive peoples by the Western standards of scientific rationality.[67] Against this position Habermas follows McCarthy, who argues that, although the critics of Winch's relativism are right in arguing that some elements of scientific thought are universal, they fail to make their case because they are not aware that those universal scientific elements must be 'stressed, developed, and expanded' as they have been in our culture, and that this involves practical considerations as to 'which areas of life should be dealt with in which way', which 'cannot itself be decided by appeal to principles of scientific reasoning'. So the case against relativism cannot be won by reducing reason to scientific reason; it requires Habermas's more comprehensive notion of communicative rationality.[68] But, at the same time, it requires acceptance of the fact that 'the mastery of the ability to reason argumentatively and reflectively about truth and rightness claims represents a developmentally advanced stage of species-wide cognitive and moral competences.'[69]

Habermas's anti-relativist arguments against ethnocentrism are also reflected in his approach to the issue of cultural identity which he treats from the same universalistic point of view. He starts from the premise that one should not construct the German identity purely in terms of national history because that is too particularistic and has the danger of issuing in ideas of racial supremacy, as happened with Nazism. In all forms of national consciousness there is a tension between universalistic elements (democracy and the rule of law) and particularistic elements which come from the national history. The balance between these elements was broken in Germany during Nazism, thus freeing national egoism from any universalistic ties. This is why he proposes that the new post-war construction of German identity has become, rather, an allegiance to constitutional democratic and universalistic principles, or 'constitutional patriotism'. Germans have made a conscious effort to dissociate themselves from their past conceived purely in terms of national history. Only a patriotism informed by universal principles could escape from triumphal continuities and comprehend the profound ambivalence of all national traditions.[70]

This happened in post-war Germany directly as a consequence of Nazism, but increasingly the other European nations too 'have developed in such a way that integration at the level of the nation state has lost significance and relevance. These countries, too, are on the way to becoming "post-national" societies',[71] as is shown by the process of European integration. They too have been able to question their own national traditions and their apparent unquestionable continuity. This does not mean that Habermas is arguing in favour of a purely universalistic kind of identity which renounces all the historical and traditional elements. All identities, Habermas argues, are particular and concrete. What Habermas cannot accept is that national traditions should be uncritically accepted, because not all that comes from the past of a nation is necessarily good and normal. Because national traditions are ambivalent it is possible, and indeed necessary, to decide which traditions to follow and which to abandon.[72] This position acquires all the more importance in the wake of German reunification as Habermas has had to face up to a wave of right-wing terrorist attacks against immigrants, the attempts to abolish asylum rights and generally a resurgent nationalism, which show that Germany has still to settle accounts with its xenophobic past.[73] All these issues set the stage for the next chapter, where the problem of cultural identity will be tackled.

6

Cultural Identity, Globalization and History

Introduction

Most universalistic theories critical of ideology were constructed in western Europe and implicitly operated with a concept of instrumental reason developed since the Enlightenment. This concept was seen as opposite to the religious and metaphysical world-view typical of the old European feudal societies. But it was also contrasted with what was simultaneously happening in other parts of the world. Most of these theories held conceptions of the non-European, of the 'other', which emphasized the contrast between the chaotic and irrational ways of the 'other' and a rather triumphalistic and optimistic notion of their own rational European cultural identity. This identity conceived of itself as the centre where history was being made and it was able to place and recognize everybody else as peripheral. Reason was to liberate humankind from unhappiness. Knowledge and science were the keys to education and progress. It is not surprising, then, that the world beyond Europe was conceived as the world of unhappiness, since instrumental reason and science were not well developed there. In that vast world outside, Europe had a mission to accomplish. Just as the bourgeoisie had managed to impose its calculating reason in Europe, it was also necessary to civilize those countries which by comparison seemed backward or 'non-improving'. The struggle against the deceptions of ideology had to continue in other lands.

Of course, it is possible to interpret this self-appointed mission as a thinly disguised economic interest in exploiting the raw materials and new markets of distant countries. But even Marx saw this European expansion abroad as inevitable and in certain respects necessary. Thus his famous idea that England had to fulfil a double mission in India: one destructive, the abolition of the old modes of production; and the other regenerating, the introduction of capitalism, which would lead to development and progress. So even in the eyes of Marxism, the most thorough critique of capitalism, Europe's mission entailed conquest and destruction for the sake of progress. The motives could be vile, but historical laws were acting through them.

It is in this context that most theories of development, accompanied by their respective critiques of ideology, encountered and contructed the 'other' that had to be saved from its traditional pattern of backwardness and stagnation. Nevertheless, as I explained in the first chapter, modernity and its universalistic and totalizing theories were criticized from the very beginning by historicist accounts which emphasized difference over uniformity, cultural relativism as against objective truth and historical discontinuity as against unilineal and teleological conceptions of history. Yet these positions did not necessarily cease to construct Europe as the centre and the non-European 'other' as peripheral and inferior. While the universalistic theories of modernity looked at the 'other' from the perspective of the European rational subject, thus reducing all cultural differences to its own unity, historicist theories looked at the 'other' from the perspective of its unique and specific cultural set-up, thus emphasizing difference and segmentation. If the former may neglect the other's specificity, the latter may lead to the construction of the 'other' as so different as to be inferior and less than human.

It is important to understand that in the construction of European cultural identities from the sixteenth century onwards the presence of the non-European other was always crucial. The discovery and conquest of America in particular played a very important role because it coincided with the beginning of capitalism and the formation of the European nation-states. The formation of cultural identities presupposes the notion of the 'other'; the definition of the cultural self always involves a distinction from the values, characteristics and ways of life of others. In the case of Europe emerging into modernity these alternative values were provided not only by Europe's own feudal past but also by the present reality of America, Africa and Asia.

In the encounter between cultures, power is always involved, especially if one culture possesses a more developed economic and military basis. Whenever there is a conflictive and asymmetric encounter between different cultures, be it by means of invasion, colonization or extensive forms of communication, the issue of cultural identity arises. The question of cultural identity does not usually arise in situations of relative isolation, prosperity and stability. For identity to become an issue, a period of instability and crisis, a threat to the old-established ways, seems to be required, especially if this happens in the presence of, or in relation to, other cultural formations. As Kobena Mercer has put it, 'identity only becomes an issue when it is in crisis, when something assumed to be fixed, coherent and stable is displaced by the experience of doubt and uncertainty.'[1] This provides us with a clue as to what is normally meant by identity. The main ideas associated with it seem to be those of permanence, cohesion and recognition. When we talk of identity, we usually imply a certain continuity, an overall unity and self-awareness. Most of the time these characteristics are taken for granted, unless there is a perceived threat to an established way of life.

The issue of cultural identity is closely related to the issue of personal identity in two senses. On the one hand culture is assumed to be one of the main determinants of personal identity. But on the other hand culture usually entails such a great variety of ways of life, such a rich diversity of social relations that one can speak of its continuity, unity and self-awareness only by analogy with personal identity. This analogy is not exempt from serious problems and can become ideological when it is used, for instance, to construct exclusivist versions of the national culture which conceal diversity and difference and deprive important cultural components of representation.

In this chapter I shall explore some issues relating to the notion of cultural identity, the different ways in which it could be conceived, its connections with conceptions of personal identity developed by modern philosophical thought, and its relationships with the concept of reason and ideology and with the process of globalization which continues to be polarized into centre and periphery.

Modernity and Personal Identity

One of the main philosophical characteristics of modernity is that it made the human being the centre of the world, the measure of all things, as against the old theocentric world-view which prevailed in medieval times. The human being became 'the subject', the basis of all knowledge, the master of all things, the necessary point of reference for all that goes on. But originally this conception of the subject was abstract and individualistic, separated from history and social relations, that is to say deprived of a sense of change and of its social dimension. It was conceived as an inherent essence. This is why the modern philosophical conception of identity was based on the belief in the existence of a self or inner core which emerges at birth, like a soul or essence, and which, in spite of being able to develop different potentialities in time, remains basically the same throughout life, thus providing a sense of continuity and self-recognition.

This given or *a priori* self was what Descartes tried to prove irrefutably by arguing that if there is thought there is bound to be something that thinks: *cogito ergo sum*. Although Locke was sceptical about the Cartesian dualism and denied all importance to identity conceived as a sameness of metaphysical substance, his own philosophy also emphasized the point of view of the subject from a different angle. His account sought to show that, beyond metaphysics, identity mattered because moral responsibility depended on it. Locke defined the self as 'that conscious thinking thing . . . which is sensible or conscious of pleasure and pain, capable of happiness or misery, and so is concerned for itself as far as that consciousness extends'.[2] The continuity of consciousness over time was crucial in the constitution of the subject. Personal identity depended on memory. Locke argued that 'as far as this consciousness can be extended backwards to any past action or thought, so far reaches the identity of that *person*.'[3] The continuity or sameness of consciousness allowed identity to exist, and such an identity was the basis of moral accountability.

Unlike Locke, Leibniz argued that personal identity required an identity of metaphysical substance, but he also insisted, following Locke, on the importance of consciousness in shaping a morally responsible subject:

> the intelligent soul, knowing what it is and being able to say this 'I' which says so much, does not merely remain and subsists metaphysically (which it does more fully than the others), but also remains morally the same and constitutes the same personality. For it is the memory or knowledge of this 'I' which makes it capable of reward and punishment.[4]

It is true that in later writings Leibniz seems to doubt the necessity of consciousness for identity, since one may learn from others about events of one's preceding life of which one is not conscious because of illness or forgetfulness. However, awareness of the past proves moral responsibility. All human beings retain impressions (minute perceptions) of what happens to them and, even if afterwards they do not immediately remember them, they might some day. It is not reasonable to assume that memory could be lost beyond any possibility of recovery:

the very existence of those perceptions provides the means of a possible recovery.[5]

From Descartes to Leibniz, therefore, a conception is developed of an individual and isolated subject which is also the point of departure of many eighteenth-century philosophers. However, in Kant, the subject assumes an even more abstract and transcendental character, becoming more than a concrete individual: the subject becomes consciousness in itself. For Kant, human beings belong to both the world of phenomena (nature) and the world of noumena (the intelligible). But what constitutes the true self is the latter, that is to say, the ability to go beyond the world of senses in order to conform with the practical moral laws provided by reason. So, ultimately, reason is the creator of the subject; by establishing the moral law it unifies the self and makes the self responsible and accountable.[6] The subject is therefore an ought-to-be, a being which becomes a true self by obeying moral law.

The Kantian notion of the subject was ahistorical, supra-temporal and abstract. Hegel added to it the historical dimension and the reference to the other: the world is conceived as a unity referred to the subject, but it is in constant historical change. The subject may still be absolute consciousness or the Idea, but it is a subject in movement, in a journey through which it manifests itself in a variety of forms, including nationally differentiated folk spirits, progressively reproducing its identity at a higher level. Additionally for Hegel self-consciousness entails a necessary reference to the other: 'Self-consciousness exists in itself and for itself, in that, and by the fact that it exists for another self-consciousness; that is to say, it *is* only by being acknowledged or "recognized".'[7]

Marx was one of the first authors within modernity to attack both the individualistic conception of the subject typical of the old materialism and the idealist conception of Hegel. According to Marx, Hegel reduced the subject to thought, and failed to posit real subjects as the starting point. This resulted in an inversion whereby the real subjects became only results and consciousness became the real subject:

> Hegel makes the predicates, the objects, autonomous but he does this by separating them from their real autonomy, viz. their subject. The real subject subsequently appears as a result, whereas the correct approach would be to start with the real subject and then consider its objectification. The mystical substance therefore becomes the real subject, while the actual subjects appear as something else, namely a moment of the mystical substance.[8]

Marx also attacked the individualistic conception of the subject as an illusion derived from the 'Robinsonades' of 'eighteenth-century prophets'.[9] He criticized Feuerbach for abstracting from the historical process and presupposing 'an abstract – isolated – human individual'. If there is a human essence, this is in its reality 'the ensemble of the social relations' and not an 'abstraction inherent in each single individual'.[10] Marx detects the paradox that 'the epoch which produces this standpoint, that of the isolated individual, is also precisely that of hitherto most developed social . . . relations.'[11] Kant failed to realize that the pure self-determination according to reason is abstracted from the material relations of production which condition the bourgeois individual, which is the true model of Kant's idea of subject.[12] Human beings can individuate themselves only in the midst of society;[13] they 'become individuals only through the process of history'.[14] This means that subjects do not act entirely according to their free will; they are conditioned by the objectified products of their own practice; they are socially determined. However, although circumstances condition human beings, human beings can change circumstances.

The idea of a subject produced in interaction with a variety of social relations became crucial for sociologists and social psychologists. G. H. Mead is one of its most distinguished representatives. He argued that the conception of the self as a soul with which the individual was born had to be abandoned in order to study the 'self in its dependence upon the social group to which it belongs'.[15] The self is not given but develops in an individual as a result of his/her social experiences. This is why the formation of the self presupposes the prior existence of the group. Unlike Locke or Leibniz, for whom the memory of sensory perceptions was crucial for a sense of identity, Mead emphasized the role of language and communication:

> The thinking or intellectual process – the internalization and inner dramatization, by the individual, of the external conversation of significant gestures which constitutes his chief mode of interaction with other individuals belonging to the same society – is the earliest experiential phase in the genesis and development of the self.[16]

However, the internalization of external attitudes does not make the self totally passive and purely receptive. The self is more than the mere organization of social attitudes. This is what Mead expresses through his distinction between the 'I' and the 'me'. The 'I' is the response, the reaction of the individual to the attitudes of the others; the 'me' is the organized set of attitudes of others which is constitutive of the self.[17] Mead accepts that because the self arises in the context of a variety of social experiences it is very complex, full of aspects or parts which make reference to certain social relations and not to others. That is why it is even possible to speak of a variety of selves:

> We carry on a whole series of different relationships to different people. We are one thing to one man and another thing to another. There are parts of the self which exist only for the self in relationship to itself. We divide ourselves up in all sorts of different selves with reference to our acquaintances. . . . There are all sorts of different selves answering to all sorts of different social reactions.[18]

However, there is also a complete self which responds to the community as a whole. The unity and structure of the complete self reflect the unity and structure of the totality of the social processes in which the individual participates: 'the various elementary selves which constitute, or are organized into, a complete self are the various aspects of the structure of that complete self answering to the various aspects of the structure of the social process as a whole.'[19]

Most sociological and social-psychological conceptions recognize the social character of individual identities, as they are shaped and formed in interaction with a variety of social relations. They are therefore aware of the immense complexity and variability within the self (elementary selves for Mead). However, it is normally assumed that the complete self, the socially constructed inner core, more or less successfully integrates the various aspects and therefore is coherent and consistent in its tendencies and activities. This is precisely the assumption which will be put into question in late modernity by poststructuralist and postmodernist theories. However, the critique of the idea of the subject did not start with them.

In effect, from the very beginning, the modern conception of the subject and of identity was doubted in a more radical manner, not just as an individual essence, but as identity as such. One of the first sceptical approaches came from David Hume, who maintained that personal identity was a fiction in so far as it was incompatible with the notion of change. As most things and human beings change over time, we can only impute identity to them in an improper sense, by means of an operation of the imagination. Identity is always ascribed by the imagination by feigning 'the continued existence of the perceptions of our senses, to remove the interruption; and run into the notion of a *soul, and self*, and *substance*, to disguise the variation'.[20] Identity is thus entirely fictitious, and cannot be introspectively apprehended: 'when I enter most intimately into what I call *myself*, I always stumble on some particular perception or other, of heat or cold, light or shade, love or hatred, pain or pleasure. I never can catch *myself*, at any time without a perception, and never can observe any thing but the perception.'[21] Hume seems to be claiming that perceptions are ontologically different from a true self, and that what we call self is nothing but a bundle of perceptions on which the imagination has bestowed some continuity. But of course such perceptions cannot be constant and invariable in reality, so their continuity is a fiction contrived by the imagination.[22]

A strikingly similar line of thought was taken by Nietzsche, who argued that ' "the subject" is the fiction that many similar states in us are the effect of one substratum.'[23] In reality 'the "subject" is not something given, it is something added and invented and projected behind what there is.'[24] Nietzsche opposed Descartes's idea that because there is thought then there must be a subject that thinks, an 'I' which is the cause of thought. The belief in an underlying thinking substance is habitual and it may even be an indispensable condition of life, but it is none the less pure fiction, an imaginary construct.

From a different perspective Freud's theory of the unconscious and of its importance in the formation of the self was clearly a new challenge to the whole tradition which had understood the self as a conscious subject, fully in command. Freud revealed that the subject was shaped by forces of which it was not conscious, and this, of course, introduced the doubt about its postulated coherence and integration. Starting from Freud, Lacan will later speak of the subject 'in process', always incomplete, always being formed. Structuralism, especially in its connection with Saussurean linguistics, constituted another stage in the process of the dissolution of the subject, precisely because it proposed to study unconscious structures and not conscious phenomena in order to explain cultural products. The subject within structuralism loses its explanatory ability, its position as the creator of meanings, the ultimate cause of knowledge and culture. Rather than being the creator, the subject is deemed to be constructed by the external structure. As Lévi-Strauss argues, 'it is vain to go to historical consciousness for the truest of meanings': 'this supposed totalizing continuity of the self . . . seems to me to be an illusion sustained by the demands of social life – and consequently a reflection of the external on the internal – rather than the object of an apodictic experience.'[25]

As is well known, the dissolution of the subject even penetrates Marxist theory through the work of Althusser. In trying to rid Marxism of all vestiges of humanism and historicism Althusser claims that ideology is a profoundly unconscious phenomenon which conditions individuals as a structure, not via their consciousness. Individuals are thus constituted as subjects in the process of being interpellated by ideology.[26] Poststructuralism may be critical of structuralism on many counts, but none the less it continues with the radical critique of the subject. Foucault is the first author to speak of the 'decentring of the subject', an occurrence which for him has been brought about by the researches of psychoanalysis, linguistics and ethnology.[27] The subject is constituted, not the starting point. Under the influence of both Nietzsche and Freud, Foucault argues that 'the individual is not a pre-given entity which is seized on by the exercise of power. The individual, with his identity and characteristics, is the product of a relation of power exercised over bodies.'[28]

Postmodernism is just the last stage in the onslaught against the subject. In the work of Laclau and Mouffe the very term subject is replaced by the notion of 'subject positions' in order to indicate that a subject can only arise within a discursive structure, and that, consequently, it is eminently dependent, contingent and temporal. Every discourse constitutes its own subject positions.[29] Similarly, Lyotard argues that 'a *self* does not amount to much, but no self is an island; each exists in a fabric of relations that is now more complex and mobile than ever before . . . a person is always located at "nodal points" of specific communication circuits.'[30] Baudrillard in his turn argues that the position of the subject has become untenable since it can no longer control the world of objects as it used to. The objects are now in control, and this must be recognized by what he calls 'fatal theory'. The difference between a traditional, banal theory and the new, more adequate, fatal theory is that

> in the former the subject always believes itself to be more clever than the object, while in the latter the object is always taken to be more clever, more cynical, more ingenious than the subject, which it awaits at every turn. The metamorphoses, tactics and strategies of the object exceed the subject's understanding.[31]

From Hume and Nietzsche's attack on the 'subject' as a fiction, through the Althusserian conception of the subject as produced in and by ideology, to Foucault's idea that subjects are the product of power relations and Lyotard's conception of the subject as the 'nodal points' of communication networks, there is a consistent line of thought which has systematically doubted the possibility of an underlying unity or substance in human beings which is responsible for knowledge and practice. So scepticism about the subject has accompanied the development of modernity from the beginning. Yet for a long time this contestation of the primacy of the subject was marginal and by no means pervaded most of the intellectual spheres of society.

Since the appearance of structuralism, poststructuralism and postmodernism as dominant forms of thinking in contemporary times, the problems of the idea of the subject have dramatically multiplied to the point that it could be said to be in crisis. But this is not just the consequence of new intellectual positions becoming dominant; the crisis of the subject responds to accelerated changes in advanced societies, which have led to the belief that modernity itself is being surpassed. The crisis of the subject as a given unity and efficient cause is no longer a mere philosophical discussion about the possibility of an underlying substance; it is now perceived to be the result of unintended complex processes of rapid and chaotic change which seem to control individuals, rather than the other way around. And of course the crisis of the subject is bound to be lived and experienced as a crisis of identity, of the sense of self. To the non-unitary subject corresponds a decentred or fragmented identity. Sociological and social-psychological theories had already recognized the existence of a variety of elementary selves in any individual, but had assumed that they were more or less integrated in the complete self. What the new postmodernist positions seem to be saying is that in contemporary times the elementary selves, although still co-existing, have become incompatible and impossible to integrate. Hence the complete self has become dislocated, decentred, incapable of unity.

Sometimes there is a certain lack of precision in the description of the implications which postmodernity has had for identity and too much of a radical rupture is ascribed to it. For instance, Stuart Hall argues that the postmodern subject has no fixed or permanent identity, that the subject assumes different identities at different times, that there are contradictory identities which cannot be unified.[32] That the subject has no fixed, biologically determined identity and that it may assume different identities at different times is not new and has been recognized since the early twentieth century, for instance in the work of Mead. What may be more authentically new and a product of the postmodern times is the fact that these various identities lack a coherent or integrated self, lack a unity. What for Mead and others were exceptional cases of dissociated personalities would seem now to be the normal situation. What would be the causes of such change? Well, the answer which is normally given alludes to the new forms of globalization, time–space compression and acceleration of change in late modernity which seem to be able to dislocate the sense of self.

Globalization and Time–Space Compression

Globalization can be defined as 'those processes, operating on a global scale, which cut across national boundaries, integrating and connecting communities and organizations in new space–time combinations, making the world in reality and in experience more interconnected'.[33] This is another way of expressing Giddens's idea that globalization refers to 'the intensification of worldwide social relations which link distinct localities in such a way that local happenings are shaped by events occurring miles away and vice versa'.[34] Globalization has existed for a long while but in recent times it has intensified and the pace of change it has been able to induce everywhere has accelerated. Marx and Engels were already aware of the dramatic changes that capitalism was bringing about by the mid-nineteenth century:

> Constant revolutionizing of production, uninterrupted disturbance of all social conditions, everlasting uncertainty and agitation distinguish the bourgeois epoch from all earlier ones. All fixed, fast-frozen relations, with their train of ancient and venerable prejudices and opinions, are swept away, all new-formed ones become antiquated before they can ossify. All that is solid melts into air, all that is holy is profaned.[35]

This often quoted passage, by referring to uncertainty, quick dissolution of relations and rapid change, seems to justify the idea that the socially dependent self must have also lost the sense of continuity and identity which characterized the traditional society. Very few authors quoting this passage, though, remember to add the continuation, where Marx and Engels said, 'and man is at last compelled to face with sober senses, his real conditions of life, and his relations with his kind.' This seems to discard the idea of a dislocated identity; rather, it forces human beings to face their real conditions of life and their relations to others. It seems to be a moment of discovery of how things and relations work, and hence a discovery of how one's own identity is shaped. But then a postmodernist will argue that the world Marx and Engels knew has substantially changed and that the present forms of globalization and change are much more radical in their effects upon the individual.

What are these radical changes which have eroded the notion of a well-integrated identity? First, there is the increasing pace and rapidity of change. New forms of organization and new technologies emerge within shorter and shorter spans of time, thus increasing the obsolescence and ephemerality of products, ideas, labour processes, fashions and all sorts of practices. The turnover times of capital have greatly accelerated. Second, there is what David Harvey has called the time–space compression. Modernity typically privileged time as the main category through which progress and development could be understood, and space was taken for granted. Now, as spatial barriers have been drastically reduced, spatial categories have come to dominate over time categories, and time has become spatialized:

> Time–space compression is the concept which indicates processes that so revolutionize the objective qualities of space and time that we are forced to alter, sometimes in quite radical ways, how we represent the world to ourselves. The word compression is used because the history of capitalism has been characterized by speed-up in the pace of life, while so overcoming spatial barriers that the world sometimes seems to collapse inwards upon us.[36]

Similarly, Giddens has spoken of the 'emptying of time', which is the result of the separation of space from place: 'The advent of modernity increasingly tears space away from place by fostering relations between "absent" others, locationally distant from any given situation of face-to-face interaction.'[37]

Thus, for instance, the collapse of communism in eastern Europe and the dissolution of the Soviet Union have not only produced the break-up of the old bipolar world which dominated the post-war international scene, but have also deeply affected the internal politics of Latin America. The level of German interest rates has decisively affected the value of the British pound in New York and Tokyo. The United States' free-trade agreements with Canada and Mexico have been determinant for the Chilean international economic strategy, and so forth. All over the world, what happens in one corner affects the situation in another faraway corner in practically no time.

Third, there has been an acceleration of the process of globalization of economic phenomena which affects all countries and regions of the world. This entails a decline of the nation-state and the growing trend towards the internationalization of the economy. Both the financial and productive spheres are increasingly controlled by multinational companies and are globally oriented and internationally articulated. Important developments particularly noticeable in this area are the extraordinary growth in international trade coupled with a spectacular growth of an increasingly globalized capital market and the deregulation of many national capital markets. Also noticeable are the marked growth in the role of multinational companies and the process of accelerating technological change.

Most important is the change from the so-called Fordist pattern of capital accumulation based on huge firms with rigid patterns of organization and labour towards a more 'flexible regime of accumulation' based on smaller firms and flexible work systems including part-time, temporary and sub-contracted labour.[38] Of equal importance is the tendency to strengthen international financial organizations which acquire a greater power to intervene in the life of countries given the wider support they enjoy and the tendency to form big trading areas presided over by a powerful nation. Thus, for instance, the United-States-controlled free-trade area including Canada, Mexico and now possibly Chile; the Japanese-controlled trade zone in the Pacific Ocean; and the European Economic Community where the German economy has primacy. All these changes and developments make it more difficult for any state with an open market economy to operate economic policies that are significantly out of line with those of the rest of the developed world.

In fourth place, the process of globalization also affects communications, politics and culture which have become more and more interconnected and interdependent throughout the world. The new form of global mass culture is certainly dominated by American influences and manifests itself principally in television and film. Entertainment and leisure are now dominated world-wide by electronic images. Stuart Hall has argued that the most important characteristic of this form of global culture is its peculiar form of homogenization, its ability to recognize and absorb cultural differences within a larger overarching framework which is essentially an American conception of the world.[39] Hence, for instance, the world-wide predominance of neo-liberalism, which is adopted everywhere in different forms.

All these important changes occurring in the late twentieth century, their rapid pace and their global impact are supposed to have a distinct disintegrating effect on personal identity. Although I am convinced of the importance of all these changes I have doubts as to whether they are in any way responsible for a totally decentred subject. I accept that the quicker the pace of change in all sorts of relations the more difficult it is for the subject to make sense of what is going on, to see the continuity between past and present, and therefore the more difficult it is for the subject to form a unitary view of itself and to know how to act. But from this to accept the total fragmentation of the subject there is a big jump. The alleged decentring of the subject corresponds to the supposed triumph of objectivity, the supposed victory of unconscious structural forces which totally destroy the sense of unity of the individual. But to accept this is to accept the final loss of agency and purpose, the inability of the subject to attempt to change the circumstances, its inability to posit any rational alternative future.

I do not believe that this has irreversibly happened or may ever totally happen, although I accept that it is more difficult than before for individuals to understand all changes and to have a sense of direction. I regard this idea of decentring and the announced demise of the subject as being suspiciously close to and corresponding with the conservative neo-liberal emphasis on the supremacy of the blind forces of the market which on no account should be interfered with. Classical economists already believed that the problem before capitalism had been the construction of artificial institutions which encroached on the free markets, but at least they recognized that human beings could politically interfere and destroy the 'natural' system. Contemporary neo-liberal positions continue to warn against the idea that human agents can construct the world as they wish and reject any tampering with the market, but what is new is that now they count on the postmodernist philosophical outlook as a powerful ideological weapon which seeks to convince people that it is impossible for human beings to act politically with effect on society as a total entity. The rapidly changing world which has lost a sense of direction, purpose and unity has finally undermined, so we are told, the very ability of the individual to know what he or she wants or how he or she could act. In times of confusion and mind-boggling changes this is a most dangerous and insidious ideology.

Globalization and National Identity

In forming their personal identities, most individuals share certain group allegiances or characteristics such as religion, gender, class, ethnicity, sexuality and nationality, which help to specify the subject and its sense of identity. This is how the idea of cultural identities emerges. In modern times the cultural identity which has had the most important influence on the formation of subjects is the notion of national identity. As I have said, I have doubts as to whether the changes occurring in late modernity, although spectacular and far-reaching, have really totally decentred and fragmented the subject so as to make its unitary identity impossible. Yet one has to recognize that these changes have indeed more deeply affected many cultural identities, especially national identity. The decline of the nation-state and the acceleration of globalization and time–space compression processes have certainly affected national allegiances and identities. But it would be a mistake to believe that the effects are simply a tendency to dissolve nationalisms, localisms and regionalisms.

As Hall has argued, the more profound the universalizing tendencies are, the more particular peoples, ethnic groups or sections of society seek to reaffirm their difference and the more they become attached to their locality.[40] One has only to look at the dissolution of the Soviet

Union and of Yugoslavia to realize that nationalism is not dead in the early 1990s. National identities in those countries were strengthened as a form of resistance to the monolithic central power which used to rule those countries. Yet from another point of view it is also true that the cultural homogenization implicit in the globalization of culture is eroding national identities, and such tendencies can be clearly seen at work in the European Community.

In more general terms globalization can be said to affect cultural identities in a variety of ways which ought to be studied in their historical specificity. That is to say, just as it could be argued that in late modernity it is eroding national identity, during earlier phases of modernity it could be said to be contributing to the success of certain versions of national identity. In this sense globalization is a complex process which assumes different forms at different times and which is by no means entirely new. Its pace accelerated with the emergence of capitalism. Capitalism brought about vastly improved means of transport and communication and hence it spread quickly throughout the world and created the so-called world market. Globalization not only assumes different forms in history, but could also be said to be a process led and dominated by the prevailing cultural patterns of a powerful international country. One of the characteristics of the new forms of globalization is, as we have already indicated above, that it is a process where the influence of the United States and its cultural forms plays a dominant role.

But it was not always like that. In earlier epochs of the process of globalization it was Britain that played the dominant role as the leading industrial and commercial world power. As Hall has argued, it is almost impossible to think about the formation of British society outside this process of globalization. From the very beginning Britain was very much present in the early forms of globalization and became the main agent of the expansion of the capitalist market. The construction of the empire was just a manifestation of a process of globalization led by British cultural forms. So, until the beginning of the twentieth century, Britain was at the centre of the process of globalization. It can be argued that through that process Britain contributed to the formation of other cultural identities, the identities of many peripheral nations; but Britain's own cultural identity too was formed in and shaped by the process in which it played a leading role. Stuart Hall has described the nature of such cultural identity as a strongly centred, highly exclusive and exclusivist form of cultural identity. It knows itself as the centre and is able to place everything else as the 'other', be it the colonized other or any less powerful other.[41]

After the Second World War, Britain hoped that with the defeat of Germany and Japan and the start of the cold war against the Soviet Union the United States would accept the strengthening of its empire and thus Britain's identity as a leading world power would be maintained. As we know, the plan failed because the North Americans, the newly emerging international power, in exchange for aid and international support demanded the end of the colonial system. A process of decolonization started. Simultaneously, and connected with decolonization, a long process of economic decline set in. It is therefore not very surprising that for the British dominant classes these changes threatened their preferred sense of identity too.

The same can be said of the United States, which replaced Britain as the main power after the Second World War. The cold war allowed the construction of an American identity as the most powerful nation in the world both economically and militarily, and as the defenders of freedom and justice. Just as Britain saw its imperial identity eroded by the loss of empire, so the United States' self-conception as the defender of the free world and the most powerful nation lost ground after the collapse of the Soviet Union and the industrial and commercial challenge mounted by Japan and by an increasingly united Europe. In both countries, therefore, there has been a search for a new role, a new sense of identity, which at points desperately tries to rekindle the past. Hence Margaret Thatcher's Falklands War and George Bush's Gulf War became opportunities where they attempted to reassert a lost sense of identity.

In fact George Bush's idea of a 'New World Order', produced on the occasion of the Gulf War, was a reaffirmation of the United States' dominant role in the world, a reaffirmation of its belief that its vision of the world has a mission to accomplish, not only to redeem humankind from its mistakes, but also to remake the world in its own image. In a speech at Maxwell Airforce Base War College on 13 April 1991, Bush declared that the New World Order was 'a responsibility imposed by our successes'. 'What defines this nation,' he went on, 'what makes us American is not our ties to a piece of territory or bonds of blood. What makes us American is our allegiance to an idea that all people everywhere must be free.' The United States, he concluded, was not a country in the traditional sense, it was 'a promise to the world' implicit in the words of its own declaration of independence.[42] It was quite clear that the concept of the New World Order was being used by Bush in order to recapture a sense of identity lost at the end of the cold war. Suddenly the United States had lost its archenemy, the 'other' in relation to which it defined its own identity.

Now with the emergence of Saddam Hussein and of other Third World dictators and warlords, the United States can continue to be the guardian of morality and defender of democracy and freedom in the world. The military interventions in Grenada and Panama, and more recently in Iraq and Somalia, are just the latest examples. As Noam Chomsky has put it, 'the new enemy is the Third World.'[43]

It is important to realize that the processes of globalization, just as much in the past as nowadays, are simultaneously processes of domination and power in which the cultural patterns prevalent in the leading society become paradigmatic, a *desideratum* which others must strive for and around which some forms of homogenization occur. The most important distinction affecting the construction of national identities, which originated in the nineteenth century and which is still valid today, is that of centre and periphery. This terminology is normally used in development studies and is recognized as a basic economic distinction which even Marx anticipated:

> By ruining handicraft production in other countries, machinery forcibly converts them into fields for the supply of its raw material. In this way East India was compelled to produce cotton, wool, hemp, jute, and indigo for Great Britain . . . foreign lands . . . are thereby converted into settlements for growing the raw material of the mother country; just as Australia, for example, was converted into a colony for growing wool. A new and international division of labour, a division suited to the requirements of the chief centres of modern industry, springs up, and converts one part of the globe into a chiefly agricultural field of production, for supplying the other part which remains a chiefly industrial field.[44]

However, it is important to realize that this economic distinction is also the basis for the construction of national identities: those countries which have been at the centre of the process of globalization as leading powers have normally constructed their national identities as being central, predominant, with a mission, able to name all other cultures as peripheral and inferior. Equally, peripheral countries are conceived as culturally subordinate and dependent on central countries. In many ways they also see themselves in that way. For instance, it is not pure coincidence that the theories of dependency were conceived in Latin America.

Cultural Identity and Essentialism

There are at least two possible ways of conceiving of cultural identity – one essentialist, narrow and closed, the other historical, encompassing and open. The former thinks of cultural identity as an already accomplished fact, as an already constituted essence. The latter thinks of cultural identity as something which is being produced, always in process, never fully completed. Hall has defined the essentialist concept in terms of 'a sort of collective "one true self", hiding inside the many other, more superficial or artificially imposed "selves", which people with a shared history and ancestry hold in common.'[45] A process of dehistoricization is employed whereby 'an original history . . . is frozen as the historic, as heritage, as tradition. Such essences can be mislaid or lost but will surely be restored, fundamentally unchanged.'[46] According to this definition there is an essence, some shared experience of 'oneness', which provides a stable set of meanings, codes and frames of reference which underlie the more superficial differences and historical changes of the people. This essence must be discovered, excavated from a privileged reservoir, which could be an ethnic or geographical background, popular religiosity, a regional or national language, and so on.

A good example of an essentialist conception of cultural identity is provided by Pedro Morandé's analysis of the Latin American identity. This approach propounds the idea that what is typical of the Latin American cultural identity was formed in the meeting of Indian cultural values and the Catholic religion brought by the Spanish. This cultural pattern emerges not as a form of written culture, because the Indians did not know writing, but as a more vital founding experience which occurs in orality, as an ethos. An ethos is a common experience, a shared understanding born out of the meeting of human beings; it is not a form of coherent argument or ideology but a shared experience which lives off its constant memory.[47] The true subject of this founding experience was the mestizo, a mixture of Spanish and Indian.

Morandé argues that in order to understand the cultural synthesis born out of the encounter between Indians and Spaniards one has to privilege more the relationships of participation and belongingness than the relationships of difference and opposition.[48] The latter, originated in Hegel's dialectic of master and slave, are usually emphasized in those accounts which describe the Spanish as dominating and subordinating the Indians, but Morandé finds them inadequate. First, the confrontation was not between the Spanish on one side and the Indians on the other. The Indians were culturally very diverse, and many of them fought alongside the Spaniards. Second, even if there was domination, it is not clear that such domination is crucial to the Latin American identity. Much more important than the fact of domination were other common experiences. For instance, rather than construing the mestizo as the result of the violation of Indian women by the Spanish, as Octavio Paz has suggested, it must be understood that, since the Indian social organization was based on kinship, it was the Indian chiefs themselves who offered the Spanish their daughters in order to establish alliances.[49] The fact that the Indian cultures had a cultic and ritual conception of life more or less fitted in with some of the Spanish Catholic rites. Both the Indian and the Catholic cultic practices were based on ritual sacrifice carried out or represented in temples.

There are three other aspects in which important coincidences or continuities between the two types of culture can be ascertained.[50] First, there is the tributary character of work. The Spanish Crown only wanted gold and tributes from America, just as the Indian empires were organized on the basis of tribute exaction from the dominated nations. Even the *encomienda* system was a way for the king to get tributes which the *encomendero*, as a tribute collector for the Crown, had to extract in advance from the Indians. Thus, according to Morandé, an idea of work develops in which payment of the tribute is more important than personal profit or personal duty. Another cultural continuity was provided by the religious organization of the time through liturgical calendars. In both Spain and the Indian empires work was organized by the liturgical calendar in accordance with the seasons. The agricultural cycle corresponded with the religious cycle. Finally, there is also a common interest in dance, theatre, liturgy and rituals which are especially noticeable in the fiestas or religious festivities around which the year is organized. Representation, liturgy and theatre, according to Morandé, synthetized the encounter between the Spanish written culture and the Indian oral culture. This means that the place of the encounter, the cradle of the Latin American culture, is sacred. Hence the conclusion that 'Latin American culture has a real Catholic substratum. This substratum is constituted between the sixteenth and the eighteenth centuries.'[51]

One of the intriguing aspects of Morandé's approach is that after patiently tracking down and putting together the main elements of the Latin American cultural synthesis he comes to the conclusion that this synthesis 'was not valued by the process of formation of the national states as its own patrimony'.[52] The elite which conducted the Latin American process of independence from Spain, very much influenced by a written culture brought from Europe, tended to assimilate the oral tradition to barbarism and Spanish domination. Thus the Latin American ruling classes and intellectuals never assumed their true identity and rejected their own mestizo origins. They found refuge in the European rational illuminist pattern, especially through the university system. But in doing so they became alienated from their own roots and made their countries embark on totalizing programmes which could not succeed. The thesis is, then, that Latin America has suffered since its independence from a cultural break. If the rational illuminist cultural pattern adopted by the Latin American elites is an alienation, where then can the true cultural synthesis be found? In popular religiosity, Morandé suggests. While the enlightened European reason praises the modernizing rationalistic elites and decries the backward religious beliefs of the alienated masses, Morandé praises the authenticity of the popular religious traditions and decries the failed modernizing attempts of a culturally alienated elite. According to Morandé, popular religiosity

> is one of the few expressions – although not the only one – of the Latin American cultural synthesis which goes across all its epochs and covers simultaneously all its dimensions: work and production, human settlements and lifestyles, language and artistic expression, political organization, everyday life. And, precisely in its role as the reservoir of cultural identity, it has had to undergo, perhaps more than any other institution, the attempts by modernity to subordinate particular cultures to the dictates of instrumental reason.[53]

Contrary to the Protestant ethic and the need to save and invest as a proof of salvation, the Latin American cultural pattern put an emphasis on work as sacrifice and on religious festivities as ritual squandering. Hence the attempt to repeat Weber's rationalization process was bound to fail, whether it took the form of modernization, the form of bureaucratic socialism or the form of the self-regulating market. Basically, Latin Americans are not supposed to be motivated by technical progress, and the subordination of their ethos to instrumental rationality was a form of alienation, a mistake punished by chronic failure. The Latin American cultural ethos has, according to this view, four important features: (1) it was shaped before the Enlightenment and therefore instrumental rationality does not form a part of it; (2) it has a necessary Catholic underlying structure; (3) it privileges the heart (sentiments) and its intuition, thus preferring sapiential to scientific knowledge; (4) it is best expressed in popular religiosity.[54]

The Latin American cultural identity is not necessarily anti-modern, Morandé argues, but it was constituted before modernity arrived. What threatens this identity is not just any kind of modernity but the modernity stemming from the Enlightenment, the modernity which entails a process of secularization. In view of the Catholic substratum of this identity, secularization is not just a threat to the church but more fundamentally a threat to Latin American culture itself. This threat succeeded in converting the Latin American elites, the Creoles, to instrumental reason, but it did not succeed against the popular religiosity of the mestizos, which has resisted all attacks to remain until today the most spontaneous and genuine expression of the cultural ethos.

Morandé's intellectual edifice is certainly impressive, argued passionately and with great conviction and persuasiveness. It certainly goes beyond many other analyses of the Latin American cultural identity, at least in all that has to do with the exploration of the encounter between the Spanish and the Indians. The great problem with his more general approach is that it reduces the problematic of Latin American cultural identity to that originating moment. In effect, it is difficult to accept that the Latin American cultural identity was fixed once and for all in the sixteenth century, in a pattern which fundamentally opposes the Enlightenment. It is also difficult to accept that academics and intellectuals in Latin America have always been profoundly alienated from their roots just because they have been educated in the values of reason which the first Indo-Iberian cultural synthesis did not privilege.

Morandé introduces a totally unjustified cleavage in Latin America's history. Up to the moment of independence there is the process of constitution of the Latin American identity which is finally consolidated and fixed once and for all. From then onwards history stops, or rather becomes the travesty of what history should have been; it becomes the history of a big alienation, the history of the total failure and betrayal of elites, intellectuals and rulers. If everything is not lost it is just because the torch of the true identity has been safeguarded in the realms of popular religiosity where it has resisted and waits to be rescued by Catholic intellectuals who one day might convince the rest of society, and especially the elites, that their true heritage and identity has an ineluctable Catholic substratum which is different from instrumental reason. Nothing of what the elites have done since independence, nothing of their intellectual production and ideological projects can affect or change the Latin American identity. All the complex history of development since 1810 does not really count for Latin American culture, or, if it does, it is only as alienation. What is behind this conception is a form of essentialism supported by a narrow conception of cultural identity.

Cultural Identity, History and Diversity

There is a more appropriate historical conception of cultural identity. Stuart Hall has described it in terms which can hardly be improved:

> Cultural identity, in this second sense, is a matter of 'becoming' as well as of 'being'. It belongs to the future as much as to the past. It is not something which already exists, transcending place, time, history and culture. Cultural identities come from somewhere, have histories. But like everything which is historical, they undergo constant transformation. Far from being eternally fixed in some essentialized past, they are subject to the continuous 'play' of history, culture and power. Far from being grounded in a mere 'recovery' of the past, which is waiting to be found, and which, when found, will secure our sense of ourselves into eternity, identities are the names we give to the different ways we are positioned by, and position ourselves within, the narratives of the past.[55]

Going back to the example of essentialism given in the last section, only the historical conception of cultural identity allows us to arrive at an understanding of the Latin American identity which does not exclude the best part of the last two centuries of Latin America's history. No doubt the first cultural synthesis produced out of the original encounter between Indians and Spanish is crucially important, but it has not remained the same; it has undergone transformations, not least the impact of Enlightenment thought since the time of independence. These new contributions which have helped shape what Latin America is today are not forms of alienation or betrayal of our 'true self'; they are just new important inputs and transformations that have to be taken into account if we want to understand anything about our present cultural identity. It may well be true that the first Latin American cultural synthesis had a Catholic substratum. But it is equally true that in all probability that cultural feature has lost importance relative to other aspects. This is not a problem of alienation, it is a problem of change, it is the result of the Latin American identity being permanently constructed and reconstructed.

Paraphrasing Colls and Dodd, one can say that cultural identities are not obvious and natural propensities of the peoples that live in a certain territory and share a common culture, even if they are old nations. One can trace some phases in the history of an identity, but it is wrong to believe that these phases simply flow one into another with logical unilinear continuity, or that the cultural identity they have produced has always stood for the same things, or that a particular people or nation can boast about having a resolved identity. Cultural identity is permanently being made and re-made within available practices and relationships and existing symbols and ideas. The fact that there are recurrent symbols and ideas used to define a cultural identity does not ensure that their meaning has always been the same or that it does not change in the context of new practices.[56]

However, to uphold a historical concept of cultural identity does not suffice. The very term 'identity' may lead one to believe that there is a single received version of it, that one can somehow determine with some precision what belongs to it and what does not, irrespective of whether one conceives of it as an immutable essence or as a historical construct. In fact, the enormous complexity and diversity of social practices and cultural forms of a particular people differ from what publicly counts as being typical of its identity. According to Richard Johnson, the public versions of identity and the enormous variety of ways of life in a country or region are two moments of an identity circuit which ought to be distinguished but which feed on each other.[57] This is illustrated in the figure.

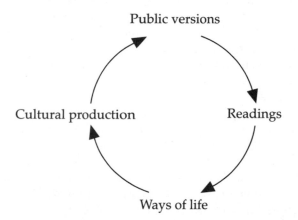

Public versions

Cultural production

Readings

Ways of life

At the basis there is a complex society with an increasingly diversified culture and a huge variety of ways of life. From this big complex reservoir, cultural institutions such as the media, churches, educational and political apparatuses produce some public versions of identity which select only some features that are considered to be representative, and exclude others. These public versions in their turn influence the way in which people see themselves and the way they act through a process of reading or reception which is not necessarily passive and uncritical. Public versions are constructed from ways of life but also constitute sites of struggle which shape the plurality of ways of life.[58] One has to accept that there are always several 'versions' of what constitutes the contents of a cultural identity. This is a result of the fact that cultural identities are not only historically constructed but also constructed around the interests and world-views of some classes or groups in society by a variety of cultural institutions. The criteria for defining cultural identity are always narrower and more selective than the increasingly complex and diversified cultural habits and practices of a people. In the public versions of cultural identity diversity is carefully concealed behind a supposed uniformity.

This narrowing process in the discursive construction of a cultural identity is achieved through certain mechanisms.[59] Thus one can typically find a process of selection whereby only some features, symbols and group experiences are taken into account and others are excluded. There is also a process of evaluation whereby the values of certain classes, institutions or groups are presented as national values and others are excluded. So a moral community with supposedly shared values is constructed which leaves out other values. A process of opposition is also frequently resorted to whereby some groups, ways of life and ideas are presented as outside the national community. Cultural identity is defined as against these other groups: thus the idea of 'us' as opposed to 'them' or to the 'others'. Differences are exaggerated. Finally, one finds processes of naturalization whereby certain cultural features are presented as naturally given in the national character. One can see some of these processes implicitly operating in Morandé's version. Thus, for instance, it selects mestizos as the crucial cultural subjects in Latin America, but tends to exclude the black slaves, the Indian communities and the European immigrants and their millions of descendants. Catholicism is selected and its values are defended, but the deep and increasing penetration of Pentecostalism and other Protestant sects in wide popular sectors of Latin America is excluded or undervalued.

All this goes to show that the discursive process of constructing a cultural identity can easily become ideological if it conceals real diversities and antagonisms in society. All attempts at fixing once and for all the contents of a cultural identity and all pretensions to having discovered the 'true' identity of a people are likely to become ideological forms which are used by certain groups or classes for their own benefit. However, it is also true that certain versions of cultural identity, especially those developed by oppressed or discriminated groups in society, perform the role of being a means of resistance in the face of domination and exclusion and cannot therefore be considered ideological. Unlike the dominant versions, they do not conceal but highlight the contradictions. This is true not only of the internal politics of a society but also of the international relations between societies. Colonialism and other more subtle forms of dependency allow one to speak of whole countries or nationalities being oppressed. In this case too the specific versions of cultural identity developed by oppressed peoples have the role of resisting the oppressor nations, and in that sense they are not ideological. Yet it is possible to find versions of cultural identity which, while constituting a form of resistance against a foreign power, conceal at the same time internal divisions and exclude certain dominated groups.

This shows the inherent ambiguity of the concept of cultural identity. On the one hand it may try to mask diversity; on the other it may serve as a means of resistance. The ruling versions usually fall into the first category, the dominated versions into the second. However, in the case of relations between nations, ruling versions of dependent countries frequently share both aspects. Here one should bring to bear Habermas's ideas about the profound ambivalence of national traditions and about their projection into the future. Identity, Habermas argues, 'is not something pregiven, but also, and simultaneously, our own project.'[60] The very fact that identity is inherently selective allows the possibility that, although a nation cannot choose its traditions, it can at least politically select how to continue or not to continue with some of them. This idea of identity as a project is rich in possibilities and allows Habermas to propose identities more fully informed by universalistic values:

> What does universalism mean, after all? That one relativizes one's own way of life with regard to the legitimate claims of other forms of life, that one grants the strangers and the others, with all their idiosyncrasies and incomprehensibilities, the same rights as oneself, that one does not insist on universalizing one's own identity, that one does not simply exclude that which deviates from it, that the areas of tolerance must become infinitely broader than they are today – moral universalism means all these things.[61]

This is, of course, a most appealing proposal which argues in favour of integration and tolerance of differences. Habermas's example is the European Community. However, we should not forget that side by side with the European example we have so many others (including the very European attitude towards the Third World) where disregard and neglect if not oppression and domination prevail, and where resorting to national traditions seems to be the only way of resisting exclusion, destruction or assimilation. Nevertheless, even in these cases,

Habermas's ideas are extremely valuable. Identity is not so much what one is as what one wants to be, and in the construction of the future not all of one's own historical traditions are equally valid. This idea applies to any country, and certainly to European countries where the ugly face of a deeply rooted racism is emerging again.

In fact, Habermas's more or less optimistic remarks about German and European identities have been more recently tinged with concern in the wake of German reunification and the wave of nationalism and xenophobia which swept through Germany in 1992. Habermas fears that the quest for national identity and self-assertion has regained importance in comparison with issues concerning democratic freedoms.[62] The government's complicity in the campaign to abolish asylum rights and the increasingly aired idea that Germany has become 'normal again' and should re-establish itself as a leading power greatly worry Habermas. Arguments such as Arnulf Baring's – that Germany must accept its relative supremacy in Europe and that 'we must relearn to look after our *own* interests, how to make *unreasonable demands* plausible to our fellow-citizens, how to develop a *healthy* national feeling'[63] – make Habermas think that Germany has not yet settled accounts with its past. Yet he sees some hope in the public demonstrations and protests against right-wing terror and in the fact that true democrats and republicans are breaking away from those who emphasize ethnicity over citizenship.

From a different perspective, Third World countries too should be aware of these problems of identity because the road ahead in a world increasingly divided into three powerful blocs, from which they are excluded, is not only difficult and uncertain, but also surrounded by neo-historicist and essentialist temptations.

Notes

Chapter I Ideology, Reason and the Construction of the Other

1 H. Barth has introduced a useful distinction between historicism as a 'method which seeks to understand man, his culture, and society in their historical uniqueness' and philosophical historicism which arose as a consequence of the former: 'the conception of man as the historic being par excellence began to invalidate ideas that assumed human reason to be essentially unchangeable. Truth became relativized: every epoch, every unified social group, every nation or culture was said to have its own truth.' See H. Barth, *Truth and Ideology* (Berkeley: University of California Press, 1976), p. 181.

2 I do not mean to argue that universalistic theories typical of modernity do not recognize any kind of historical discontinuities. Of course they do, as Marx's theory of modes of production and revolutionary changes clearly shows. The point, though, is a different one and has not got to do with conceiving history as evolving smoothly, for, although Marx anticipated revolutionary breaks, he still saw history as having an overall direction. It is this sense of direction that historicism questions.

3 K. Marx, 'A Contribution to the Critique of Hegel's Philosophy of Right: Introduction' , in K. Marx, *Early Writings*, ed. L. Colleti (Harmondsworth: Penguin, 1975), p. 244.

4 Ibid.

5 K. Marx and F. Engels, *The German Ideology*, in K. Marx and F. Engels, *Collected Works* (London: Lawrence & Wishart, 1976), vol. 5, p. 41.

6 Ibid., p. 36n.

7 K. Marx, *Capital* (London: Lawrence & Wishart, 1974), vol. 3, p. 45.

8 For a full treatment of Marx's concept of ideology, see J. Larrain, *The Concept of Ideology* (London: Hutchinson, 1979) and *Marxism and Ideology* (London: Macmillan, 1983).

9 K. Marx, *Wage, Labour and Capital*, in *Selected Works in One Volume* (London: Lawrence & Wishart, 1970), p. 82.

10 K. Marx, *Grundrisse* (Harmondsworth: Penguin, 1973), p. 541.

11 Marx, *Capital*, vol. 1, p. 542.
12 J. B. Thompson, *Studies in the Theory of Ideology* (Cambridge: Polity Press, 1984), p. 4.
13 J. B. Thompson, *Ideology and Modern Culture* (Cambridge: Polity Press, 1990), p. 7.
14 Thompson, *Studies in the Theory of Ideology*, pp. 81 and 194.
15 Ibid., p. 142.
16 By globalization I understand roughly what Giddens has proposed: 'the intensification of worldwide social relations which link distinct localities in such a way that local happenings are shaped by events occurring miles away and vice versa'. A. Giddens, *The Consequences of Modernity* (Cambridge: Polity Press, 1990), p. 64.
17 Marx and Engels, *The German Ideology*, p. 447.
18 Ibid., p. 455.
19 G. Lukács, *The Destruction of Reason* (London: Merlin Press, 1980), pp. 16 and 99.
20 C. Mongardini, 'The Ideology of Postmodernity', *Theory, Culture and Society*, 9, 2 (1992), p. 57.
21 See J. B. Say, *Cours complet d'économie politique pratique* (Rome: Edizioni Bizzarri, 1968), part 4, ch. 26, p. 311, quoted in J. P. Platteau, *Les Economistes classiques et le sous-développement* (Namur: Presses Universitaires de Namur, 1978), vol. 1, p. 192: 'It is "in the interest of the human species" that the advanced European nations must keep and even increase their influence in Asia . . . it is evident that "with its despots and superstitions, Asia has no good institutions to lose" but "she could receive many good ones from the Europeans."'
22 T. R. Malthus, *An Essay on Population* (London: Dent, 1952), vol. 2, book 3, ch. 4, p. 30.
23 T. R. Malthus, *Principles of Political Economy* (London: International Economic Circle, Tokyo and the London School of Economics and Political Science, 1936), book 2, section 4, pp. 337–41.
24 J. Mill, *The History of British India* (London: Baldwin, Cradock & Joy, 1820), vol. 2, book 2, ch. 10, p. 195.
25 D. Ricardo, letter to J. Mill, 6 January 1818, in *The Works and Correspondence of David Ricardo*, ed. P. Sraffa (London: Cambridge University Press, 1951), vol. 7, p. 243.
26 G. W. F. Hegel, *Lectures on the Philosophy of World History* (Cambridge: Cambridge University Press, 1986), pp. 162–71.
27 Ibid., p. 167.
28 K. Marx, letter to F. Engels, 2 December 1854, in K. Marx and F. Engels, *Materiales para la Historia de América Latina* (Mexico: Cuadernos de Pasado y Presente, 1980), pp. 203–4 (my translation).
29 F. Engels, 'Democratic Pan-Slavism', *Neue Rheinische Zeitung*, 15 February 1849, in K. Marx, *The Revolutions of 1848*, ed. D. Fernbach (Harmondsworth: Penguin, 1973), p. 230.
30 F. Engels, 'Die Bewegungen von 1847', *Deutsche Brüsseler Zeitung*, 23 January 1848, in Marx and Engels, *Materiales para la Historia de América Latina*, p. 183 (my translation).
31 See K. Marx, 'The Future Results of the British Rule in India', in K. Marx, *Surveys from Exile*, ed. D. Fernbach (Harmondsworth: Penguin, 1973).

32 Ibid., p. 324.
33 K. Marx, 'Bolívar y Ponte', *The New American Cyclopaedia*, vol. 3 (1858), in Marx and Engels, *Materiales para la Historia de América Latina*, pp. 76–93.
34 K. Marx, letter to F. Engels, 20 November 1862, in Marx and Engels, *Materiales para la Historia de América Latina*, p. 286.
35 E. Said, *Orientalism* (London: Penguin, 1985), p. 13.
36 D. Hume, 'Of National Characters', in D. Hume, *Essays: Moral, Political, and Literary*, ed. T. H. Green and T. H. Grose (London: Longmans, Green and Co., 1875), vol. 1, p. 252.
37 J. Locke, *Two Treatises of Civil Government* (London: Dent, 1955), book 2, ch. 4, sections 23 and 24, p. 128. See also section 85, p. 158.
38 See M. Horkheimer, *Eclipse of Reason* (New York: Seabury Press, 1974).
39 Ibid., p. 19.
40 Ibid., p. 24.
41 Ibid., p. 25.
42 D. Hume, *A Treatise of Human Nature* (Oxford: Oxford University Press, 1978), p. 457.
43 Ibid., p. 458.
44 J. Locke, *An Essay concerning Human Understanding* (London: Dent, 1948), book 4, ch. 17, section 1, p. 325.
45 Ibid., pp. 325–6.
46 Ibid., ch. 18, section 2, p. 334.
47 See on this R. Echeverría, *El Buho de Minerva* (Santiago: Programa Interdisciplinario de Investigaciones en Educación (PIIE), 1988), pp. 65–71.
48 Locke, *An Essay concerning Human Understanding*, book 4, ch. 6, section 7, p. 282.
49 H. M. Bracken, 'Essence, Accident and Race', *Hermathena*, 116 (1973), p. 84.
50 W. Outhwaite, *Understanding Social Life* (London: Allen & Unwin, 1975), p. 19. The sections in inverted commas are quotations from J. Wach, *Das Vertehen* (Tübingen: Mohr, 1926), vol. 1, pp. 39 and 37.
51 J. G. Herder, *Ideas for a Philosophy of the History of Mankind*, book 7, section 1, in *J. G. Herder on Social and Political Culture*, ed. F. M. Barnard (Cambridge: Cambridge University Press, 1969), p. 311.
52 Ibid., p. 284.
53 J. G. Herder, *Yet Another Philosophy of History*, section 2, in *J. G. Herder on Social and Political Culture*, pp. 186–7.
54 I. Berlin, 'Herder and the Enlightenment', in E. R. Wasserman (ed.), *Aspects of the Eighteenth Century* (Baltimore: Johns Hopkins University Press, 1965), p. 76.
55 Ibid., p. 74.
56 Ibid., p. 47.
57 Lukács, *The Destruction of Reason*, p. 125.
58 F. W. Schelling, *Introduction a la Philosophie de la Mythologie* (Paris: Aubier, 1945), vol. 2, p. 279 (my translation).
59 Ibid., p. 286 (my translation).
60 Ibid., pp. 292–3 (my translation).
61 H. A. R. Gibbs in the Haskell Lectures, University of Chicago, 1945, quoted in Said, *Orientalism*, p. 107.

62 Ibid., p. 45.
63 T. Todorov, *La Conquista de América: el Problema del Otro* (México: Siglo XXI, 1989), p. 259 (my translation).

Chapter 2 Ideology and the Assault on Reason

1 G. Lukács, *The Destruction of Reason* (London: Merlin Press, 1980), p. 104.
2 F. Jameson, 'Postmodernism, or the Cultural Logic of Late Capitalism', *New Left Review*, 146 (1984), pp. 53–93.
3 A. Schopenhauer, *El Mundo como Voluntad y Representación* (Buenos Aires: Aguilar, 1960), vol. 2, section 21, p. 110. (This and the other quotations from Schopenhauer have been translated by me.) The English version, *The World as Will and Representation* (New York: Dover Publications, 1969), does not always coincide with the Spanish version.
4 Ibid., vol. 2, section 18, pp. 70 and 71.
5 Ibid., vol. 2, section 27, p. 150.
6 Ibid., pp. 151–2.
7 Ibid., vol. 3, section 55, p. 28.
8 Ibid., vol. 2, section 19, p. 83.
9 Ibid., p. 84.
10 Ibid., p. 100.
11 Ibid., p. 83.
12 Ibid., vol. 2, section 22, p. 136.
13 Ibid., vol. section 2, 31, p. 279.
14 Lukács, *The Destruction of Reason*, pp. 232–3.
15 Ibid., p. 203.
16 F. Nietzsche, *The Will to Power* (New York: Vintage Books, 1968), section 612, p. 329.
17 F. Nietzsche, *On the Genealogy of Morals* (New York: Vintage Books, 1989), section 12, p. 119.
18 Nietzsche, *The Will to Power*, section 423, p. 227.
19 Ibid., section 480, p. 266.
20 Ibid., section 262, p. 151.
21 F. Nietzsche, *Beyond Good and Evil* (New York: Prometheus Books, 1989), section 4, pp. 8–9.
22 Ibid., section 39, pp. 53–4.
23 F. Nietzsche, *La Gaya Ciencia* (*The Gay Science*) (Buenos Aires: Ediciones del Mediodia, 1967), section 11, p. 27.
24 Ibid., section 354, p. 206. (All translations from this work are mine.)
25 Nietzsche, *The Will to Power*, section 674, p. 355.
26 Ibid., section 707, p. 376.
27 Ibid., section 584, p. 314.
28 F. Nietzsche, *Human all too Human* (Cambridge: Cambridge University Press, 1986), section 31, p. 28.
29 Nietzsche, *The Will to Power*, section 537, p. 291.
30 Ibid., section 452, p. 248.
31 Ibid., section 552, p. 298.
32 Nietzsche, *La Gaya Ciencia*, section 265, p. 141.
33 Ibid., section 110, p. 103.

34 Nietzsche, *The Will to Power*, section 493, p. 272.
35 Ibid., section 507, pp. 275–6.
36 Ibid., section 455, pp. 249–50.
37 Ibid., section 457, pp. 250–1.
38 Ibid., section 534, p. 290.
39 Nietzsche, *On the Genealogy of Morals*, section 25, p. 153.
40 Nietzsche, *La Gaya Ciencia*, section 344, p. 189.
41 Nietzsche, *On the Genealogy of Morals*, section 20, p. 147.
42 Ibid., section 24, p. 151.
43 Ibid., p. 152.
44 Ibid.
45 Ibid., p. 153.
46 Nietzsche, *The Will to Power*, section 853, p. 451.
47 Ibid., section 584, pp. 314–15.
48 Ibid., section 853, p. 451.
49 Ibid., section 55, pp. 36–7.
50 Ibid., section 853, p. 452.
51 Ibid., section 583, p. 314.
52 Ibid., section 544, p. 292.
53 Nietzsche, *Beyond Good and Evil*, section 2, p. 7.
54 Nietzsche, *The Will to Power*, section 968, p. 507.
55 Nietzsche, *On the Genealogy of Morals*, section 10, p. 36.
56 Ibid., p. 37.
57 Ibid., p. 38.
58 Ibid., section 13, p. 46.
59 Ibid., section 10, p. 38.
60 Ibid., p. 36.
61 Nietzsche, *The Will to Power*, section 351, p. 191.
62 Ibid., p. 192.
63 Ibid., pp. 192–3.
64 Ibid., section 400, p. 216.
65 Ibid., section 55, p. 37.
66 Ibid., section 362, p. 198.
67 Ibid., section 685, p. 364.
68 Ibid., section 373, p. 201.
69 Nietzsche, *On the Genealogy of Morals*, section 16, pp. 84–5.
70 Ibid., p. 85.
71 Ibid., section 15, p. 127.
72 Ibid., p. 128.
73 Ibid.
74 Ibid., section 16, pp. 129–30.
75 Ibid., section 17, p. 131; section 18, pp. 134 and 135; section 19, p. 136.
76 Ibid., section 20, pp. 140–1.
77 See on this Lukács, *The Destruction of Reason*, p. 354.
78 Nietzsche, *The Will to Power*, section 942, p. 496.
79 Ibid., section 954, p. 501.
80 Nietzsche, *Beyond Good and Evil*, section 261, p. 233.
81 Ibid., section 259, p. 226.
82 Nietzsche, *On the Genealogy of Morals*, section 1, p. 76.
83 Ibid., section 12, p. 78.

84   Ibid., section 14, p. 122.
85   Ibid.
86   Ibid., p. 124.
87   Nietzsche, *Beyond Good and Evil*, section 239, pp. 187, 188 and 189.
88   Nietzsche, *The Will to Power*, section 943, p. 497.
89   V. Pareto, *A Treatise on General Sociology*, ed. A. Livingstone (New York: Dover Publications, 1963), p. 198.
90   Ibid., p. 7.
91   Ibid., p. 36.
92   Ibid., p. 8.
93   Ibid., pp. 178–9.
94   Ibid., p. 171.
95   Ibid., p. 200.
96   Ibid., p. 511.
97   Ibid., p. 591.
98   Ibid., p. 885.
99   Ibid., p. 899.
100   Ibid., p. 891.
101   Ibid., p. 24.
102   Ibid., p. 1104.
103   Ibid., p. 1011.
104   Ibid., p. 1024.
105   Ibid., p. 1121.
106   Ibid., p. 1185.
107   Ibid., p. 1423.
108   Ibid., p. 1430.
109   Ibid., p. 2192.
110   Ibid., p. 1281.
111   Ibid., p. 1299.
112   Ibid., p. 1300.
113   M. Horkheimer, *Eclipse of Reason* (New York: Seabury Press, 1974), p. 19.
114   M. Horkheimer and T. Adorno, *Dialectic of Enlightenment* (London: Verso, 1979), p. xiv.
115   J. Habermas, *The Philosophical Discourse of Modernity* (Cambridge, Mass.: MIT Press, 1987), pp. 118–19.
116   T. Adorno, *Negative Dialectics* (London: Routledge & Kegan Paul, 1973), p. 197.
117   Quoted in D. Held, *Introduction to Critical Theory* (London: Hutchinson, 1980), p. 186.
118   See on this Horkheimer and Adorno, *Dialectic of Enlightenment*, pp. 120–67.
119   T. Adorno, 'Culture Industry Reconsidered', *New German Critique*, 6 (1975), p. 19.
120   Horkheimer, *Eclipse of Reason*, p. 93.
121   Horkheimer and Adorno, *Dialectic of Enlightenment*, p. 26.
122   Ibid., p. 13.
123   Frankfurt Institute for Social Research, *Aspects of Sociology* (London: Heinemann, 1973), p. 190.
124   Ibid., p. 199.
125   T. Adorno, *Prisms* (London: Neville Spearman, 1967), p. 29.

126 Frankfurt Institute for Social Research, *Aspects of Sociology*, pp. 202–3.
127 H. Marcuse, *One Dimensional Man* (London: Abacus, 1972), p. 24.
128 Ibid., p. 130.
129 H. Marcuse, *Negations* (Harmondsworth: Penguin, 1972), pp. 223–4.
130 Habermas, *The Philosophical Discourse of Modernity*, pp. 112, 113 and 119.
131 J. Habermas, *Toward a Rational Society* (London: Heinemann, 1972), p. 89.
132 Ibid., p. 87.
133 J. B. Thompson, *Ideology and Modern Culture* (Cambridge: Polity Press, 1990), p. 105.

Chapter 3   Structuralism and the Dissolution of Althusserianism

1 D. Lecourt, *Marxism and Epistemology* (London: New Left Books, 1975), p. 12.
2 L. Althusser, *Lenin and Philosophy and other Essays* (London: New Left Books, 1971), pp. 123–41.
3 Ibid., p. 169.
4 L. Althusser, *For Marx* (London: Verso, 1977), pp. 167 and 171.
5 Ibid., p. 213.
6 L. Althusser and E. Balibar, *Reading Capital* (London: New Left Books, 1975), p. 97.
7 See Althusser, *Lenin and Philosophy*, pp. 150–1; J. Mepham, 'The Theory of Ideology in *Capital*', in J. Mepham and D. H. Ruben (eds), *Issues in Marxist Philosophy* (Brighton: Harvester Press, 1979), vol. 3, pp. 144–5, and N. Poulantzas, *Political Power and Social Classes* (London: New Left Books, 1973), p. 20.
8 K. Marx and F. Engels, *The German Ideology*, in K. Marx and F. Engels, *Collected Works* (London: Lawrence & Wishart, 1976), vol. 5, pp. 36 and 60.
9 Althusser, *Lenin and Philosophy*, p. 150.
10 Poulantzas, *Political Power and Social Classes*, p. 205.
11 G. Stedman Jones, 'The Marxism of the Early Lukács: An Evaluation', *New Left Review*, 70 (1971), pp. 53–4 and 48–9.
12 Althusser, *For Marx*, p. 233.
13 L. Althusser, *La Filosofía como Arma de la Revolución* ('Philosophy as a Weapon of Revolution') (Córdoba: Cuadernos de Pasado y Presente, 1970), p. 55 (my translation).
14 Althusser, *Lenin and Philosophy*, p. 150.
15 Ibid., p. 152.
16 Althusser, *La Filosofía como Arma de la Revolución*, p. 56.
17 Ibid., pp. 56–7 and 48–9 (my translations).
18 Althusser, *Lenin and Philosophy*, p. 148.
19 See L. Althusser, *Essays in Self-Criticism* (London: New Left Books, 1976).
20 L. Althusser, 'Nota sobre los Aparatos Ideológicos de Estado' ('Note on Ideological State Apparatuses'), in L. Althusser, *Nuevos Escritos* ('New Writings') (Barcelona: Editorial Laia, 1978), p. 99.
21 Ibid., p. 100 (my translation).
22 A. Gramsci, *Selections from the Prison Notebooks*, ed. and trans. Quintin Hoare

(London: Lawrence & Wishart, 1971), p. 331: the philosophy of practice must base itself initially on common sense 'in order to demonstrate that "everyone" is a philosopher and that it is not a question of introducing from scratch a scientific form of thought into everyone's life, but of renovating and making "critical" an already existing activity.'

23 Althusser, 'Nota sobre los Aparatos Ideológicos de Estado', p. 102 (my translation).

24 I do not know of any English translation of the collection of articles published in Spanish under the title *Nuevos Escritos* ('New Writings').

25 See M. Godelier, 'Fétichisme, religion et théorie générale de l'idéologie chez Marx', in *Annali* (Rome: Feltrinelli, 1970), pp. 22–39. See also *Rationality and Irrationality in Economics* (London: New Left Books, 1972) and *Horizon, trajets marxistes en anthropologic* (Paris: Maspero, 1973).

26 See E. Terray, *Marxism and 'Primitive' Societies* (New York: Monthly Review Press, 1972).

27 See G. Dupré and P. P. Rey, 'Reflections on the Pertinence of a Theory of the History of Exchange', *Economy and Society*, 2, 2 (1973), pp. 131–63.

28 See P. P. Rey, *Les Alliances de Classes* (Paris: Maspero, 1978).

29 See J. Taylor, *From Modernization to Modes of Production* (London: Macmillan, 1979).

30 See Poulantzas, *Political Power and Social Classes*.

31 See E. Laclau, *Politics and Ideology in Marxist Theory* (London: New Left Review, 1977) and ' "Socialism", the "People", "Democracy": the Transformation of Hegemonic Logic', *Social Text*, 7 (1983), pp. 115–19.

32 See C. Mouffe, 'Hegemony and Ideology in Gramsci', in C. Mouffe (ed.), *Gramsci and Marxist Theory* (London: Routledge & Kegan Paul, 1979), pp. 168–204; see also E. Laclau and C. Mouffe, *Hegemony and Socialist Strategy* (London: Verso, 1985).

33 See S. Hall, 'Some Problems with the Ideology/Subject Couplet', *Ideology and Consciousness*, 3 (1978), pp. 113–21; 'Cultural Studies: Two Paradigms', in T. Bennett et al. (eds), *Culture, Ideology and Social Process* (London: Batsford Academic, 1981), pp. 19–37; 'The Whites of their Eyes, Racist Ideologies and the Media', in G. Bridges and R. Brunt (eds), *Silver Linings* (London: Lawrence & Wishart, 1981), pp. 28–52; 'The Problem of Ideology–Marxism without Guarantees', in B. Matthews (ed.), *Marx, 100 years on* (London: Lawrence & Wishart, 1983), pp. 57–85; and 'The Toad in the Garden: Thatcherism among the Theorists', in C. Nelson and L. Grossberg (eds), *Marxism and the Interpretation of Culture* (London: Macmillan, 1988).

34 See P. Macherey, *A Theory of Literary Production* (London: Routledge & Kegan Paul, 1978).

35 See T. Eagleton, *Marxism and Literary Criticism* (London: Methuen, 1976).

36 C. Sumner, *Reading Ideologies, an Investigation into the Marxist Theory of Ideology and Law* (New York: Academic Press, 1979).

37 See Mepham, 'The Theory of Ideology in *Capital*'.

38 See B. Hindess and p. Hirst, *Pre-Capitalist Modes of Production* (London: Routledge & Kegan Paul, 1975); B. Hindess and P. Hirst, *Mode of Production and Social Formation: An Auto-Critique of 'Pre-Capitalist Modes of Production'* (London: Macmillan, 1977); A. Cutler et al., *Marx's Capital and Capitalism Today* (London: Routledge & Kegan Paul, 1977); B. Hindess, 'The Concept of Class in Marxist Theory and Marxist Politics', in J.

Bloomfield (ed.), *Class, Hegemony and Party* (London: Lawrence & Wishart, 1977), and P. Hirst, *On Law and Ideology* (London: Macmillan, 1979).

39 J. Kristeva, 'La Sémiologie: science critique et/ou critique de la science', in *Tel Quel* (eds), *Théorie d'ensemble* (Paris: Éditions du Seuil, 1968), pp. 80–93.

40 J. L. Baudry, 'Écriture, fiction, idéologie', in *Tel Quel* (eds), *Théorie d'ensemble*, pp. 127–47.

41 P. Sollers, 'Écriture et révolution', in *Tel Quel* (eds), *Théorie d'ensemble*, pp. 67–79, and *Sur le matérialisme* (Paris: Editions du Seuil, 1974).

42 R. Coward and J. Ellis, *Language and Materialism* (London: Routledge & Kegan Paul, 1977).

43 D. Adlam et al., 'Psychology, Ideology and the Human Subject', *Ideology and Consciousness*, 1, (1977), pp. 5–56.

44 M. Pêcheux, *Les Vérités de la Palice* (Paris: Maspero, 1975). There is an English version entitled *Language, Semantics and Ideology: Stating the Obvious* (London: Macmillan, 1982).

45 Poulantzas, *Political Power and Social Classes*, p. 207.

46 Mepham, 'The Theory of Ideology in *Capital*', p. 152.

47 Godelier, 'Fétichisme, religion et théorie générale de l'idéologie chez Marx', p. 23.

48 Ibid., p. 35.

49 Pêcheux, *Les Vérités de la Palice*, p. 81 (my translation).

50 Ibid., pp. 128–9.

51 Ibid., p. 145.

52 Hall, 'Cultural Studies: Two Paradigms', p. 32.

53 Laclau, *Politics and Ideology in Marxist Theory*, p. 108.

54 Ibid., p. 101n.

55 Hall, 'The Whites of their Eyes, Racist Ideologies and the Media', p. 31.

56 Ibid., pp. 31–2.

57 Laclau, *Politics and Ideology in Marxist Theory*, pp. 108–9.

58 Ibid., p. 160.

59 Hall, 'The Problem of Ideology – Marxism without Guarantees', p. 60.

60 Ibid., p. 61.

61 Ibid., pp. 67–73.

62 Ibid., p. 76.

63 N. Mouzelis, 'Ideology and Class Politics: A Critique of Ernesto Laclau', *New Left Review*, 112 (1978), p. 53.

64 Hall, 'The Toad in the Garden: Thatcherism among the Theorists', p. 42.

65 See Poulantzas *Political Power and Social Classes*, p. 202, and Laclau, *Politics and Ideology in Marxist Theory*, pp. 160–1.

66 Hall, 'The Toad in the Garden: Thatcherism among the Theorists', p. 42.

67 Ibid., p. 43.

68 Ibid., p. 44.

69 Ibid., p. 46.

70 Ibid., p. 44.

71 See Hall, 'The Problem of Ideology – Marxism without Guarantees'.

72 Hall, 'The Toad in the Garden: Thatcherism among the Theorists'.

73 'F. Engels, letter to Franz Mehring in Berlin, 14 July 1893, in K. Marx and F. Engels, *Selected Correspondence* (Moscow: Progress, 1975), p. 434.

74 K. Marx, *Capital* (London: Lawrence & Wishart, 1974), vol. 1, p. 172.

75 Marx and Engels, *The German Ideology*, p. 59.
76 Hall, 'The Toad in the Garden: Thatcherism among the Theorists', pp. 44–5.
77 Apart from Hall and Laclau, see, for instance, Hirst, *On Law and Ideology*, and J. McCarney, *The Real World of Ideology* (Brighton: Harvester Press, 1980). For a critique of this position, see J. Larrain, *Marxism and Ideology* (London: Macmillan, 1983), pp. 94–121.
78 Coward and Ellis, *Language and Materialism*, p. 69.
79 Adlam et al., 'Psychology, Ideology and the Human Subject', p. 17.
80 Ibid., p. 16: 'in that ideology consists in representations, it has a material existence.'
81 Ibid., p. 22.
82 Coward and Ellis, *Language and Materialism*, p. 73.
83 Ibid., p. 71
84 Ibid., p. 2.
85 S. Hall, 'Some Problems with the Ideology/Subject Couplet', *Ideology and Consciousness*, 3 (1978), p. 116.
86 Marx and Engels, *The German Ideology*, p. 42.
87 Coward and Ellis, *Language and Materialism*, p. 91.

Chapter 4   Poststructuralism and Postmodernism

1   R. Boyne and A. Rattansi, 'The Theory and Politics of Postmodernism: By Way of an Introduction', in R. Boyne and A. Rattansi (eds), *Postmodernism and Society* (London: Macmillan, 1990), pp. 10–11.
2   M. Poster, *Foucault, Marxism and History* (Cambridge: Polity Press, 1984), p. 1.
3   M. Foucault, *The Archeology of Knowledge* (London: Tavistock, 1977), p. 10.
4   M. Foucault, 'Truth and Power', in C. Gordon (ed.), *Michel Foucault, Power/Knowledge* (Brighton: Harvester Press, 1980), p. 114.
5   M. Foucault, 'Lecture 7 January 1976', in Gordon (ed.), *Michel Foucault, Power/Knowledge*, p. 98.
6   M. Foucault, *The History of Sexuality* (Harmondsworth: Penguin, 1984), vol. 1, pp. 93 and 92–4.
7   M. Foucault, 'Prison Talk', in Gordon (ed.), *Michel Foucault, Power/Knowledge*, p. 39.
8   M. Foucault, 'Body/Power', in Gordon (ed.), *Michel Foucault, Power/Knowledge*, p. 60.
9   M. Foucault, 'Théories et institutions pénales', *Annuaire du Collège de France, 1971–1972* (Paris, 1971), quoted in A. Sheridan, *Michel Foucault, the Will to Truth* (London: Tavistock, 1980), p. 131.
10 M. Foucault, *Discipline and Punish* (Harmondsworth: Penguin, 1977), p. 27.
11 Foucault, *The Archeology of Knowledge*, p. 186.
12 Foucault, 'Truth and Power', p. 131.
13 Foucault, *Discipline and Punish*, p. 25.
14 Foucault, *The History of Sexuality*, vol. 1, p. 139.

15　M. Foucault, 'Questions on Geography', in Gordon (ed.), *Michel Foucault, Power/Knowledge*, p. 77.
16　M. Foucault, 'Lecture 14 January 1976', in Gordon (ed.), *Michel Foucault, Power/Knowledge*, p. 102.
17　Foucault, 'Truth and Power', p. 133.
18　Foucault, 'Théories et institutions pénales', p. 131.
19　Foucault, 'Body/Power', p. 58.
20　Foucault, 'The History of Sexuality: Interview', in Gordon (ed.), *Michel Foucault, Power/Knowledge*, p. 186.
21　Foucault, 'Truth and Power', p. 118.
22　Foucault, *The Archeology of Knowledge*, p. 48.
23　Ibid., p. 115.
24　Foucault, 'Lecture 14 January 1976', p. 97.
25　Foucault, 'Lecture 7 January 1976', p. 79.
26　Foucault, 'Lecture 14 January 1976', p. 105.
27　Ibid., p. 106.
28　Foucault, *The History of Sexuality*, vol. 1, p. 86.
29　Ibid., p. 91.
30　See on this M. Cousins and A. Hussain, *Michel Foucault* (London: Macmillan, 1984), p. 238.
31　A. Cutler et al., *Marx's Capital and Capitalism Today* (London: Routledge & Kegan Paul, 1977), vol. 1, pp. 216–17.
32　P. Hirst, *On Law and Ideology* (London: Macmillan, 1979), pp. 62–3.
33　B. Hindess and P. Hirst, *Mode of Production and Social Formation: An Auto-Critique of 'Pre-Capitalist Modes of Production'* (London: Macmillan, 1977), pp. 13–14.
34　B. Hindess, 'The Concept of Class in Marxist Theory and Marxist Politics', in J. Bloomfield (ed.), *Class, Hegemony and Party* (London: Lawrence & Wishart, 1977), p. 104.
35　Hindess and Hirst, *Mode of Production and Social Formation*, p. 59.
36　For more extensive critiques of Hindess and Hirst's attack on epistemology, see J. Larrain, *Marxism and Ideology* (London: Macmillan, 1983), pp. 185–93; J. B. Thompson, *Studies in the Theory of Ideology* (Cambridge: Polity Press, 1984), pp. 96–8; T. Benton, *The Rise and Fall of Structural Marxism, Althusser and his Influence* (London: Macmillan, 1984), pp. 179–99; and G. Elliott, 'The Odyssey of Paul Hirst', *New Left Review*, 159 (1986), pp. 81–105.
37　I have borrowed this expression from H. Meiksins Wood, *The Retreat from Class: A New 'True' Socialism* (London: Verso, 1986), p. 55n.
38　E. Laclau and C. Mouffe, *Hegemony and Socialist Strategy* (London: Verso, 1985), p. 107.
39　Ibid., p. 109.
40　Ibid., pp. 112–15.
41　Ibid., p. 136.
42　Ibid., p. 151.
43　E. Laclau, ' "Socialism", the "People", "Democracy": the Transformation of Hegemonic Logic', *Social Text*, 7 (1983), p. 116.
44　Meiksins Wood, *The Retreat from Class*, p. 62.
45　P. Anderson, *In the Tracks of Historical Materialism* (London: Verso, 1983), p. 48.

46　Laclau and Mouffe, *Hegemony and Socialist Strategy*, p. 176.
47　Ibid., pp. 154–5.
48　Ibid., p. 178.
49　D. Harvey, *The Condition of Postmodernity* (Oxford: Blackwell, 1989), p. 53.
50　Ibid., p. 9.
51　J.-F. Lyotard, *La Fenomenología* ('Phenomenology') (Buenos Aires: EUDEBA, 1973), p. 56 (my translation).
52　J.-F. Lyotard, *¿Por qué filosofar?* ('Why Philosophy?') (Barcelona: Paidós, 1989), p. 148.
53　Ibid., p. 150 (my translation).
54　J.-F. Lyotard, *Les Dispositifs pulsionnels* (Paris: Christian Bourgeois, 1980), p. 40 (my translations throughout).
55　Ibid., p. 144.
56　Ibid., p. 55.
57　J.-F. Lyotard, *Économie libidinale* (Paris: Editions de Minuit, 1974), p. 117 (my translations throughout).
58　Ibid., p. 102.
59　Ibid., p. 101.
60　Ibid., p. 128.
61　Ibid., p. 287.
62　W. van Reijen and D. Veerman, 'An Interview with Jean-François Lyotard', *Theory, Culture and Society*, 5, 2–3 (1988), p. 278.
63　J.-F. Lyotard, *The Postmodern Condition: A Report on Knowledge* (Manchester: Manchester University Press, 1984), pp. 37, 15 and 40.
64　J.-F. Lyotard and J.-L. Thébaud, *Just Gaming* (Manchester: Manchester University Press), 1985, p. 10.
65　Ibid., p. 98.
66　Lyotard, *The Postmodern Condition*, p. 82.
67　R. Rorty, 'Habermas and Lyotard on Postmodernity', in R. J. Berstein (ed.), *Habermas and Modernity* (Cambridge: Polity Press, 1985), p. 161.
68　J. Baudrillard, *The System of Objects*, in *Selected Writings*, ed. M. Poster (Cambridge: Polity Press, 1988), p. 18.
69　J. Baudrillard, *Consumer Society*, in *Selected Writings*, p. 46.
70　Ibid., p. 50.
71　J. Baudrillard, *For a Critique of the Political Economy of the Sign*, in *Selected Writings*, p. 70.
72　Ibid.
73　Ibid., p. 71.
74　Ibid., p. 76.
75　Ibid.
76　Ibid., p. 77.
77　Ibid., p. 78.
78　Especially in *Mythologies* (London: Cape, 1972) and *Elements of Semiology* (London: Cape, 1967).
79　R. Barthes, *S/Z* (London: Cape, 1974), p. 9.
80　Baudrillard, *For a Critique of the Political Economy of the Sign*, in *Selected Writings*, p. 89.
81　Ibid., p. 90.
82　J. Baudrillard, *The Mirror of Production*, in *Selected Writings*, p. 98.

83 J. Baudrillard, *Symbolic Exchange and Death*, in *Selected Writings*, p. 125.
84 Ibid., pp. 126 and 128.
85 Ibid., p. 120.
86 Ibid.
87 J. Baudrillard, *Simulacra and Simulations*, in *Selected Writings*, p. 170.
88 Ibid., p. 182.
89 Lyotard, *Économie libidinale*, p. 42.
90 Van Reijen and Veerman, 'An Interview with Jean-François Lyotard', p. 279.
91 J. Keane, *Democracy and Civil Society* (London: Verso, 1988), p. 231.
92 Ibid., pp. 234–5.
93 Ibid., p. 235.
94 Ibid., p. 236.
95 A. Callinicos, *Against Postmodernism: A Marxist Critique* (Cambridge: Polity Press, 1989), pp. 147–8.
96 Baudrillard, *Simulacra and Simulations*, in *Selected Writings*, p. 172.
97 Ibid.
98 Ibid., p. 173.
99 Ibid., pp. 176–7.
100 J. Baudrillard, *Cool Memories* (Paris: Éditions Galilée, 1987), p. 286.
101 Ibid.
102 Ibid., p. 226.
103 D. Kellner, *Jean Baudrillard: From Marxism to Postmodernism and Beyond* (Cambridge: Polity Press, 1988), p. 62.
104 D. Kellner, 'Postmodernism as Social Theory: Some Challenges and Problems', *Theory, Culture and Society*, 5, 2–3 (June 1988), p. 246.
105 Baudrillard, *The Mirror of Production*, in *Selected Writings*, pp. 98 and 104.
106 J. Baudrillard, *Oublier Foucault* (Paris: Éditions Galilée, 1977), pp. 13 (my translations throughout).
107 Ibid., p. 81.
108 Ibid., p. 15.
109 J. Baudrillard, *La Gauche Divine* (Paris: Grasset, 1985), pp. 98 and 101. Quoted in Kellner, *Jean Baudrillard: From Marxism to Postmodernism and Beyond*, pp. 193–4.
110 J. Habermas, *The Philosophical Discourse of Modernity* (Cambridge Mass.: MIT Press, 1987), p. 97.
111 Harvey, *The Condition of Postmodernity*, p. 116.

Chapter 5 Habermas and the New Concept of Reason

1 J. Habermas, *Toward a Rational Society* (London: Heinemann, 1971), pp. 99–101.
2 Ibid., p. 114.
3 Ibid., p. 89.
4 Ibid., p. 88.
5 H. Kunneman, 'Some Critical Remarks on Habermas's Analysis of Science and Technology', *Theory, Culture and Society*, 7, 4 (1990), p. 124.
6 Ibid., pp. 119–20.

7   K. Marx, *Theories of Surplus Value* (London: Lawrence & Wishart, 1969), vol. 1, p. 391.

8   K. Marx, *Grundrisse* (Harmondsworth: Penguin, 1973), pp. 699–700.

9   J. Habermas, 'Remarks on the Discussion', *Theory, Culture and Society*, 7, 4 (1990), p. 132.

10 J. Habermas, *The Theory of Communicative Action*, vol. 1 (London: Heinemann, 1984), p. 392.

11 Ibid., p. 390.

12 J. Habermas, *Communication and the Evolution of Society* (London: Heinemann, 1979), p. 5.

13 Habermas, *The Theory of Communicative Action*, vol. 1, p. 287.

14 J. Habermas, *Legitimation Crisis* (London: Heinemann, 1976), p. 108.

15 Ibid., p. 110.

16 J. Habermas, 'Towards a Theory of Communicative Competence', *Inquiry*, 13, 4 (1970), p. 372.

17 Habermas, *Toward a Rational Society*, p. 111.

18 J. Habermas, *Knowledge and Human Interests* (London: Heinemann, 1972), p. 311.

19 J. Habermas, 'Vorbereitende Bemerkungen zu einer Theorie der kommunikativen Kompetenz', in J. Habermas and N. Luhmann, *Theorie der Gesellschaft oder Sozialtechnologie–Was leistet die Systemforschung?* (Frankfurt: Suhrkamp, 1971), quoted in T. McCarthy, 'A Theory of Communicative Competence', in P. Connerton (ed.), *Critical Sociology* (Penguin, Harmondsworth, 1976), pp. 477–8.

20 J. Habermas, 'On Systematically Distorted Communication', *Inquiry*, 13, 3 (1970), p. 207.

21 Habermas, *Legitimation Crisis*, p. 113.

22 Habermas, *The Theory of Communicative Action*, vol. 1, p. 398.

23 G. Lukács, *History and Class Consciousness* (London: Merlin Press, 1971), p. 51.

24 Habermas, *Legitimation Crisis*, p. 113.

25 D. Held, *Introduction to Critical Theory* (London: Hutchinson, 1980), p. 398.

26 T. Eagleton, *Ideology* (London: Verso, 1991), p. 131.

27 See, for instance, H. G. Gadamer, 'Replik', in J. Habermas et al. (eds), *Hermeneutik und Ideologiekritik* (Frankfurt: Suhrkamp, 1971), pp. 294–5; H. J. Giegel, 'Reflexion und Emanzipation', in Habermas et al. (eds), *Hermeneutik und Ideologiekritik*, pp. 278–9; P. Ricoeur, *Hermeneutics and the Human Sciences*, ed. and trans. J. B. Thompson (Cambridge: Cambridge University Press, 1981), p. 85; P. Ricoeur, *Lectures on Ideology and Utopia*, ed. G. H. Taylor (New York: Columbia University Press, 1986), pp. 245–53; Held, *Introduction to Critical Theory*, p. 394; T. McCarthy, *The Critical Theory of Jürgen Habermas* (Cambridge: Polity Press, 1984), pp. 205–7.

28 J. Habermas, *Theory and Practice* (London: Heinemann, 1974), pp. 32–3.

29 Ricoeur, *Lectures on Ideology and Utopia*, p. 248.

30 Held, *Introduction to Critical Theory*, p. 394.

31 J. Habermas, *The Theory of Communicative Action*, vol. 2 (Cambridge: Polity Press, 1989), p. 343.

32 Ibid., p. 350.

33 A. Giddens, *Studies in Social and Political Theory* (London: Hutchinson, 1977), p. 152.

34 Habermas, *The Theory of Communicative Action*, vol. 2, p. 348.
35 K. Marx and F. Engels, *The German Ideology*, in *Collected Works* (London: Lawrence & Wishart, 1976), p. 30.
36 Habermas, *The Theory of Communicative Action*, vol. 2, p. 355.
37 Ibid.
38 J. B. Thompson, *Ideology and Modern Culture* (Cambridge: Polity Press, 1990), p. 301.
39 See J. Habermas, *The Philosophical Discourse of Modernity* (Cambridge, Mass.: MIT Press, 1987).
40 D. Kellner, 'Postmodernism as Social Theory: Some Challenges and Problems', *Theory, Culture and Society*, 5, 2–3 (1988), p. 265.
41 T. McCarthy, 'Introduction', in Habermas, *The Philosophical Discourse of Modernity*, p. xv.
42 Habermas, *The Philosophical Discourse of Modernity*, p. 96.
43 Ibid., p. 336.
44 Ibid., p. 314.
45 Habermas, *The Theory of Communicative Action*, vol. 1, pp. 285–7.
46 McCarthy, *The Critical Theory of Jürgen Habermas*, p. 30.
47 Habermas, *The Philosophical Discourse of Modernity*, p. 315.
48 Habermas, *The Theory of Communicative Action*, vol. 2, p. 304; see also vol. 1, p. 240.
49 J. Habermas, 'Questions and Counterquestions', in R. J. Berstein, (ed.), *Habermas and Modernity* (Cambridge: Polity Press, 1985), p. 197.
50 Habermas, *The Theory of Communicative Action*, vol. 1, p. 240.
51 Habermas, *Communication and the Evolution of Society*, pp. 119–20.
52 A. Giddens, 'Reason Without Revolution? Habermas's *Theorie des kommunikativen Handelns*', in Bernstein (ed.), *Habermas and Modernity*, p. 114.
53 A. Wellmer, 'Intersubjectivity and Reason', in L. H. Hertzberg and J. Pietarinen (eds), *Perspectives on Human Conduct* (Leiden: E. T. Brill, 1988), p. 128. The quote is taken from I. Kant, *The Critique of Judgment* (Oxford: Clarendon Press, 1952), p. 152.
54 A. Callinicos, *Against Postmodernism: A Marxist Critique* (Cambridge: Polity Press, 1989), p. 111.
55 Wellmer, 'Intersubjectivity and Reason', pp. 157–8.
56 Ibid., p. 158.
57 Callinicos, *Against Postmodernism: A Marxist Critique*, p. 111.
58 See on this McCarthy, *The Critical Theory of Jürgen Habermas*, p. 304.
59 Ibid., p. 307.
60 Quoted in ibid., p. 308.
61 Wellmer, 'Intersubjectivity and Reason', p. 159.
62 Ibid., p. 163.
63 Habermas, 'Questions and Counterquestions', p. 192.
64 Ibid., p. 194.
65 Ibid., p. 195.
66 Habermas, *The Theory of Communicative Action*, vol. 1, pp. 66–7.
67 See p. Winch, 'Understanding a Primitive Society', in B. R. Wilson (ed.), *Rationality* (Oxford: Blackwell, 1970), pp. 78–111.
68 McCarthy, *The Critical Theory of Jürgen Habermas*, p. 319.
69 Ibid., 321.
70 J. Habermas, 'Historical Consciousness and Post-Traditional Identity:

The Federal Republic's Orientation to the West', in J. Habermas, *The New Conservatism* (Cambridge, Mass.: MIT Press, 1989), pp. 253–7.

71 J. Habermas, 'The Limits of Neo-Historicism', interview with J. M. Ferry, in J. Habermas, *Autonomy and Solidarity* (London: Verso, 1992), p. 240.

72 Habermas, 'Historical Consciousness and Post-Traditional Identity', p. 263.

73 See on this J. Habermas, 'The Second Life Fiction of the Federal Republic: We Have Become "Normal" Again', *New Left Review*, 197 (January/ February 1993).

Chapter 6 Cultural Identity, Globalization and History

1 K. Mercer, 'Welcome to the Jungle: Identity and Diversity in Postmodern Politics', in J. Rutherford (ed.), *Identity, Community, Culture, Difference* (London: Lawrence & Wishart, 1990), p. 43.

2 J. Locke, *Essay concerning Human Understanding* (London: George Routledge, 1948), book 2, ch. 27, section 17, p. 251.

3 Ibid., section 9, p. 247.

4 G. Leibniz, *Philosophical Writings* (London: Dent, 1973), p. 44.

5 Ibid., pp. 156–7. For a good discussion of Locke's and Leibniz's conceptions of personal identity, see H. Noonan, *Personal Identity* (London: Routledge, 1989), chs 2 and 3.

6 See H. Goldman, *Max Weber and Thomas Mann* (Berkeley: University of California Press, 1988), pp. 121–5.

7 F. Hegel, *The Phenomenology of Mind* (London: George Allen & Unwin, 1971), p. 229.

8 K. Marx, *Critique of Hegel's Doctrine of the State*, in *Early Writings*, ed. L. Colletti (Harmondsworth: Penguin, 1975), p. 80.

9 K. Marx, *Grundrisse* (Harmondsworth: Penguin, 1973), Introduction, p. 83.

10 K. Marx, 'Theses on Feuerbach', in *The German Ideology*, in K. Marx and F. Engels, *Collected Works* (London: Lawrence & Wishart, 1976), vol. 5, thesis VI, p. 29.

11 Marx, *Grundrisse*, p. 84.

12 Marx and Engels, *The German Ideology*, in *Collected Works*, pp. 193–6.

13 Marx, *Grundrisse*, p. 84.

14 Ibid., p. 496.

15 G. H. Mead, *Mind, Self, and Society* (Chicago: University of Chicago Press, 1974), p. 1.

16 Ibid., p. 173.

17 Ibid., p. 175.

18 Ibid., p. 142.

19 Ibid., p. 144.

20 D. Hume, *A Treatise of Human Nature* (Oxford: Oxford University Press, 1978), p. 254.

21 Ibid., p. 252.

22 For a good discussion of Hume's sceptical approach to identity, see Noonan, *Personal Identity*, ch. 4.

23 F. Nietzsche, *The Will to Power* (New York: Vintage Books, 1968), section 485, p. 269.

24 Ibid., section 481, p. 267.
25 C. Lévi-Strauss, *The Savage Mind* (London: Weidenfeld & Nicolson, 1974), pp. 254 and 256.
26 L. Althusser, *Lenin and Philosophy and other Essays* (London: New Left Books, 1971), pp. 160–70.
27 M. Foucault, *The Archeology of Knowledge* (London: Tavistock, 1977), p. 13.
28 M. Foucault, 'Questions on Geography', in C. Gordon (ed.), *Michel Foucault, Power/Knowledge* (Brighton: Harvester Press, 1980), pp. 73–4.
29 E. Laclau and C. Mouffe, *Hegemony and Socialist Strategy* (London: Verso, 1985), p. 115.
30 J.-F. Lyotard, *The Postmodern Condition: A Report on Knowledge* (Manchester: Manchester University Press, 1984), p. 15.
31 J. Baudrillard, *Fatal Strategies*, in *Selected Writings*, ed. M. Poster (Cambridge: Polity Press, 1988), p. 198.
32 S. Hall, D. Held and T. McGrew, *Modernity and its Futures* (Cambridge: The Open University and Polity Press, 1992), p. 277.
33 Ibid., p. 299.
34 A. Giddens, *The Consequences of Modernity* (Cambridge: Polity Press, 1990), p. 64.
35 K. Marx and F. Engels, *Manifesto of the Communist Party*, in *Selected Works in One Volume* (London: Lawrence & Wishart, 1970), p. 38.
36 D. Harvey, *The Condition of Postmodernity* (Oxford: Basil Blackwell, 1989), p. 240.
37 Giddens, *The Consequences of Modernity*, p. 18.
38 See on this Harvey, *The Condition of Postmodernity*, pp. 147–56.
39 S. Hall, 'The Local and the Global: Globalization and Ethnicity', in A. King (ed.), *Culture, Globalization and the World-System* (London: Macmillan, 1991), p. 28.
40 Ibid., p. 33.
41 Ibid., pp. 20–1
42 Quoted in F. Biancardi, 'President Bush's "New World Order"', discussion paper presented at the Nottingham Trent University Communication Forum on Ideology, 3 November 1992, pp. 3–4. I am indebted to Biancardi's paper for some excellent ideas on the New World Order.
43 N. Chomsky, 'From Cold War to Gulf War', *Living Marxism*, 29 (March 1991), p. 21.
44 K. Marx, *Capital* (London: Lawrence & Wishart, 1974), vol. 1, pp. 424–5.
45 S. Hall, 'Cultural Identity and Diaspora', in J. Rutherford (ed.), *Identity, Community, Culture, Difference* (London: Lawrence & Wishart, 1990), p. 223.
46 R. Johnson, 'Towards a Cultural Theory of the Nation: A British–Dutch Dialogue', MS, Department of Cultural Studies, University of Birmingham. (To appear in B. Henkes et al., *Images of the Nation* (Amsterdam: Rodopi, 1993), p. 22.)
47 P. Morandé, 'Latinoamericanos: Hijos de un Diálogo Ritual', *Creces*, 11/12 (1990), p. 10.
48 P. Morandé, 'La Síntesis Cultural Hispánica Indígena', *Teología y Vida*, 32, 1–2 (1991), pp. 43–5.
49 That was the way, for instance, in which 'la Malinche' and nineteen other young women slaves were offered to Hernán Cortés.

50 P. Morandé, 'La Síntesis Cultural Hispánica Indígena', p. 48.
51 P. Morandé, *Cultura y Modernización an América Latina*, Cuadernos del Instituto de Sociología (Santiago: Universidad Católica de Chile, 1984), pp. 139–40 (my translation).
52 P. Morandé, 'La Síntesis Cultural Hispánica Indígena', p. 51 (my translation).
53 P. Morandé, *Cultura y Modernización an América Latina*, p. 129 (my translation).
54 Ibid., pp. 144–5.
55 Hall, 'Cultural Identity and Diaspora', p. 225.
56 See on this R. Colls and P. Dodd (eds), *Englishness, Politics and Culture 1880–1920* (London: Croom Helm, 1986), Preface.
57 See Johnson, 'Towards a Cultural Theory of the Nation: A British–Dutch Dialogue', p. 9.
58 Ibid., p. 23.
59 Ibid.
60 J. Habermas, 'The Limits of Neo-Historicism', interview with J. M. Ferry, in J. Habermas, *Autonomy and Solidarity* (London: Verso, 1992), p. 243.
61 Ibid., p. 240.
62 See J. Habermas, 'The Second Life Fiction of the Federal Republic: We have become "Normal" Again', *New Left Review*, 197 (January/February 1993), p. 58.
63 Ibid., p. 64.

Index

Index by Margaret Cronan